DIGITALLY
CURIOUS

DIGITALLY CURIOUS

YOUR GUIDE TO NAVIGATING THE FUTURE OF AI AND ALL THINGS TECH

ANDREW GRILL

WILEY

This edition first published 2025

This book was produced in collaboration with Write Business Results Limited. For more information on their business book and marketing services, please visit www.writebusinessresults.com or contact the team via info@writebusinessresults.com.

Registered Office(s)
John Wiley & Sons, Inc., 111 River Street, Hoboken, NJ 07030, USA
John Wiley & Sons Ltd, The Atrium, Southern Gate, Chichester, West Sussex, PO19 8SQ, UK

For details of our global editorial offices, customer services, and more information about Wiley products visit us at www.wiley.com.

Wiley also publishes its books in a variety of electronic formats and by print-on-demand. Some content that appears in standard print versions of this book may not be available in other formats.

Library of Congress Cataloging-in-Publication Data is Available:

ISBN 9781394211258 (Cloth)
ISBN 9781394217014 (ePDF)
ISBN 9781394217007 (ePub)

Cover Design: Jon Boylan
Cover Image: © graficriver_icons_logo/Shutterstock
Author Photo: © Tilde Lennaárd

Set in 11/14pt and MinionPro by Straive, Chennai, India

SKY10086327_100124

For Mum, Dad, Carolanne, and Madeleine

CONTENTS

Introduction: Are You Digitally Curious?   1

1   Becoming Digitally Curious   7
2   Why Being Digitally Curious is Good for Your Career and
        Your Business   15

PART I   CURIOUS ABOUT … AI   **25**
3   From Turing to Transformers   29
4   Deploying AI in the Workplace   39
5   Tools to Get You Started with AI   53

PART II   CURIOUS ABOUT … TECHNOLOGY   **59**
6   The Promise of 5G   63
7   Let's Talk – The Power of Voice   73
8   Cloud Computing   83
9   The Internet of Everything   99

PART III   CURIOUS ABOUT … THE INTERNET   **109**
10 The New Internet   113
11 The Metaverse   125
12 Bitcoin and Blockchain   137
13 Tokenisation and NFTs   147

PART IV   CURIOUS ABOUT … YOUR DATA   **157**
14 Your Digital First Impression   159
15 Staying Safe in the Age of AI   169
16 Creating Your Digital Legacy   179
17 Data Privacy and Regulation   185

CONTENTS

PART V   CURIOUS ABOUT ... THE FUTURE   **193**

18   The Future of AI   195
19   The Future of Work   205
20   Quantum Computing   213
21   Sovereign Identity   225
22   Everything as a Service   235

Conclusion: Curious About ... What's Next?   243
Glossary   257
Resources   277
Notes   291
Acknowledgements   305
About the Author   311
Index   313

INTRODUCTION: ARE YOU DIGITALLY CURIOUS?

In the age of Generative AI (GenAI) and ChatGPT, it is probably more important than ever to point out that a human has written this book. When I started writing in late 2022, I never expected to have to completely rewrite this introduction, and many other sections, due to the speed at which AI technologies have developed. I've used several AI tools throughout, which I will highlight in the following chapters and explain how you too can leverage the power of AI.

It is fair to say that the launch of ChatGPT version 3.5 to the public on 30 November 2022 was a watershed moment not only for the AI movement but also for the broader effects that AI will have on society long after this book has been published. It has also helped me to promote my mantra and encourage readers of this book, listeners of my podcast, and audience members at my talks to become "digitally curious" and actively experiment with each new tool that appears.

GenAI platforms such as ChatGPT have removed the friction and allowed us to be even more digitally curious about new technologies and their effect on business and society.

When I suggest the need to be digitally curious to my audiences, I encourage them to actively use the tools and platforms I am discussing. In most cases, they agree that only by trying these new tools can you truly understand how the power of new technologies can help you in your business and your personal life.

If you've picked up this book and been intrigued by the cover contents, then you're on the path to becoming more digitally curious!

This book is for anyone who has heard phrases such as blockchain, crypto-currency, cloud computing, quantum computing, GenAI, or 5G and wondered what they mean and, more importantly, what they mean for you and your business. To help you better understand these terms, I've also created an extensive Glossary at the back of the book.

Why This Book, and Why Now?

I've been trying to write a book since 2009, way back when Twitter was a new tool. I was commissioned to write a book entitled *Twitter for Business*, which I never finished because I became so busy working for several demanding startups.

Fast forward to 2016, when I joined the professional speaker collective Speaking Office.[1] My speaking agent, Michael Levey, encouraged me to once again look at writing a book like this to explain to audiences of any type the powerful impact technology can have on business and society.

It was a daunting task to create a 60,000-word book from scratch, so Michael suggested I start a podcast series to interview the brightest minds worldwide on various technology topics and turn these interviews into chapters for the book. This is the work you now hold in your hands.

You'll find a mix of my thoughts and experiences here, coupled with over 60 experts from The Digitally Curious Podcast,[2] which can be found at www.podc.st, where you can listen to the episodes in full, all referenced from the relevant chapters here.

You'll also benefit from my experience delivering over 550 keynote presentations on new technologies and concepts as a professional keynote speaker.[3] I've spoken to corporate audiences in over 40 countries. The questions I'm asked at each event have helped sharpen my thinking and test these new concepts and ideas on a corporate audience hungry to hear about what's next.

In my keynote talks, as soon as I take the stage, I start off by asking: "Are you digitally curious?"

Then I ask my audience six simple questions:

1. Have you Googled yourself lately?

2. Do you consume your newspapers and magazines digitally?

3. Do you bank with an app-only bank?

4. Do you use two-factor authentication on everything?

5. Have you tried ChatGPT?

6. Have you bought some Bitcoin?

I start by asking the entire audience to stand, and then to continue standing if they are doing each of these things. It provides me with an excellent opportunity at the start of each talk to "read the room" and better understand their digital curiosity. By the last question, I normally have just three audience members standing.

How many of these six could you claim to be doing?

Each of them demonstrates an increasing level of digital curiosity. Let me briefly take you through each one.

Googling yourself – this is to do with your "digital first impression", which we will cover in Chapter 14. A potential client will type your name into Google, or LinkedIn, to find out more about you and what you are known for. Do you know what they will find?

Consuming newspapers and magazines digitally tells me that you're hungry for a wide range of news and information while on the move and like to have it in your device rather than printed out.

If you bank with an app-only bank such as Monzo, N26, or Revolut, then you're interested in seeing the future of financial services from these challenger or "Neo" banks.

Turning on two-factor authentication (2FA) is key if you want to stay safe online, a topic covered in Chapter 15, and reduces the risk from being hacked.

Trying out ChatGPT is something most audiences claim they have done. The challenge is integrating it into our daily workflow, which is covered in Chapter 4.

The final test, buying Bitcoin, tells me that you are interested in new Web 3.0 services, such as cryptocurrencies, which are covered in more detail in Chapter 12.

By the end of this book, I hope you could stay standing at one of my talks for each of these six questions.

My training as an engineer will also come into play. Those engineers reading this will know that we are schooled in the art of thinking from "first principles" – going back to the root cause of an issue and better understanding how to fix the problem at hand. In the case of the advice I deliver from stage, and here, married with the fact I have styled myself as "The Actionable Futurist", you can be assured that the advice contained in these pages is entirely practical and actionable.

Curious Five

As I am The Actionable Futurist, at the end of each chapter I will present the "Curious Five" – five tips and resources to help you put what you've read into action. I've also included links to a specially created website allowing you to continue your journey after each chapter: www.curious.click.

Notably, the list of technologies covered here is not exhaustive; I've selected the ones my corporate audiences ask me about the most to ensure the book focuses on what's essential for you and your business now and next year.

Over the following chapters, we will look at the benefits of becoming more digitally curious, the technologies you should be looking at now, and a view of what's coming next.

This book is written in seven sections to satisfy your curiosity across a range of subjects.

- **Introduction: Are You Digitally Curious?**

  Here I will outline what it means to be digitally curious, and why digitally curious leaders can be more successful.

- **Part I: Curious About ... AI**

  The subject that is all over the news. We will look at the history of AI, deploying it in the enterprise and tools you can use to your advantage.

- **Part II: Curious About ... Technology**

  In this section we look at a range of technologies that you will have heard about and be curious about.

- **Part III: Curious About ... The Internet**

  The internet has been around for more than 30 years, but what does the next chapter look like and where do Web 3.0, blockchain, and NFTs fit in?

- **Part IV: Curious About ... Your Data**

  Consumers still seem not to be aware of the power of their own data. Here we will look at what you can do to put your best foot forward online, stay safe, secure your digital legacy, and how regulation will impact your personal data.

- **Part V: Curious About ... The Future**

  This section looks at some of the technologies that are new or under development, but that you need to be aware of now, ahead of them going mainstream in 5–10 years' time.

- **Conclusion: Curious About ... What's Next**

  Finally, I'll guide you as to what your next steps to become more digitally curious should be.

I encourage you to make use of the www.curious.click links that I've provided as notes throughout the chapters. The format of the links is simple to use – just type it into your browser. I've chosen to do this for several reasons:

- While the general approach for quoting links is to use a long-winded full link, using this in a book is complicated. After all, it is much easier to type "curious.click/fluency" into your phone than https://bankingblog .accenture.com/boosting-digital-fluency-becoming-more-agile.

- Specific links online don't last forever – some might change or be removed. Using www.curious.click, I can monitor these links. If the link changes or is removed, I can update them so that you can always rely on the links to send you to where you need to go.

- I've created a snapshot of each page, so if they do disappear from the internet, you will still have access to the resources mentioned on the book's dedicated website via www.curious.click.

I hope that with the help of this book, you will become and stay digitally curious...

CHAPTER 1
BECOMING DIGITALLY CURIOUS

So, why am I uniquely qualified to be your co-pilot along this digitally curious journey?

I have been digitally curious for my whole life. My digitally curious journey into the world of electronics and technology began when I was 6 years old. My father helped me with scientific experiments that I would write up by hand in a small exercise book. I remember him encouraging me to think critically about why changing the connection between three lamps would make the lamps glow dimly or shine brightly.

Once I had started, I never stopped being curious about technology.

I had my first computer in 1980, the Sinclair ZX-80. Back then, it had just 1 kilobyte of random access memory (RAM) for storing programs and 4 kilobytes of read-only memory (ROM) that kept the BASIC computing interpreter used to programme the device. In comparison, the average size of a photo taken on a mobile phone is around 2 megabytes (MB). A lot has changed since then.

In my public talks, I ask for a show of hands as to who was born after 1983, then remark that I've been online longer than some of my audience has been alive. By 1983, I was "dialling up" (remember those dial-up tones) the bulletin board system (BBS) at the Angle Park Computing Centre in Adelaide and was connecting at a blistering 300 bits per second (yes, BITS, not megabits or gigabits – imagine if your phone today was that slow).

I was so fascinated by this new online world that my father had to install a second telephone line because I was always "online", and no one could get through to our house as I had the phone line permanently tied up.

Starting life as someone who is naturally digitally curious has helped me greatly. At each stage of my career, my love of technology has helped me get promoted and be presented with opportunities I never thought possible. One pivotal moment was in 1991 when I was studying for an engineering degree at the University of South Australia in Adelaide. By being the only student (on a campus of 5000) to attend an information session run by the late Professor Mike Miller about a plan to construct a new research building at the university, I landed a position as a research assistant. Over the next 2 years, I gained valuable experience around satellite engineering while studying for my degree. When I later applied to study for a Master of Engineering degree as part of the newly formed Australian Information Technology Engineering Centre (AITEC), this experience helped me gain one of only 18 places.

I believe this also helped me get selected for a 5-month work placement with British Aerospace Australia to work on an innovative portable satellite earth station for the Australian Army – Project Parakeet.[1] I gained broad practical experience on this project. It covered everything from simulating the equipment in a tropical environment at 60°C and 100% humidity, through to recreating the forces exerted when a train runs into a flatbed carriage during a rail shunting exercise. This "real-world" engineering experience only contributed to my digital curiosity.

Straddling the engineering and business worlds has greatly enhanced my career and business opportunities. Being able to "talk tech" with engineers in one moment, then explain the complex workings of a solution to a room full of non-technical board members the next has proved invaluable.

Technology is all around us. Being able to deeply understand how something works, and then explain that to a decision-maker looking to spend money with you or your firm is, I believe, the sweet spot today.

As GenAI has taken off, I've seen many commentators who were talking about social media, then bitcoin, then the metaverse, re-engineer themselves as AI

Figure 1.1 The ZX80 is displayed behind a glass cabinet in the Science Museum in London, such is its place in the history of computing. Credit: Andrew Grill

experts. I'm hoping that my "real-world" engineering training, and experience in the field with large-scale projects, has allowed me to understand any new technology that emerges, and then work out a way to explain it to non-technical audiences.

I hope that you feel I am therefore well qualified to lead you on this journey to becoming more digitally curious.

What is an Actionable Futurist?

Many have also asked why I call myself "The Actionable Futurist". The origins of this date back to 1985, when I was completing my final year of high school. For our final English exam, we had to source four books and write about them under the umbrella of a single topic. I chose "The Future" and reviewed four classic books on the future:

- *Brave New World* by Aldous Huxley – published 1932.

- *Animal Farm* by George Orwell – published 1945.

- *1984* by George Orwell – published 1949.

- *A Clockwork Orange* by Anthony Burgess – published 1962.

Each book takes a very dystopian and futuristic view of how life might unfold in the future. I've never found the essay I wrote all those years ago, but what stuck with me is that I've always had a fascination with the future. I have always loved looking at the art of the possible, and making life easier for work and play using technology.

This fascination has stayed with me throughout my life, shaped many of my decisions, and enabled many of my successes. In 2000, I appeared on a webinar for my then employer, Telstra, to talk about "Visions for the Future" and was introduced as a "Futurist" for the very first time.[2]

I've been responsible for the launch of a new high-speed data network for Optus in Australia, as well as a commercial property website, PropertyLook, which was a joint venture between four of the largest property companies in Australia.[3] I was also behind the launch of a new mobile location company in Europe with Vodafone, which is the reason why I have lived in London since moving from Sydney in 2006.

Figure 1.2   Andrew Grill presenting in Dubai in 2023. Credit: Nik Moore

My deep connection with new and ground-breaking technologies has kept me digitally curious over the years. I'm always trying out new technologies to explain them to corporate audiences.

For the last 20 years, my experience presenting to corporate audiences about emerging technologies, often at the most senior levels of an organisation or industry, has allowed me to fine-tune my message and understanding around what matters most when it comes to the application of technology in business and society.

What are the Traits of the Digitally Curious?

The digitally curious are often innovators who think outside the box. They are constantly looking for creative solutions to problems that apply digital technologies in new and creative ways. Their curiosity drives them to experiment until they find the most effective ways to improve processes, create new products, or enhance the personal and professional lives of everyone around them.

Being digitally curious is also about being eager to learn. The digitally curious have a strong desire to acquire new knowledge and skills in a continuing pursuit of growth and personal development. They frequently engage in online courses, webinars, and other educational opportunities to enhance their digital skills.

Digital curiosity requires being aware and also critical of the information being consumed. It is vital to stay aware of the possible impacts and risks of new technologies. The critical approach the digitally curious take to new information helps them navigate through misinformation and identify trustworthy data.

Digitally curious individuals are adaptable and open to changing technologies and digital landscapes. They embrace new digital innovations and are not intimidated by the rapid pace of technological change. They value the potential of digital platforms to connect with others, share ideas, and collaborate on projects. This drives them to engage in online communities, participate in forums, and use social media effectively.

Such individuals use digital resources to solve problems, whether it's Googling a question, participating in online forums for advice, or using specialised software. They are also confident in leveraging digital tools to express themselves creatively, from digital art to content creation on social media.

Therefore, this is increasingly recognised as a valuable trait, as it facilitates lifelong learning, enhances employability in a tech-driven economy, and supports personal growth and adaptability in a rapidly changing, AI-enabled digital world.

How to Assess Your Digital Curiosity

I've broken the main traits of individuals with high digital curiosity down into six areas. These individuals are often characterised by their:

1. Willingness to experiment

2. Proactive learning

3. Engagement with digital trends

4. Problem-solving

5. Creativity and innovation

6. Adaptability

To self-assess your level of digital curiosity, give yourself a score of between 1 (just starting out) and 5 (I consider myself an expert) for each of the six areas I've just set out. When you've finished this book, return to this chapter and re-evaluate your score.

Curious Five

What can you do today, to become digitally curious?

1. Set aside some time, at least an hour each week, to investigate the items in this book. Over 22 chapters, there are more than 100 tips for you to investigate – decide how you will make time to do this.

2. To keep you curious, decide to share some of these tips with your friends and family. You will be surprised how quickly you become the "go-to" person with a range of new technical knowledge gleaned from these pages.

3. Set up a separate email address (perhaps your name.curious@gmail .com) to use for all of the new services you will be signing up for, to keep them separate from your work and personal emails so they won't get buried.

4. Start a notepad entry on your phone or computer with the tips you've learned in this book as a way to reinforce them and come back to the ones that make you the most curious.

5. Visit www.curious.click to see the latest updates, or ask the book's own AI a question, and visit the links presented in each section.

CHAPTER 2
WHY BEING DIGITALLY CURIOUS IS GOOD FOR YOUR CAREER AND YOUR BUSINESS

In the promotion for this book, I coined a phrase that sums up what I hope you can achieve from reading it:

"Digitally Curious: A self-help book for the technically overwhelmed."

When I shared this with friends and colleagues, they agreed that they too seemed "technically overwhelmed". While I grew up playing with technology, studied it, and made it a career, I am sensitive to the fact that as technologists, we tend to overwhelm people. When friends receive a new piece of technology, such as a Wi-Fi router, and struggle to set it up, they end up turning to me for help. I often wonder why companies assume that everyone has the same level of technical proficiency.

Recently, I read an interesting quote in an IBM report[1] about AI and the impact it might have on jobs:

"AI won't replace people – but people who use AI will replace people who don't."

Rewriting this to be more generic:

"New technologies won't replace people. People who regularly use and are comfortable with technology will replace people who don't."

In my technology career spanning over 30 years, I've been in more board-room presentations than I care to remember, and the common theme is that senior leaders seem reluctant to get "hands-on" experience and play with new technologies. They feel that they have IT teams to worry about the technology and don't want to touch the tech themselves, possibly because of a fear of the unknown or their experience with new technologies being somewhat overwhelming.

My aim with this book is to remove the mystery and encourage you to experiment with new technologies so that they seem less intimidating.

I have seen first-hand how senior executives experience an "ah-ha!" moment when I slowly and carefully unpack a new technology or platform and explain what it means for them and their business.

In writing this book, I was inspired by a 2013 report from Capgemini and MIT Sloan,[2] which talked about how digital leaders outperform their peers in every industry. The paper discusses companies having digital maturity, which they define as a combination of two separate but related dimensions.

1. *Digital intensity*: Investment in technology-enabled initiatives to change how the company operates, its customer engagements, internal operations, and business models.

2. *Transformation management intensity*: Helping to create the leadership capabilities necessary to drive digital transformation in the organisation.

Both dimensions can be applied to individuals and measured as a level of digital curiosity, especially the second dimension.

My view is that digital curiosity is good for your career and your business – and I will explain throughout these chapters how it has worked for me, and how it can work for you too.

The Starbucks Test

I have an unofficial "Starbucks test", where technologies that I have been investigating start to be discussed in my local Starbucks. I remember the time in

2009 when I overheard someone talking about Twitter, and I knew then that it would become popular. When a technology becomes well known enough that everyone is talking about it, it is a good sign that it is entering the mainstream.

Being digitally curious is a great way to be aware of a technology before this point – or even be the one starting conversations about it over coffee! When you are aware of a technology before it goes mainstream, it means that you and your business can be ready for it, and potentially gain a competitive advantage.

ChatGPT will be used frequently in this book as an example of a watershed technology – something that people in coffee shops are talking about thanks to widespread exposure in the media. However, as I will explain in Chapter 3, the technology was out there long before November 2022.

The challenge for technologies such as this is to "cross the chasm"[3] from early adopters to early majority. While it is a good start to try out a new piece of technology or online platform, people who are truly digitally curious integrate this technology into their daily workflows, and then encourage their teams and colleagues to do the same.

Winning New Business Thanks to AI

I was humbled by a recent interaction with a new friend I met at a party in France. When I was introduced, we spoke about what I do as a Futurist, and my new friend, an interior designer, was fascinated about how AI could be used in her industry.

Fast forward two months later. When we met again, she told me that our discussion had prompted her to be more digitally curious, and to seek out a course run by a university around the use of AI in interior design.

She is now using Midjourney, an AI tool that creates hyper-realistic images from text descriptions to provide visualisations of proposed designs for client proposals. Her success rate for new business is now close to 100% because she is able to provide clients with a better view of what their finished project might look like, down to the grain used in the marble finish.

This is exactly what I hope this book will do for you – give you that small push towards learning more about new technologies to the point where they positively impact your business or life, which then leads to you adopting them into your daily routine.

At a recent talk in Dubai to a group of business leaders,[4] I asked for a show of hands from those who had tried ChatGPT. I then asked the audience to raise their hands if they used it daily. Not surprisingly, most hands went down. While we may sign up for a new tool such as ChatGPT or download an app someone has mentioned, it will remain foreign to you unless you work out how to integrate it into your daily workflow.

One of the slides I present in my keynote talks, shown below, I have named the "Scary Slide".[5]

It's called scary because by showing this mix of jargon and technical terms, I want to scare the audience into feeling quite uncomfortable that they may not know about all the items listed.

Take a moment to review the words on this slide. If you don't know what they all mean, then that's expected. Tonight or tomorrow, play "Wikipedia bingo"

Andrew Grill Actionable Futurist	6G	Metaverse	Chatbots
Super Apps	Personal Digital Twin	Fusion Teams	AGI
			XaaS
	Meeting Equity	Dynamic Predictions	GPT-6
Smart Contracts			
	BYOID	API	Deepfake
Quantum Computing	Explainability	2FA	Ambient Tech
		Sovereign Identity	Web3
XDR	NFT	RFID	
Nano Tech	IoT	Blockchain	Distributed Ledger

Figure 2.1 The "Scary Slide"

and look up what these words mean and what they mean for your business. If you don't want to do this, just ask a young person, as they will likely tell you what they all mean.

Pause for thought here. How uncomfortable did it make you not knowing what some of these items meant? If I told you that these phrases will impact your business in the next 6 to 9 months, would that make you more interested in discovering more?

Going Digital or Born Digital?

For several years now I've been speaking about the "two tribes" that exist in every organisation – those "Going Digital", very experienced executives whose digital skills are developing; and those "Born Digital", whose first toy was a smartphone. The latter tribe live and breathe digital and are hungry to try new technologies and platforms. In many ways, this tribe could be seen as "permanently curious" when it comes to digital.

The two tribes can benefit from each other. At the end of all my talks, I suggest companies run a "hackathon". Once the reserve of software development teams to solve complex technical problems, hackathons can be used to solve broader business problems, with both the Born Digital and the Going Digital in the same room, sharing their very different perspectives to solve the same business problem.

Hackathon – A short, focused, and intensive period of collaboration with the goal to create functioning software or hardware by the end of the event.

The word "hackathon" is a portmanteau of the words "hack" and "marathon", where "hack" is used in the sense of exploratory programming.[6]

Whether you fall into the "Going Digital" or the "Born Digital" camp, I'm assuming – as you have bought this book – that you are already digitally literate, or making a concerted effort to become so. However, many people, particularly those heading up organisations, are not yet fully digitally literate. I've witnessed first-hand situations where a technology investment proposal – a request for funding sometimes numbering into the millions – is presented to a board or a management team. From the limited questioning of the presenter, I can tell that those charged with making these investment decisions perhaps did not fully realise what they were being asked to approve.

If it's a new cloud platform to help grow the business, why is no one asking where the data will be hosted, who the provider is, what the redundancy strategy is, and how DevOps will be undertaken? With new GenAI platforms being pitched to boards, are they asking about how the Large Language Models (LLMs) were developed, what data was used to train the model, if the risk and legal teams were involved, and whether it has been warranted to be safe from the threat of extreme harm?

A digitally curious board or management team would know enough about the technology from making enquiries, reading widely, speaking with technical teams, and reading this book to ask these questions and more.

Digital transformation involves technology and culture, so digital literacy must start at the top of the organisation. Studies have shown[7] that digitally literate boards and management teams make far better technology investment decisions than those who are not digitally literate.

What is Your Technology Quotient (TQ)?

First, there was the intelligence quotient (IQ), then the emotional quotient (EQ), and now there's the technology quotient (TQ).[8] This is the skills piece of the digital fluency puzzle, and when done well, it unlocks workers' enthusiasm, expertise, and value.

Accenture research in 2022[9] pointed out that nearly three-quarters (72%) of the banking workforce say their employers consider digital skills necessary. However, another survey suggested that only 1 in 10 banking board directors has tech expertise. They also argue: "A digital foundation supports flexibility, and flexibility enables agility, which is essential for business performance today and in the future."[10] This all points to the need for digital curiosity.

So, if the workers' digital skills are essential, then the leadership and management teams' digital skills and digital literacy are even more critical. The path to enhanced digital skills and understanding starts with digital curiosity.

The Capgemini MIT Sloan survey mentioned earlier highlighted that digital leaders outperform their peers in every industry. They argue that: "Digital maturity matters. It matters in every industry. And the approaches that digitally mature companies use can be adopted by any company with the leadership drive to do so." The report[11] defines four types of digital maturity:

- *Beginners:* These firms do very little with advanced digital capabilities but may use more traditional systems such as ERP or e-commerce. They are unlikely to have a digitally savvy leadership team in place.

- *Fashionistas:* Companies that have implemented or experimented with many "sexy" digital applications – some creating value and others not. They most likely have not implemented these digital initiatives with a real strategy linking them all together because most are experiments or pilots – or perhaps are just "ticking the boxes".

- *Conservatives:* Digital conservatives favour prudence over innovation. While they understand the need for a robust digital vision, governance, and culture to match, they are not there yet. While they spend wisely, they are missing the advantages that can be realised from digital.

- *Digerati:* These companies are digital stars. They understand how to drive value with digital transformation and combine this with exemplary leadership, governance, and culture to accelerate their work with digital technologies. In short, these companies have a robust digital culture and drive actual revenue.

Digitally curious executives operate at least in the Fashionista mode – they are willing to try new things and are open to new technologies. This is something you should aspire to on completion of this book.

An MIT Sloan article,[12] "The New Elements of Digital Transformation", revisits some ground-breaking work from 2013, looking at what it takes to become a digital leader and outperform your peers.

It requires that companies become what we call digital masters and cultivate two key traits: *digital capability*, which enables them to use innovative technologies to improve elements of the business, and *leadership capability*, which enables them to envision and drive organisational change in systematic and profitable ways.

These two traits allow a company to transform digital technology into a business advantage. The "Curious Five" at the end of each chapter will help you increase your digital and leadership capabilities, so set aside some time to try at least one of the suggestions in each chapter.

As outlined in the Introduction, I've been a technologist since the age of 6, and I've had a mantra for the last 30 years: "To get digital, you've got to be digital." By this, I mean that if you are to truly understand digital technologies and effect a proper digital transformation in your business, then you must *be digital* and use the technologies that your teams, competitors, and customers are also using.

Being digitally curious or digitally literate doesn't mean that you need to study for an engineering degree, as I have done. Far from it. The intent behind this book is that each of the sections will provide you with enough of an overview to help you ask the right questions and work out if you need to dive deeper by reading more articles or enrolling in a short course, better to understand the impact of the technology on your business now and in the near term.

Curious Five

Here are five steps you can take to become more digitally curious.

1. Listen to technology-focused podcasts – why not start with Digitally Curious at www.podc.st?

2. Read the technology section of leading newspapers.

3. Subscribe to technology journals such as *Wired*[13] and *The Information*.[14]

4. Consider a short course to learn more about a specific technology, such as the Oxford Artificial Intelligence Programme.[15]

5. Seek out your more tech-savvy colleagues and ask them how they stay up-to-date with new trends.

PART I
CURIOUS ABOUT ... AI

Why Am I Curious About AI?

I've been fascinated by AI for a number of years, but was never able to really get my head around how it mattered to me personally. I was comfortable talking about AI, but not being an AI programmer; I wasn't able to easily build my own AI tools and models.

Until ChatGPT burst onto the stage on 30 November 2022, the whole concept of AI and its uses seemed quite far off. My view of AI, pre-ChatGPT, was that large companies would invest a lot of time in training such platforms for specific roles.

This had been borne out in my time at IBM, where the legacy of the 2011 *Jeopardy!* win was omnipresent. For those who don't remember this feat, the IBM computer (Watson) beat two *Jeopardy!* champions.[1] In 2013, the then-CEO Ginni Rometty announced a new commercial division – IBM Watson. This was when I knew that we were on the cusp of something really interesting.

Back in the Watson days, the promise of AI was possibly overstated by IBM and a number of other vendors. This was all pre-GenAI, so the more traditional machine learning and deep learning techniques were much harder to observe in action.

In an interview with Goldman Sachs after she had left IBM, Rometty commented that, "when making a market, people have to trust the technology".[2]

At the time, Rometty tasked the IBM Watson team to focus on oncology, one of the most challenging and ambitious areas to apply AI.

At IBM, I was a Global Managing Partner in the consulting group, and was often called to present and sell the benefits of AI to the boards and management teams of some of IBM's largest customers. This was challenging because, at the time, it was very hard to show a team of executives exactly how AI worked, and what the benefits might be. All we had were a few formative case studies, as this application of AI was very new.

This kept me curious, yet at the same time frustrated that we couldn't easily demonstrate the technology. We could talk about case studies after the fact, and after months of training and analysis, but clients couldn't play with the technology themselves, the way that ChatGPT operates today.

So, the concept of AI and its promise has existed for quite some time, and I've been continually curious about where it might go next. Tools that I've mentioned elsewhere, such as Grammarly[3] and Otter.ai,[4] are powered by AI. Over the years I have been a user of each tool and have seen how they have improved as the AI technology evolves.

With the advent of GenAI, my curiosity has been piqued once again. Now I can simply programme and train AI systems as easily as you would have a conversation with an AI developer. I've possibly never been quite as curious as I am now about AI and I've been experimenting with AI around text, images, video, and voice.

I've just created my own customised AI avatar, which is a clone of my face and voice, using Veed.io.[5] To train the system, I read a script in front of a camera for just 9 minutes, and now I can use my avatar everywhere, and create endless versions of myself.

You can see my avatar in action at https://curious.click/avatar.

I've also created a ChatGPT interface specifically for this book. If you head to https://curious.click/gpt then you can ask the tool any question you care to about the book, the author, or what has happened since publication. As part of my own digital curiosity, I will be updating and retraining this GPT on a regular basis as the technology and industry evolves.

Why Should You Be Curious About AI?

There is possibly no better example of why and how you need to be digitally curious than GenAI. The fact that governments are rushing to regulate it, the media is discussing it ad nauseum, and companies are racing to implement it, to me feels like the early days of the internet when people were asking, "do we need to be on the internet?"

Finally, 70-plus years after the notion of artificial intelligence was first discussed by Dr Alan Turing and others, we are now at a point where the friction for AI experimentation and adoption has been removed and these platforms are available to anyone with a device connected to the internet.

One of the ways I satisfied my own curiosity about this subject was to read as widely as possible. One example was a paper written by Stephen Wolfram, entitled "What Is ChatGPT Doing . . . and Why Does It Work?".[6] This paper both educated me and challenged my thinking on AI. It gave me a way to explain how ChatGPT works: "it predicts the next word in a sentence", and it also challenged my thinking about how close AI will get to being able to think more like a human over time.

Wolfram's paper dives deep into neural networks, way above my pay grade and experience, highlighting how complex the human brain is, and why it is so difficult to emulate it. In many ways, this is the perfect example of digital curiosity. Wolfram's thinking made me deeply curious about a subject I thought I already knew a lot about.

What reading his paper made me curious about was how much more structure and simplicity there is in the human language than we ever knew, and the fact that there are actually simple rules that describe how language can be assembled.

As AI is being discussed everywhere, including in the boardrooms and management teams of every organisation, it won't be long until you are asked for your opinion on AI. As I say elsewhere in this book: "AI won't replace people – but people who use AI will replace people who don't." The same is true here. Your promotion prospects are likely to be much more interesting if you're up with the latest technology tools and techniques.

When it comes to deploying AI in the enterprise, the measure of success of the project will likely come down to one thing – the quality of the data available to train and update the AI model. Your curiosity should lead you to explore the data you have today, what you need next and where from, and how you will source it. Finally, to stay digitally curious around AI, you will need a range of tools that you constantly use, to flex the curious side of your mind.

CHAPTER 3
FROM TURING TO TRANSFORMERS

This has been one of the most challenging chapters of the book to write. When I started writing in late 2022, ChatGPT was something that only engineers were playing with – using a vastly different interface than we see today. As I write this chapter, OpenAI, the company behind ChatGPT and DALL-E, which provides a text-to-image service, has just launched Sora. This is a text-to-video service that will revolutionise how moving images are created.[1]

Even as a futurist, it's hard to predict what OpenAI will do next. As I've been working on this book, I've witnessed:

- The launch of ChatGPT 3.5, ChatGPT 4, ChatGPT 4o and ChatGPT 5, which is likely to be live by the time you read this.

- Sam Altman be ousted as CEO, only to be reinstated days later.

- Microsoft hire Mustafa Suleyman, DeepMind and Inflection Co-founder, as CEO of a new division: Microsoft AI.[2]

- OpenAI's video-to-text tool, Sora, be out in the open.

By the time this book is published, there will be many more twists and turns in the AI world. Not just from OpenAI, but from Google with Gemini, Amazon with their investment in Anthropic, or another player that no-one has considered yet.

The problem I face, as an author of a physical book about the use of emerging technologies, including GenAI, is how I can keep up with the latest trends between submitting my manuscript and the publication date and beyond.

In the printed pages here, I will review what has come so far and make some broad predictions about what will likely happen over the next few months, but please bear with me if some of these are wide of the mark, or have already happened when you are reading this. I will also maintain a digital record of important technologies and advances that I will keep updated as things change and advance.

As I explained previously, all www.curious.click links will direct you to an up-to-date link for that citation. The link https://curious.click/latest will provide an update on what has happened since manuscript submission and publication, and any relevant updates and corrections since you bought the book.

One constant in the AI story is the history of how we got here. With the latest interest in GenAI, many forget that AI has been around since 1950. This is, therefore, an excellent place to start.

The History of AI

I want to take you on a short history lesson about how we got here with AI, from Turing to transformers. In 1950, Mathematician Dr Alan Turing wrote a paper entitled "Computing Machinery and Intelligence".[3] The very first line of this paper asks the question: "Can machines think?" As we get closer to the AI, we know today that this question is becoming easier to answer.

In 1952, Arthur Samuel developed a program to play checkers, which was the first to ever learn the game independently.[4]

If we fast forward to 1956, John McCarthy, also a grandfather of the AI movement, held a 6-week summer workshop – the "Dartmouth Summer Research Project"[5] – widely considered the founding event of artificial intelligence as a field.

In 1957, McCarthy created LISP (acronym for List Processing), the first programming language for AI research, which is still in popular use to this day.[6]

In 1959, Samuel created the term "machine learning" when speaking about how to teach machines to play chess better than the humans who programmed them.[7]

In 1966, ELIZA, an early natural language processing computer program, was developed by Joseph Weizenbaum at MIT to explore communication between humans and machines.

Weizenbaum was surprised and shocked that individuals, including his own secretary, attributed human-like feelings to the computer program. This led to the "Eliza effect",[8] where humans started to believe that an AI system had human characteristics.

James L. Adams created the Stanford Cart in 1961, which became one of the first examples of an autonomous vehicle. In 1979, it successfully navigated a room full of chairs without human interference.[9]

Some examples you may be more familiar with include the 1997 win by IBM's Deep Blue against world chess champion Garry Kasparov.[10] In 1997, the Dragon Dictate speech recognition system (mentioned in more detail in Chapter 7) was released.

In 2011, the same year that IBM Watson won *Jeopardy!*, Apple released Siri. Then, in 2017, a Google research team developed the concept of transformers with a paper entitled "Attention Is All You Need".[11] This formed the basis of the GenAI systems we're now all familiar with.

The reason I share this history of AI with you is because I believe it's important that we realise this is not "brand new" technology. It has been in the making for decades – and as such it is going to stick around.

Clarifying Terms in AI

Have you heard terms like "machine learning", "LLM", or "deep learning" in conversations about AI? How do they make you feel? I could likely make a "Scary Slide" for AI alone!

At this point I should pause for a second to define the important terms and concepts you might need to know.

The phrase "artificial intelligence" describes the field of computer science focused on creating machines that can mimic human-like behaviour. When people mention "AI", it's deliberately a very broad topic.

The important thing to remember is that no matter how advanced an AI, not one of them thinks in the same way as a human does. They are still computers and specialise in processing data as binary "yes-or-no" (to put it simply – we'll get to quantum computing in Chapter 20). What makes an AI more or less advanced, or a specific tool better or worse at a given task, is how it "thinks". For our purposes, let's divide these into two categories: machine learning and deep learning.

Machine Learning (ML)

Have you ever tried logging into something and been asked to do a task like "mark every box with a car in it"? Did you know that this is helping train AI?[12] A human can look at two different brands of car in two different colours and recognise that they are both still cars. A computer can't do that so well.

They are amazing at sifting through large amounts of data to find patterns. They can then improve on that data to make decisions or predictions. However, categorising the data and sifting through it are two different steps. In machine learning, the AI tool needs to organise the data before it can do anything with it. This requires human input at first to help the tool correctly identify and sort the data.

Financial Times journalist Madhumita Murgia in her book *Code Dependent: Living in the Shadow of AI* provides some truly disturbing examples of how humans are used to train AI systems for very low wages in countries such as Kenya, Uganda, and India, and without such human effort, many of the GenAI systems we take for granted today would never have launched.

Deep Learning (DL)

Deep learning, on the other hand, is a subset of machine learning designed to let a machine train itself to do a task. This is done by using neural networks – systems that are designed to emulate how the human brain thinks and operates.

In deep learning, the task of identifying and categorising gets broken down into smaller steps. This allows the AI to copy how humans look at the world and make connections between things before reacting to them. It is important to note that these are still computers though. Deep learning does not make computers capable of fully human-like thought, it merely allows a computer to solve a problem more efficiently.

Bret Greenstein, PwC Partner and Generative AI leader, spoke to me on the podcast while in a previous role about Evolutionary Artificial Intelligence:[13]

> "What we really have is the simulation of intelligence. When you look at AI that can recognise what's in a picture, read an X-ray, understand language, or produce understandable text or speech, it feels intelligent. But it's really pattern recognition, and simulation of us the same way that mechanical turks[14] and systems for hundreds of years have represented how people behave in a way that can feel and appear to be real.
>
> There are companies now, for example, that are training AI systems on what we individually say, to create a virtual version of us. William Shatner recently, for his birthday, had himself recorded so people can interact with the virtual version of himself for generations to come. And it'll talk as if he were talking, but it's not him and it's not actually intelligent. It's mimicking the patterns of what people do – the same way that parrots sound like people, but they've learned how to respond in a way that we respond to."
>
> —Bret Greenstein, PwC

Many readers will remember when, in 1997, Chess Champion Garry Kasparov lost to IBM's Deep Blue.[15] Or when, in 2011, IBM Watson won *Jeopardy!*, as I've already mentioned.[16] These achievements are not because these AI were smarter than a human in general. Instead, they were successfully trained on how to do a specific "narrow" task well enough to match a human.

GenAI

The final term you might have heard of is Generative AI (GenAI). GenAIs are a category of AI tools that can apply advanced techniques like deep learning to create things. For example, generating "new" content like text, images, videos, and voice.

When we talk about "AI", we're normally talking about some form of GenAI – for example, ChatGPT or AI image generation tool Midjourney[17]. Due to how deep learning works, the ability to generate content requires a massive amount of training data. In the context of AI tools that generate text, the combination of dataset and AI algorithm is called a "Large Language Model" (LLM).

In the case of ChatGPT 3.5, experts believe it was trained on datasets such as the open internet, Wikipedia, and unpublished academic texts.[18]

The way these work is similar to how predictive texting works. Based on what has already been said, the prompt, and the context, the AI generates the next most likely word. Due to the sheer size of the dataset, this means it is highly likely that the output will read or seem correct. However, this is not always the case.

Hallucinations

GenAI systems like ChatGPT are designed to generate answers based on a prompt and confidently present them as fact. However, these answers are not always correct or entirely accurate – a phenomenon known as "hallucination".

This is easiest to see in images created with GenAI. Small details like fingers or teeth might appear correct from a distance, but are a bit "off" on closer inspection. In text, it is more subtle. Facts might sound correct, but be wrong if you check more carefully.

There can be several causes of this. The nature of deep learning means that a GenAI can recognise the form of the right answer and produce something accordingly. But since an AI does not have the ability to think like a human, nor is a GenAI designed to fact check its own responses (something that would require another tool to be running at the same time), it can't catch when the response is wrong.

Similarly, in a public LLM, not every piece of data has been cross-checked as correct. ChatGPT's function is to communicate like a human across a range of topics and it has been trained accordingly. This, in fact, is what makes the design and personalisation of your own specific LLMs so important. We'll talk about this more in the next chapter.

The Rise of GenAI

To better understand why GenAI systems are so popular, it is worth looking more closely at how they've evolved. First off, what does the "GPT" in Chat-GPT actually mean? It stands for <u>G</u>enerative <u>P</u>re-trained <u>T</u>ransformer.

- *Generative*: We've already covered this. This simply means that it can generate its own sentences and paragraphs.

- *Pre-trained*: Without a dataset, no AI can work. A pre-trained AI means that it has undergone some form of machine learning process to process enough data to function. In ChatGPT's case, it comes with its own LLM already – no need to feed it any data before it can start working.

- *Transformer*: As a human, you instinctively know what the important parts of a sentence or question are without help. A transformer is a system designed to help the AI understand what to pay attention to so it can understand the prompt and generate a relevant response.

As I mentioned earlier, the genesis of GenAI as we know it today was a 2017 Google research paper entitled "Attention Is All You Need".[19] This paper discusses transformers and how they can help an AI system make sense of what it reads and how it answers.

From there, OpenAI's GPT model went through three main stages:

- **GPT-1** in June 2018. This was the first iteration of the GPT series and consisted of 117 million parameters. This model demonstrated the power of unsupervised learning in language-understanding tasks, using books as training data to predict the next word in a sentence.

- **GPT-2** in February 2019. This represented a significant upgrade from GPT-1, with 1.5 billion parameters. It showcased a dramatic improvement in text-generation capabilities and produced coherent, multiparagraph text.

- **GPT-3** was a giant leap forward in June 2020. This model was trained on around 175 billion parameters. Its advanced text-generation capabilities led to widespread use in various applications, from drafting emails and writing articles to creating poetry and even generating programming code. It also demonstrated an ability to answer factual questions and translate between languages.

Building on ChatGPT 3, on 30 November 2022, OpenAI released ChatGPT 3.5[20] to the public. This version made the headlines because it removed the fiction from engaging with AI models. Placing a chatbot-like interface in front of ChatGPT 3.5 allowed anyone, even journalists, to play with the technology.

OpenAI's most recent GPT foundation model (at the time of writing), GPT 4o, was released on 13 May 2024. Users can access it for free with a cap on the number of queries, or via a premium version of ChatGPT called GPT Plus,[21] which costs around $20/month and allows more queries and functionality.

I'm assuming that most people reading this book have played with some variant of ChatGPT. Still, if a show of hands at each of my talks is a good representative sample, then few have integrated this tool into everyday workflows.

While ChatGPT's launch onto the world stage quickly raised the opportunity of AI systems to the general public, you may not know that you're using AI at almost every stage of your day.

When you unlock your phone with your fingerprint or your face, you're using AI embedded securely on your phone to process this in real time without sending any data away from the phone.

Suppose you use a navigation program such as Waze, Google Maps, or City-mapper to navigate from A to B. In that case, you're using AI, as these mapping platforms have to calculate the fastest route using various transport methods in real time and consider things like weather, disruption, and roadworks.

If you watch streaming TV such as Netflix, Apple TV, or Amazon Prime, then you may not know that the suggestions for what you might like to watch are all based on AI.

Increasingly, we will start seeing the programmes' thumbnails generated in real time to match your viewing preferences perfectly. This means that the thumbnail I am shown for the movie *Oppenheimer* will differ from the one you're seeing, based on my own preferences that have been discerned from my viewing habits.

Before GenAI, the ability to generate different images almost individually was unthinkable. Going forward, we can expect more personalised advertising based on our viewing and browsing preferences, which perfectly match what we like. Welcome to the power of GenAI.

What This Means for You

Thanks to these latest AI innovations, you're now armed with the most significant technological advancement since the internet: GenAI.

The whole ethos of this book is that you need to remain digitally curious. It is no longer appropriate to "wait and see" how this technology shakes out. GenAI is here; your competitors are already learning to adapt and adopt it. It is up to you to discover its value. This means that you need to sign up for an account if you haven't already, and explore the art of the possible.

In the next chapters, we will look at the responsible use of AI.

Curious Five

Start with the following steps to stay digitally curious in the age of AI.

1. Sign up for ChatGPT[22] and use the more powerful 4o model which will allow you to upload documents for analysis, create images, and issue commands by speaking.

2. Treat your GenAI tool as your intern – start using it daily to get work done and experiment with broad and complex questions. Start by asking it to compare your company with your nearest competitor. The answers it provides may surprise you.

3. Look at other AI platforms such as Claude.ai,[23] Jasper.ai,[24] Google Gemini,[25] and Amazon's Anthropic.[26] Understand how each model differs and what tools work best for your daily tasks.

4. Review or establish guidelines in your organisation about the use of AI tools.

5. Explore what other AI tools you can use in your daily work – Chapter 5 and the resources section at the end of this book provide some great examples.

CHAPTER 4
DEPLOYING AI IN THE WORKPLACE

Being curious about AI in the enterprise is essential because AI is rapidly transforming industries and business operations. It's not just about staying current with trends; it's about understanding a powerful tool that can drive significant growth, innovation, and competitive advantage.

Competitors will already be working out how to use AI to their advantage – can you be left behind? Customers are also playing with AI tools and will expect that your organisation will be embracing these tools to improve their products, services, and the way they interact with you.

Now that AI is being discussed in every boardroom, and on every media outlet, I'm sure that your senior management team (or someone like me invited to talk about AI) has asked the question: "What are we doing with AI?" Here's a little secret – AI isn't the answer for everything, and it can be prohibitively expensive for simple tasks. So, how can you spot areas in your business that could benefit from AI?

Demystifying AI: What AI Can Do vs What it Cannot Do

While AI can drive value, it also requires significant resources to implement and maintain. You may need different skill sets to interpret the data you already have to get it ready for training. GenAI systems also consume 10–1000 times the computer power of standard systems,[1] meaning your data centre or cloud provider bill is likely to increase significantly – have you budgeted for this?

Without proper planning, a senior management call to "do AI" can become complicated, expensive, and possibly divert valuable resources away from important tasks and projects. Implementing AI because it is in the news, or a competitor has adopted it, without a clear business case or value proposition, will never make business sense. AI should be used as a tool to solve specific challenges, not as a catch-all solution to solve broad business problems.

A common myth is that AI can surpass human intelligence in all areas, leading to a future where machines outsmart us. The reality is that AI excels in specific tasks that involve data processing and pattern recognition, but it lacks the general understanding and consciousness of humans.

AI cannot perform well without a large quantity of relevant, high-quality data, or infer additional context if the information is not present in the data. Therefore, while AI thrives on pattern recognition, it does not possess the intrinsic creativity and understanding of the human context needed for many tasks.

One interesting enterprise use of AI is in the legal sector. Lawyers require specific skills and depend heavily on human strengths that no AI can replicate, such as creative and strategic abilities, along with empathy and emotional intelligence. These can't be replicated by an AI. They need to understand their clients and plan around it. They then need to be able to craft and present a convincing argument in court. Implementing AI for a legal firm therefore needs to focus on what computers do far better than a human could.

A lot of a lawyer's day-to-day work is repetitive and low risk. Tasks like creating repetitive contracts, freedom of information access requests, filing paperwork, and so on. These menial tasks could all be easily automated and accelerated by AI. This could free up a lawyer's time to focus on the creative and critical thinking they specialise in.

Alternatively, no lawyer can read every piece of law ever written. However, a specifically trained LLM could find precedents that might otherwise take a long time to discover. It is important to note that due to the risks of hallucination or bias, this requires a specific AI that is focused and trained specifically on that task.

"That's where the limitations of ChatGPT and other generalist AI chatbots begin. They're not fit for purpose in very specialist fields. So take medicine, manufacturing, engineering; all of these require that same level of deep domain knowledge that legal does.

So it's important that the AI being used in those fields is able to adapt to and learn the nuanced ways in which those industries do business and make decisions. Anything less than that has the potential to do more harm than good."

—*Jaeger Glucina, Luminance AI*[2]

So, AI should not be used when tasks require human empathy, moral judgement, or complex interpersonal interactions. In areas like HR, personal counselling, or any service requiring deep emotional intelligence, a human touch is irreplaceable and vital for genuine connections.

Similarly, AI should not be considered when the problem space is poorly defined or requires a level of creativity and innovation that AI cannot (yet) replicate, such as in strategic planning or content creation. In these instances, it is best to rely on human expertise.

AI is not suitable when the cost of errors is exceedingly high and cannot be reduced to an acceptable level through AI's learning curve. In life-critical systems such as medical procedures or air traffic control, where human lives are at stake, the risk associated with AI-driven decisions may be too great.

Additionally, if the data used to train AI systems is not available, poor quality, or biased, AI can amplify these issues, leading to unreliable or unfair outcomes. It's essential to have robust, clean, and representative datasets for AI to function effectively. In the absence of such data, deploying AI can be more harmful than beneficial.

"The way that I think about looking for places where you can use general AI in a transformative way is think about it as additive. In 20, or 50, years when people are writing the story of AI, it's not going to be about its intended or substitutive applications. It's going to be the additive applications: the work that we aren't doing now because it's not economic."

—*Dr Mark Kennedy, Imperial College London*[3]

There are some quick wins in a range of areas such as customer care, marketing and communications, and HR, which will be discussed later.

Ultimately though, I go back to my show of hands at every one of my keynotes for the past 12 months. Almost everyone has tried AI tools such as ChatGPT, but few are using them in their everyday work.

Identifying opportunities for AI in your business should start with areas where intelligence and efficiency can be amplified. I like using the phrase "scale and speed" to categorise what it is that AI can do over a human. The first step is to assess tasks that are repetitive and time-consuming, which can often be automated to free up human talent for more complex work. Another area to investigate is bottlenecks and inefficiencies in your current processes.

Where Can AI Provide the Most Benefit?

- If your business generates large amounts of data, AI can provide insights and trends that would be impossible for humans to discern within a practical timeframe.

- AI can be used to optimise workflows, predict maintenance needs, and streamline operations.

- In customer service, AI chatbots can improve response times and personalise communication.

- Sales and marketing can benefit from AI's ability to predict customer behaviour, enabling tailored recommendations and dynamic pricing.

All of these use cases are predicated by having access to quality data.

AI innovation company Appen specialises in the development of human-annotated datasets for machine learning and AI, and they also have an emphasis on data quality.[4] The company highlights that the success of AI models relies heavily on the accuracy, relevance, and comprehensiveness of the training data.

"The success of your AI project depends on the quality of your data"[5]

Analysing the quality of data could be the subject of an entire book. A good place to start is asking yourself these questions:

- Do you have enough data?

- Is there data containing the information you need, even if disguised or buried?

- Is it ethical and safe to use the data?

- Do you have the right sort of data for the AI model to learn from, and do you have someone who can analyse this data to make that determination?

- Is your data accurate and consistent? If not, what cleansing processes would you need to put in place?

- Is your data complete? If it's not, how can you fill in the gaps?

- Is the task large-scale and repetitive enough that a human would struggle to carry it out?

- Would it provide information a team could use to achieve outcomes in the real world?

While these questions are not exhaustive, they should be a good start to rule in or out an AI project, and give you a way to challenge your management team as to your state of AI readiness.

Product and service innovation is another opportunity, and AI can help develop new products or services by analysing market data, customer feedback, and current trends. It can simulate and model outcomes, reducing the risk and cost of development at faster scale and speed than humans, leaving your teams to apply critical thinking to the results generated by AI.

You will also need to consider the ethical, legal, and risk implications, and ensure that AI applications align with your company's values and regulatory requirements.

"Have you involved your risk and legal teams?"

This is a question that I pose to all of my audiences. As governments introduce AI regulations, expect to have to be able to report on how your AI model performs with variables such as transparency, privacy, and fairness. Italy, in particular, has made the news multiple times over its concerns as to whether ChatGPT is compliant with GDPR and safe to use.[6] Similarly, ChatGPT has been sued over concerns as to whether its training data has used copyrighted content illegally.[7]

It might be a worthwhile exercise to engage an AI regulatory expert to brief your legal teams as to what changes with AI.

The following are some of the new terms you are likely to encounter in any new AI project.

- *Explainability*

  Explainability is driven by processes and methods that allow human users to comprehend and trust the results and output created by machine learning algorithms. Explainable AI is used to describe an AI model, its expected impact and potential biases, and answer the question: Are my AI models making the right decisions once set to work?

- *Observability*

  AI observability is the collection of statistics, performance data, and metrics from every part of a machine learning system. This answers the question: Can you monitor the cause and effect of the models, and are the models trained and tested on relevant, accurate, and generalisable datasets?

- *Fairness*

  Is the AI system deployed by users trained to implement them responsibly and without bias?

Conscious Bias

Everyone looks at a problem or situation with conscious bias. When I stand on stage to present, I know everyone will have a view on the way I stand, the clothes I am wearing, and my Australian–British accent. Our own personal views and biases around social issues, religion, politics, and gender will find their way into the way we train AI systems because we are choosing the data that algorithms use, and also deciding how the results of those algorithms will be applied.

This means you need to be careful about the source of the data used to train the AI you are using. Take an AI trained to recognise and read human expressions or emotions. If it is not properly trained on an inclusive dataset, then it might cause issues. Imagine that it encounters a type of face, with a skin colour and size or shape of eye that it was not trained to look at or recognise. It could give a false response.

This could cause huge issues that might even carry legal consequences. This is just one example to demonstrate why the data needs to be carefully monitored.

"AI companies, where someone like us, or ChatGPT, or anyone creating their own proprietary models, now need to have a Trust and Safety Department within the organisation. Their core job should be to find undesirable data that's inadvertently entering the model and take it out as soon as it's found, or cited, so that the bias is controlled."
— *Umesh Sachdev, CEO, Uniphore*[8]

The Danger of a Biased AI

A famous early example of the wrong data training an AI in the wrong direction was Google's image recognition system.[9] In 2015, a group of young, white, male programmers of Western European descent aged between 28 and 32 in Silicon Valley trained their image analysis system

(continued)

(*continued*)

on a dataset full of people who looked like them. Understandably, they didn't see the issue at the time. Their unconscious bias meant they didn't notice that most of the images were 30-year-old white men.

When the AI was deployed, it was terrible at recognising the differences between images that weren't of the programmer's demographic. This meant it was awful with images of women or other ethnicities. One of the worst examples, which ended up getting the biggest headlines, was when it would routinely confuse people of African descent with gorillas.

This was a big embarrassment for Google, who have since fixed the problem. It is also a very fitting example of why having a diverse work-force designing these AI platforms is vital, to ensure they can catch each other's biases and have diverse data.

One issue that I reinforce in my talks on the responsible use of AI is the need to employ diversity when recruiting people onto AI projects where humans are used to select, train, and review AI data.

Before OpenAI released ChatGPT 3.5, they employed Reinforcement Learning from Human Feedback (RLHF). This meant they had to employ human AI trainers who provided sample data by acting out both sides of a conversation between a human user and an AI assistant.[10]

A whitepaper from OpenAI that dives deeper into the training methods explained:[11]

> ". . . we hired a team of about 40 contractors on Upwork and through ScaleAI. Compared to earlier work that collects human preference data on the task of summarization . . . our inputs span a much broader range of tasks, and can occasionally include controversial and sensitive topics. Our aim was to select a group of labelers who were sensitive to the preferences of different demographic groups, and who were good at identifying outputs that were potentially harmful."

This is one way that OpenAI sought to reduce the impacts from conscious bias, by exposing controversial and sensitive topics to a small group of humans that had been sourced from diverse backgrounds.

Starting Small with AI Projects: Pilot Projects, Proofs of Concept, MVP

So, you've answered the questions in the previous segment with "Yes, we're ready for an AI project" – what do you do next?

My strong advice is to look at developing a pilot, prototype, or Minimum Viable Product (MVP) to test your project's viability before investing too much time and resource into a project that is not yet AI ready.

> "When these enterprises adopt any new technology, not just AI, they first start with a small proof of concept, which becomes a pilot. Then a different department is added to the pilot and the cycle continues. By the time a technology is heading to scales of 50–60,000 users, that means the technology is delivering proven return on investment and delivering on business outcomes."
>
> —*Umesh Sachdev, CEO, Uniphore*[12]

The Importance of Change Management when Implementing an AI Prototype or Hackathon

Running an AI prototype project or hackathon represents a substantial change from routine operations, involving a significant shift towards innovation and experimentation. Change management will play a crucial role in these initiatives, ensuring that the transition is smooth, the participants are fully engaged, and the outcomes are effectively integrated into the organisation's strategic vision.

Here are some things to consider in relation to people and organisational management when running a short-term AI project.

- *Enhancing participant engagement and collaboration*: It's essential to prepare participants for a shift in mindset from everyday tasks to innovative thinking. Encourage a culture of collaboration and creativity. Teamwork and open communication are key to generating innovative solutions.

- *Aligning objectives with organisational goals*: This alignment is critical for securing support from senior management and ensuring that the outcomes of these initiatives contribute to the strategic objectives of the company. Alignment also makes it easier to integrate new AI-driven innovations into existing processes and workflows.

- *Managing resistance and fostering a culture of innovation*: Resistance to change is a natural human response. In the context of AI prototypes and hackathons, it can manifest as scepticism towards new technologies or reluctance to adopt new working methods. The key to removing resistance is communicating the value and potential of AI innovations. Highlight successful case studies and provide training and support to your teams to get them onboard.

- *Ensuring sustainability and continuous improvement*: Think about the continuous improvement and integration of AI innovations into your organisational ecosystem. Use structured feedback loops, post-hackathon reviews, and ongoing support to maintain momentum.

Here are some actionable tips for initiating pilot projects and proofs of concept.

- *Define clear objectives*: Start with a specific, well-defined problem that you want AI to solve. The goals should be measurable and achievable within the scope of a small project.

- *Select the right use case*: Choose a use case that has the potential for high impact but is contained enough for a pilot. It should be a task that is representative of broader business processes to ensure the learnings are scalable. Think about quick wins in customer care, such as using GenAI to review customer calls and better understand key themes, or using it in writing and refining website copy.

- *Gather quality data*: Ensure you have access to quality data that is necessary for training your AI models. The success of the pilot often hinges on the data quality and availability. You will also need a data/business analyst that not only understands the data, but the business benefits of that data, once processed by AI.

- *Choose the right tools and platforms*: Utilise user-friendly AI platforms that require minimal setup. This allows for quicker deployment and testing without extensive upfront investment in tools and infrastructure.

- *Build a cross-functional team*: Involve stakeholders from different parts of the business to provide diverse perspectives and ensure the solution meets a range of needs.

- *Start with off-the-shelf solutions*: Consider using pre-built AI models or services to accelerate development. Custom solutions can come later, based on the outcomes of the pilot.

- *Set realistic expectations*: Understand that AI projects often require iteration. Manage expectations around immediate results and be prepared for a learning curve.

- *Monitor and measure*: Establish Key Performance Indicators (KPIs) to measure the success of the AI pilot against your objectives.

- *Scale gradually*: Use the pilot project to understand the challenges of integrating AI into your operations. Scaling up should be gradual, based on the insights and learnings from the initial project.

- *Document everything*: Keep detailed records of your methodology, challenges, results, and lessons learned. This documentation will be invaluable for scaling your AI efforts. Share this using your internal collaboration tools so the rest of the organisation can share in the learnings, and provide ideas and insights.

- *Ethical considerations*: Ensure that your AI pilot adheres to ethical guidelines and does not inadvertently promote bias or discrimination. Involve your legal, HR, and risk teams early on so they can advise on these issues, and also learn about how AI tools will impact your business.

Designing the Product

"Just because you can do something using a technology doesn't mean you should. You need to figure out why you want to do these things and what you're going to do: figure out where it's going to have the best impact, whether it's a commercial impact, customer engagement one, or loyalty one.

What we have seen over the last year or so is lots of experimentation, not very much stuff going into production. There's a scramble around which tools to use and the use cases, but without a solid business case behind the project."

—*Darshan Chandarana, PwC*[13]

Intelligent Implementation

Speaking with Julia Howes from PwC, she pointed out that getting employees on board and adopting the technology is important to get value from the project. Their interest is going to naturally rise and fall, and that might not happen at the same time for everyone.

"It's about not thinking that everyone in a certain function or a certain role that's organisational-based is going to be the same. You need to get to the individual and their own mindsets, their own history, their own background that they bring to AI, because it's a very personal change."

—*Julia Howes, PwC*

The key is to invest in the enablers – those people who might already be digitally curious and aware of the capabilities of GenAI or have experimented with it themselves. By encouraging such people across the organisation to experiment and play with any tools, they will naturally discover the use cases that might be most valuable to investigate and implement, and help socialise the opportunities of AI throughout the organisation.

If you then make this accessible to everyone, they can discover how it can apply to themselves. As Julia says: "We're seeing better success in organisations where they look at a use case and an application, for example in a function like HR. But then they start thinking about how else it could be applied and are able to apply it across the business."

Isabel Perry from Marketing Agency DEPT told me on the podcast:

"I would strongly recommend finding a partner or someone to work with mapping out one of your common workflows. For example, within DEPT, we create a lot of content. We've done a number of workshops, where we've mapped out everything from taking a brief from a client to cost estimates to come up with creative ideas, creating content, pushing that to paid media platforms and understanding which parts of that process are the most repetitive and have datasets. Then it's important to spend time with people that are actually able to automate some of that. You should also be curious within your own domain, because that's what you're an expert in."

— *Isabel Perry, VP Emerging Technology, DEPT*[14]

Curious Five

These steps are helpful for staying digitally curious when applying AI in your workplace.

1. Data – analyse what data you already have that would be suitable for an AI project. Use the questions in this chapter to query your teams about what data you have/need/would like.

2. Diversity – look at ways to staff an AI project with a diverse range of thinking and views to avoid unconscious bias.

3. Look at the areas of the business that could benefit from AI – initially as a prototype or MVP. Identify the person or team you need to approach for funding.

4. Review current and planned AI regulations with your legal and risk teams.

5. Consider a hackathon to select AI projects for your division or group.

CHAPTER 5
TOOLS TO GET YOU STARTED WITH AI

Now you've read some of the case studies and understood the right approach to AI in the enterprise, what tools should you be investigating and using on a daily basis? What tools are right for the broader business and your own personal use? And what tools should be considered for specific industries?

The list below is not exhaustive. Some are free to use, some offer a paid trial, some require an initial subscription, and some can be enabled by your IT department. I've provided a more extensive list in the resources section at the end of this book.

The issue for any manager reading this book is that your teams also have access to these tools with just a few clicks and a credit card. The research house Forrester predicted that up to 60% of staff will use personal AI tools to perform job tasks, introducing the concept of Bring Your Own AI (BYOAI).[1] This will open a flood of compliance, security, and personal data issues unless managed carefully.

Security and Data Risks

Protecting your data is vital in an enterprise environment. This means that you will have countless protocols and measures in place to make sure that private data stays private. In some fields and industries, you might even have official standards and regulations that you need to be compliant with.

Personal AI tools may not have been designed with these specific protocols and regulations in mind. Inputting data into a third-party AI tool could potentially lead to a data breach as you do not know if your data is being stored on external servers or used in ways that violate privacy policies or regulations.

While there is a "data controls" option within the consumer ChatGPT interface to restrict your data being used to train the model, this is not immediately visible, and the setting does not work across browsers or apps.[2] At the time of writing, the Enterprise version of ChatGPT provides much more control on the use of enterprise data.

Ethical and Legal Issues

In Chapter 4, I talked about the need to get your legal team onboard and aware of the risks in the tools used within the enterprise. This also goes for BYOAI tools.

If there is no standardised or official stance towards AI tools used within the enterprise, there could be legal repercussions. Using tools which are not completely fair and transparent means that there is a risk that the content produced might be biased or inaccurate, harming the reputation of the company as a result.

Additionally, using external AI tools for creating and modifying work products can raise questions about the ownership of the Intellectual Property (IP) or copyright. This could end up causing issues around whether the IP belongs to the company, the employee, or the AI tool's provider.

In fact, in early 2023, the US copyright office revoked the copyright for a comic with illustrations generated in Midjourney as they had no human author. They ruled that the artist's right to the comic was negated as they had not declared this use of AI. Instead, the artist could only claim the text and story as their IP.[3]

Quality and Reliability Concerns

Finally, if every employee is using their own preferred AI tools, this leads to a lack of standardisation across the company. As the quality of a given AI depends heavily on the specific tool used and how well the user prompts it, this can lead to huge differences in the results that are being produced.

This can result in difficulties in collaboration across the company and managing teams. It can also hurt business operations and client satisfaction.

My view is that you need to ensure the AI enablers are there to reduce the risk of BYOAI. You should also make sure that you have identified the tools and systems which best fit your enterprise's needs. Once you've done so, you need to ensure that everyone has the training and access they need to use the tool in a consistent way across the company. Imagine asking people to buy their own copy of Microsoft Office and work out how to use it to do their job.

An up-to-date list of these tools and more can be found at curious.click/tools.

GenAI Enablers

The following are some examples of GenAI enablers that I personally use – and that you have likely heard of. There is a more extensive list of tools that I recommend exploring in the Resources section at the end of this book.

ChatGPT Plus

The one everyone talks about. At the time of writing, $20/month gets you access to the latest GPT model (currently GPT-4o), as well as access to image generator DALL-E and an interface that can access the open web. I subscribe to this tool and use it daily. It has also been used to create the Digitally Curious GPT to allow you to continue your curiosity while you're reading the book.

https://curious.click/gpt

You can still use the features of ChatGPT-4o for free, but my experience is that if you're paying a monthly subscription, you're more likely to be more curious and use it on a regular basis.

Microsoft Co-Pilot

This is built into the Microsoft 365 product family, available for an additional fee, and also as a stand-alone web-based tool. When used inside Word, PowerPoint, Teams, or Outlook, it is a pervasive GPT prompt that can be used to complete tasks within the app.

https://curious.click/copilot

Grammarly

This is a grammar and syntax tool. I've been a subscriber since 2016. It's a "must-have" tool in my eyes. I use it across everything on my PC, and have used it extensively for this book to ensure I'm using the best grammar, and my spelling and syntax is correct.

https://curious.click/grammarly

Otter.ai

I've been using this tool since 2020. It is my other "must-have" tool. Not only does it do a brilliant job of transcribing and summarising meetings, but with Otter.ai chat you can interrogate the transcript to provide deeper insights. It's just like ChatGPT, but from within the app.

I have used Otter.ai extensively to transcribe all of the podcast recordings, summarise the discussions, and extract insights from the episodes – and this has made its way into the book.

Exercising Otter.ai further, the true power emerges. You can summarise long meetings and have it provide you with action items, and look at who contributed most/least to the meeting or discussion. It provides a permanent corpus of information that can then be interrogated using ChatGPT-type prompts for later analysis.

The link here will provide you with a 1-month free trial of the tool.

https://curious.click/otter

If you don't see a tool here or in the Resources section that meets your needs, then look at what you use on a regular basis, and dig deeper to see if it already has an AI feature. For example, LinkedIn now has a "rewrite using AI" button in the box when you're writing a new post.

This chapter is really what being digitally curious is all about – trying out a new tool or platform and seeing how it can work for you and your business.

With so many AI tools in the market, take some time to explore which ones are really useful and which ones you could work into your daily routine. Jump to the Resources section at the end of this book for more tools to try.

For me, ChatGPT Plus, Grammarly, and Otter.ai are the three tools that I use every day.

Curious Five

What can you do to stay digitally curious about the world of AI?

1. Contact your IT department to understand what tools are available for enterprise use, what the policies are on BYOAI and what the policy is for assessing and introducing new tools.

2. If you're not regularly using any of these tools, sign up for ChatGPT and start using it as your "always-on intern" for a week and see if you start using it more often as a result.

3. Try some of the industry-focussed tools such as Jasper.ai for marketing, Otter.ai for meeting notes, and Grammarly for writing.

4. Ask your close friends and colleagues which AI tools they are using and how they are using them.

5. Review the more extensive list of AI tools in the resources section at the end of this book and commit to trying five new tools – one per week over the next 5 weeks.

PART II
CURIOUS ABOUT ...
TECHNOLOGY

Why Am I Curious About Technology?

Having grown up in a very technically focused household, and played with technology from an early age, I've had a curious streak since childhood. As I explained in the Introduction, my early experimentation with electronic circuits, programming personal computers such as the ZX80, and dialling up bulletin boards over 40 years ago have instilled in me a permanent curiosity about all things technical. It is fair to say that my training as an engineer has prompted me to always want to know more and ask the question: "How does this work?"

Around age 13, I remember being on holiday at the seaside town of Aldinga, 45 km south of my hometown of Adelaide. I was with friends when I found an old black-and-white television that did not work. I wanted to take it apart to see if I could bring it back to life.

When I was around 22 years old, I had a part-time job with Motorola Communications while studying; my job was to repair broken two-way radios. I had to learn very quickly how to use all the diagnostic equipment to perform the right checks to fix these broken devices. I even built my own Motorola professional walkie talkie from second-hand parts.

This deep level of curiosity about technology has continued to the present day. As I write this chapter at Château Santa Anna in Saint-Jean-de-Luz, France,

I've just installed a Wi-Fi network for my friends that covers the whole property – something they had been struggling to achieve for some time.

When I arrived, I surveyed the surroundings and set to work designing and deploying an enterprise-grade network using UniFi equipment.[1] I currently remotely manage nine other Wi-Fi networks for friends, family, and a local church. I do this at no charge, as I'm interested in how to manage these networks remotely. I want to become comfortable with this commercial-grade equipment, all of which is managed through network software hosted "in the cloud". This is something I also learned to set up and manage by reading widely and watching YouTube videos. I first became aware of the UniFi product range back in 2017 on a trip to the US. I was in my favourite camera and gadget shop, B&H Photo on 9th Avenue in New York, and I came across an entirely new type of Wi-Fi setup. Googling more, I discovered security researcher Troy Hunt's blog entitled "How I fixed my dodgy WiFi"[2] and this encouraged me to investigate further and buy some devices to test.

You may be thinking by now that your author is quite the hands-on Futurist, and this is something that you would never be comfortable doing. I don't expect many of my readers to have experienced what I have, but if we step back from the deep technical side, let's think about how various technologies have transformed the way in which we work and live.

As technology is such a broad topic, in this section we will focus on 5G mobile services, voice, cloud computing, and the Internet of Things (IoT).

Why Should You Be Curious About Technology?

While I would classify myself as "extremely curious" about technology, not just as a result of my training and experience, I also like to step into the shoes of the ordinary consumer and ask myself the question: "How does this device improve my life?"

Back in 1994, I was the first of my friends to own a mobile phone. At the time, this was quite a novelty. Mobiles were considered a business tool and something that executives used, not a gadget for a poorly paid student.

As my friends found it much easier to contact me, they too realised that having a mobile phone was useful. As the technology improved, and prices came down, most of my friends purchased a mobile phone and the network effect came into play. Each of us was discovering first-hand how first-generation (1G) mobile telephony could change our lives.

Mobile technology improved and by the third generation (3G), we were able to experience reasonably fast internet connections on our devices. This further enhanced the utility of our phones, as we found more ways to use them in our daily lives and for work.

The mobile phone is probably the most used piece of technology we own. We have it on our person most of the day, so we know first-hand how useful it is, and probably are aware of most of its functions.

I've worked at Australia's two largest telecommunications companies, Telstra and Optus, in the very early days of 1G mobile phones, and have worked with every "G" since, right up to 5G. I'm constantly curious about what's coming next.

You should be too. We've already seen mobile phones transform our lives – aren't you curious to see how this technology develops in the future? Of course, mobile phones are not the only pieces of technology we should be curious about.

Since the first time I used a voice synthesiser on my Commodore 64 to translate text into speech, I've been fascinated by the power of voice. Fast forward to the era of Siri and other voice assistants such as Alexa, and as you'll know most consumers are comfortable speaking to their home appliances. My curiosity with voice has always centred on what is coming next. In the podcast episode with voice expert James Poulter, he made me even more curious by talking about "ambient listening", which we will cover in Chapter 7.

Cloud computing is another area that I've been curious about for some time. I remember the first cloud "instance" that I "spun up" on the Amazon Web Services (AWS) platform many years ago. Back then, and even today, Amazon provide anyone with 12 months of "free tier" basic cloud computing access[3] to try out their services. My first cloud project was a simple Virtual Private Network (VPN). Once I saw how easy it was to create and deploy an application "on cloud" I realised that this was a technology I should investigate further, and today I run a number of services "in the cloud" from my website, to applications that control the Wi-Fi networks mentioned earlier.

My own examples above range from simple Wi-Fi and mobile telephony, to voice and cloud services. These are technologies that you use every day at home and at work, perhaps without even giving them a thought, because they (mostly) work as expected. If you delve deeper, however, you will gain a much better insight into how these technologies work, and the benefits and issues that you may face in the future as you deploy them in your business and personal life.

My example of using a free AWS service could be a good starting point to better understand how dynamic and scalable technology can improve your business and lower your costs. Voice is another area that is easy to investigate and try out new and emerging services, especially when coupled with GenAI. If you've made it this far in the book and started putting into action the Curious Five at the end of each chapter, you're well on the way to being more digitally curious.

CHAPTER 6
THE PROMISE OF 5G

The GSM mobile standard dates back to 1987 when representatives from 13 European countries sat around a table in Copenhagen and signed the Groupe Spécial Mobile memorandum of understanding. This committed them to working together to create and deploy a digital mobile phone system across Europe. They hoped for 20 million users by the end of the century; by the time 2000 arrived, they had a quarter of a billion.

5G refers to the fifth generation of the European Global System for Mobiles (GSM) standard. According to leading consumer research agency GWI, 40% of people in the UK said they had 5G available on their phones.[1] Still, one in four say they have a poor or very poor understanding of 5G, according to a Vodafone UK report from June 2023.[2] That means millions of people are unaware of the additional, true benefits that 5G and the next phase of 5G will bring.

I've been associated with mobile technologies since before 1G, let alone 5G. Back in Australia in the late 1980s I worked for Telstra, the country's leading telecommunications company. They launched the first automated mobile service in the mid-1980s. The technology consisted of "car phones", where there was a fixed handset with a large box containing the radio transmitter in the boot.

Interestingly, these first mobile services had the dialling prefix "007", presumably because those using it would truly feel like they were James Bond.

In 1987, Telstra launched a more sophisticated mobile service using a technology called AMPS (Analogue Mobile Phone Service). This is what we would now call 1G. In the late 1990s, when I worked for Telstra's main rival in Australia – Optus, the first GSM networks were introduced.

This second generation, or 2G, network was based on the European GSM standard, which we now take for granted when we travel to a different country, switch on our phones, and it just works. It allowed voice messaging and short messaging (SMS) services between mobile users. You may not know that the humble SMS message started as a way for network engineers to send short messages, up to 160 characters, to each other. It was never designed for consumers to use for messaging.

It was 2.5G that introduced us to the very first version of the internet on our phones, using Wireless Application Protocol (WAP). But it was not until 3G and the launch of the first iPhone in 2007 that we started to understand how a mobile device could help run, and dictate, our lives by being constantly connected to the internet.

In 2003, in the UK and other countries, networks launched 3G services marketed as enabling new mobile applications such as video calling, mobile internet browsing, and mobile TV. My own experience was that the true use case for 3G was mobile internet, and I cannot recall making more than one very poor video call. I don't think I ever watched a TV show on a mobile back in the mid-2000s.

Like all mobile services, telecommunications companies need to justify the enormous expenditure on erecting towers across cities and towns and the cost of the "spectrum" – which is essentially a licence to use the very precious resource of radio airwaves. The brilliance of the GSM standard developed by the European Telecommunications Standards Institute (ETSI) in 1997 meant that it could use different radio frequencies available in a particular country.

Over the years, the switch to digital TV transmissions has made more spectrum available, clearing frequencies in the 700 MHz range, for example.

The Rise of 4G

The next generation of mobile networks was labelled 4G. They were designed with a focus on speed, providing the capability to launch new services thanks to the higher speeds. The first 4G network in the UK was launched in November 2012 by a new company called "Everything Everywhere", a joint venture between France Telecom's Orange and Deutsche Telekom's T-Mobile. The company is now called EE and became part of the British Telecom Group on 29 January 2016.

I had first-hand experience of the launch as I tried to become one of their first 4G customers. However, two incorrect SIM cards and a flurry of misdirected Tweets later, I found myself with a viral blog post with over 10,000 views, an article in the *Telegraph* newspaper, and a couple of meetings with senior people at EE.

The whole experience at the time was a lesson on how not to launch a brand new 4G network. Due to favourable licensing conditions, EE had a nearly 18-month head start on their rivals, so the network was launched very quickly to take advantage of this.

With the introduction of 5G, more bandwidth and, therefore, more radio frequency spectrum is required. The law of physics states that the higher the frequency, the more available bandwidth there is, hence the opportunity for faster speeds.

5G phones must operate in the "millimetre wave" bands between 24 and 40 GHz to deliver on the promise of fibre-like speeds. This will only be possible with very closely spaced mobile cell towers due to the very short range of these frequencies. In the US, mobile operators such as T-Mobile and Verizon are rushing to install millimetre wave technologies in football stadiums.

One of the challenges for 5G is clearing the spectrum needed for these faster services, as many of the required frequencies are already used by TV networks, governments, and the military.

This came to light in January 2022 when 5G services launched in 46 markets in the US, using frequencies in a radio spectrum called the "C-band". These frequencies can be close to those used by radio altimeters, an essential piece of safety equipment in aircraft.

To ensure this did not lead to hazardous interference, the Federal Aviation Authority (FAA) required that radio altimeters be upgraded.[3] On the day 5G C-band services were launched, hundreds of flights were cancelled, and this was resolved by introducing temporary restrictions on the operation of 5G transmitters near 50 major airports.

So, if 4G Promised Us "Broadband-Like" Speeds, is 5G Just Faster Than 4G?

Well, yes and no. The first 5G networks were built on top of the existing 4G networks, so they had to share existing infrastructure. These networks are known in the industry as Non-Standalone (NSA).

The true promise of 5G networks has always been faster speeds, massive amounts of simultaneous connections on the same base station, and a range of new services, but these can't be realised on 5G NSA networks. Instead, the next evolution of 5G networks is called Stand Alone (5G SA).

I've been working with leading mobile operator Vodafone in the UK to understand better how a range of industries might benefit from the power of "true 5G" or 5G SA.[4] Because 5G SA networks have their own infrastructure, the benefits include faster speeds, increased battery life, many more individual connections at the same time, and the ability to "slice" or reserve part of the network for specific applications such as gaming or broadcast-quality TV.

While 5G networks have been used for live news gathering for some time, they must compete for bandwidth used by mobile customers. Mobile connectivity is a challenge at a significant public event like a coronation or sporting match because of the number of users trying to compete for the same network connectivity.

In the example of live TV pictures, a "network slice" can be set to guarantee a minimum upload speed threshold so that high-definition TV content is uploaded quickly and reliably for live streaming. It also removes the risk of network congestion impacting the performance of the broadcast.

As media organisations increasingly rely on mobile networks for outside broadcasts, achieving predictable network performance has become essential. Network slicing using 5G SA gives broadcasters their private mobile network for video transmission with no extra heavy-duty equipment, planning, back-office, or spectrum licensing needed, and it can be accessed via a SIM card.

Network slicing is one way of creating a private mobile network on a public network, and the next phase of 5G also opens the possibility for a fully private 5G network to be created.

What's the Business Benefit of 5G? Why Introduce Private 5G?

Private 5G is a self-contained 5G network deployed within the boundaries of an enterprise, such as within a factory, campus, or venue. The key benefits of private 5G networks include:

- A dedicated licensed spectrum is allocated directly to the enterprise for its exclusive use, providing more control and security than a public network.

- Customisation of the network design and configuration to precisely meet the needs of the enterprise use cases and coverage requirements.

- Ultra-low-latency connectivity suitable for mission-critical industrial applications requiring real-time decision-making.

- The enterprise controls device provisioning for faster activation and more robust access controls compared to public networks.

- Prioritisation of security, reliability, and control over raw speed, making it well suited to industrial and critical infrastructure settings with sensitive data and operations.

I spoke to Shahid Ahmed from NTT on the podcast about the typical use cases for 5G.[5]

Some key use cases for private 5G networks include:

- Connecting Internet of Things (IoT)/Operational Technology (OT) devices in industrial settings like factories, mines, and ports. This includes machine vision cameras, conveyor belts, forklifts, and other equipment.

- Enabling augmented/virtual reality applications for remote assistance, equipment training, and digital twin simulations.

- Providing high-speed connectivity for mission-critical applications that require ultra-low latency, such as real-time analytics and automated decision making.

- Supporting secure communications for applications like push-to-talk radios for workers at airports, stadiums, and campuses.

- Facilitating smart city/port applications involving large numbers of connected devices like autonomous vehicles, environmental sensors, and infrastructure monitoring equipment.

- Powering private networks for venues like hospitals and enterprise campuses that need dedicated wireless connectivity within a controlled environment.

I spoke with Paul Scanlan, former CTO of Huawei, about what he saw as the benefits of 5G.[6] He sees some of the most exciting things about 5G technology as its potential to transform entire industries and drive innovation through new applications that were not previously possible in manufacturing, healthcare, transportation, and more.

The mass connectivity it enables between people and billions of devices through the IoT, which we'll discuss in Chapter 9, could create entirely new connected systems and open up new possibilities. Its low latency will be crucial for applications like autonomous vehicles, remote robotics, telemedicine, and others requiring real-time feedback.

Another benefit is 5G's significantly enhanced security features compared to 4G, which help address important privacy and data concerns about connected systems.

Finally, 5G systems benefit from improved energy efficiency, which could help reduce carbon emissions from wireless networks over time as deployment increases.

The Rise of Connected Clothing with 5G

Today, technology is increasingly used to influence how we dress and feel. However, smartwatches and fitness trackers mostly rely on the owner's mobile to be nearby to work effectively. What if everything we were wearing could measure our wellbeing, connect to other garments, provide a richer experience, and even suggest what we should wear?

With 5G SA, people can unlock the ability for the products they buy and wear to influence their style and wellbeing far beyond what is possible with today's wearables.

According to Sofia Remtulla, former Accenture retail strategy lead, a futuristic use of 5G SA in retail will be product-to-product communication, where we may see trainers talking to each other as their wearers pass in the street. Informed by the data they collect, they would then suggest which outfit to buy based on the preferences of people like them, creating brand new shopping experiences.[7]

This would also create your own personal style guide. The data collected by your clothing would tell you "what goes with what" based on what other people wear. Ultimately, thanks to connected clothing, the fashion faux pas could become a thing of the past.

However, this will only be possible with a 5G SA network, thanks to its ability to connect large numbers of devices simultaneously. While we've been using wearables such as fitness trackers to monitor our physical health and emotional wellbeing for many years, we've yet to fully leverage the social potential of wearables. With 5G SA, a wearable could help connect you with people with similar interests and styles.

Ann-Marie Tomchak, former Digital Director for British *Vogue*, thinks that we could see a time when wearable devices become a part of us and influence how we dress – whether that's helping you identify what's in your wardrobe to suit your mood or having an AI-powered personal stylist suggest what to wear and what to buy based on the data collected from your connected clothing.

In other words, personalised products "at the edge" of the network, powered by always-on 5G chips.

The existence of connected clothing could even enable us to create personalised items on demand. For example, L'Oréal-owned NYX has been testing the ability to use an app to match the colour of a garment and then enable the consumer to "print" a lipstick to match, thanks to 3D printing and AI technologies "at the edge" – that is, closer to the consumer.[8]

This can be produced on demand and adapted to seasons, moods, and styles without buying a new lipstick. Inspiration can happen anywhere. 5G SA will allow consumers to create the look that transforms them in the moment and on the go, and have it printed for them before they get home.

Frictionless Shopping Becomes the Norm

Uniqlo has pioneered using RFID tags for self-checkout, where you place all your items in a basket at the till and they're instantly scanned. Similarly, Amazon Go stores have shown frictionless shopping in action. As you walk out of the store, sensors recognise the items you've bought and charge your bank account – meaning you never have to queue. After experiencing seamless shopping at places like Uniqlo and Amazon Go, shoppers increasingly demand this experience.

However, a recent report in the *Guardian*[9] suggested that the Amazon experience relied more on humans than AI, proving how difficult it is to implement technology in a retail environment with multiple variables.

Because 5G SA allows millions of devices to be connected at once and can power 5G RFID tags that track the movement of items in a shop, it will be the trigger for making frictionless shopping a reality.

Increasingly, retailers will need to focus on the experience. Ann-Marie Tomchak believes that "the purpose of a store is no longer just to be the place where point of sale happens; it's about the experience".[10]

Curious Five

Here are five activities to help you better understand the opportunities for 5G.

1. Are you even aware you have 5G available on your phone? When not connected to Wi-Fi, try this speed test https://curious.click/speed to see what upload and download speeds your phone is capable of. Compare this with a friend's phone.

2. When next passing the retail store of your phone operator, pop in and ask them about their range of 5G phones, and plans for 5G rollout in your area. Ask them what speeds you should expect on your 5G phone.

3. Consider how a private 5G network might enhance your business operations.

4. Beyond faster speeds, think about how the other 5G benefits might improve the way you serve your customers now and in the future.

5. If you are on a 4G-enabled phone and are eligible to upgrade to a 5G phone, consider doing this so that you are using the latest mobile technologies.

CHAPTER 7
LET'S TALK – THE POWER OF VOICE

Voice technology, encompassing a broad spectrum of applications from voice recognition to natural language processing, has significantly transformed our interaction with digital devices and services. Most of us have used a voice tool at some point – Siri on Apple, Google Assistant on Android, or Alexa on an Amazon device.

I experimented with voice synthesis in my teens, using a Commodore 64 computer and playing with very early speech-to-text programs. I remember the very first time that I managed to get my computer to "speak" to me in a very robotic voice. It was exciting to think I could task a computer to mimic human behaviour.

Later, I experimented with voice transcription programs such as Dragon Dictate.[1] The technology at the time was ground-breaking but required the user to extensively "train" the software to recognise their voice. Today's systems – which require no training at all and can recognise a variety of accents, languages, and dialects – are a testament to how far this technology has come over the last 30 years.

The Voice of Apple

Apple's famous voice assistant started as a spin-off from a project developed by the SRI International Artificial Intelligence Centre, and Nuance Communications providing its speech recognition engine. It used advanced machine learning technologies to function.

(continued)

(continued)

I've had the original Australian voice of Siri, Karen Jacobsen – or "Aussie Karen" – join the podcast,[2] and I also met her when she lived in New York. The Siri project pre-dates GenAI, so Karen was hired as a voice actor to recite hundreds of words and phrases that could be combined with the technology of the time.

Karen explained on the podcast how one phone call in 2002 literally changed her life. The caller said they were looking for a native Australian female voiceover artist living in the Northeast US. She auditioned for the role and left the recording booth to be told she had secured the job on the spot.

This particular engagement took her to Ithaca, in upstate New York, for 3 weeks. Here, she was required to read a script that took about 50 hours to record. The Nuance voice engineers had specially designed the script to capture every possible combination of syllables. They then manipulated and edited these voice files to create a voice system based on her speaking voice.

Karen tells the story of a phone-book-sized script that she recorded for a maximum of 4 hours per day so that her voice did not sound fatigued. Twenty years later, the evolution of voice synthesis has come a long way thanks to GenAI.

Voice technologies are well understood by consumers. Most of us have tried Siri, Google Assistant, Alexa, but what else can we do with them in a business sense?

Voice recognition has come a long way and is now more accurate. Today's voice technologies are not limited to simple command-and-control tasks; they can conduct complex conversations, control smart home devices, make recommendations, and even book meeting rooms with "ambient" voice technologies.

The future of voice in the enterprise is likely to involve these "always listening" systems and be powered by conversational AI.

What is Conversational AI?

Conversational AI refers to technologies that enable computers to simulate real-life conversations. This encompasses a suite of AI technologies such as natural language processing (NLP), machine learning (ML), and speech recognition. At the heart of conversational AI is the ability to recognise speech and text, understand intent, decipher different languages, and respond in a way that mimics human conversation.

Conversational AI is used in chatbots, virtual assistants like Siri, Alexa, or Google Assistant, and other customer service automation. These AI systems can handle a wide range of tasks, from answering FAQs to providing real-time help or even engaging in small talk. As technology advances, conversational AI will become more sophisticated, learning from interactions to provide more accurate and helpful responses.

Speech recognition is the first step in any voice-based conversational AI system. Here, spoken language is converted into text that a computer can understand. Advanced speech recognition transcribes words and identifies the speaker's intent and context, which are crucial for the system to provide relevant responses. There are several technologies that make this technology possible:

- *Natural Language Understanding (NLU)*: After the speech is transcribed into text, NLU interprets the meaning of the text. It looks beyond the dictionary definitions of words to grasp the user's intent. This allows the AI to handle a wide variety of spoken queries, commands, and statements.

- *Dialogue management*: This involves managing the flow of the conversation. A system with good dialogue management can handle complex interactions, remember the context of a conversation, manage multiple dialogue turns, and guide the conversation naturally to the desired outcome.

- *Natural Language Generation (NLG)*: For the AI to respond to the user, it must generate human-like speech. NLG is responsible for converting the AI's decision-making process into natural-sounding spoken words.

- *Continuous learning*: Voice-based conversational AI systems often have the ability to learn from each interaction. Machine learning algorithms analyse conversations to improve the system's accuracy, understanding, and responsiveness over time.

James Poulter, co-founder of voice agency Vixen Labs, appeared on an episode of the podcast and explained the concept of ambient voice.[3]

In the context of voice assistants, ambient voice refers to an "always on" tool that is constantly listening to what is being said in a meeting. It is important to note that all meeting participants should be aware that this is occurring. I often see "OtterPilot"[4] as an additional meeting participant on Zoom and Teams calls, there to record and transcribe the meeting. This means that the concept of ambient voice is already here for virtual meetings, so we should prepare for this technology being enabled for purely in-person as well as hybrid meetings.

> "Imagine being in a meeting and being able to say 'Alexa, hey, can you rebook this meeting room this time next Tuesday for the same guests', that's something that we should just be able to do because it's such a programmable thing. We're particularly excited about voice in enterprise use cases – particularly for those of us that work in large corporates or with large corporates. It's something crazy that the average desk worker spends about three hours of their day just retrieving something that they already know exists."
>
> —*James Poulter, CEO, Vixen Labs*

The ability to do that with your voice will be game-changing. Imagine being able to ask a system like Salesforce or Zoho to provide you with data, in the same way you might ask a colleague a quick question. But that's not all.

James sees the future applications of voice in the enterprise being an assistant that is listening ambiently in that space. Because it's been given discreet authority to do so in that moment, it will be able to pick up what's required, then answer and surface that data before you even ask the question. You can then get data points like sales performance, location data of your sales team, or tracking advertising performance in an automated and frictionless way.

Google Duplex

In 2018, researchers at Google released a conversational AI tool named Duplex. I used a video of this tool for some years as an example of how digital agents might emerge and take all of the minutiae of our lives, such as booking a restaurant, away from us.[5]

In one of the videos produced by Google, a woman receives a text from her husband saying that he has secured a sitter for "date night". The woman speaks to her Google Assistant and says: "Hey, Google, book a table for two at El Cocotero on Tuesday at seven."

Google Duplex: "All right, just in case that's not available. Can I try between 7 pm and 8 pm?"

Woman: "Sure."

Google Duplex: "All right. I'll call to book under your name and phone number, and I'll update you in the next 15 minutes. Is that okay?"

The Google Duplex AI system then calls the restaurant, announces that it is an AI tool and asks the restaurant manager to reserve a table for dinner, negotiating with them until a suitable time can be agreed upon. It then confirms the booking with the woman and puts an entry in her diary for dinner.

I've been talking about the opportunity for us to use these digital agents for some time. While the Google Duplex tool provided some of the components needed, the recent development of GenAI systems has brought this closer to becoming a reality.

I would happily pay $1000 a year to have an AI-powered tool connect to all the components of my life and streamline them – perhaps we are not too far away from this.

One of my favourite examples of the power of voice is integrating What-3words with car navigation.

What3words is a proprietary geocode system designed to identify any location on the surface of earth with a resolution of about 3 m.[6] It divides the world into 3 m × 3 m squares and labels them with three words. For example, the front door of 10 Downing Street in London is identified by ///slurs.this.shark.

What3words differs from most location encoding systems in that it uses words rather than strings of numbers or letters, and the algorithm that maps locations to words is their "secret sauce". As these three words can be spoken, it lends this system to a voice interface, so you can ask your car navigation system to direct you to a What3words address.

Voice Recognition Software

Voice recognition technology has also made significant strides in accuracy and efficiency. Since the early days of Dragon Dictate, speech-to-text applications have become more sophisticated, enabling real-time transcription services that are increasingly accurate, even in noisy environments or with accented speech. This improvement is largely due to advances in deep learning and neural network architectures that mimic how human brains process language.

Dragon was developed by Nuance in 1997, a pioneer in voice technologies. In 2022, Microsoft acquired Nuance for $19.7 billion. Ahead of the acquisition being finalised, I spoke with Dr Simon Wallace, Chief Clinical Information Officer at Nuance Communications, and Umang Patel, Chief Clinical Information Officer at Microsoft, about the specific use case of voice and conversational AI in the healthcare sector.[7]

Medicine these days is more complex than ever, and medical professionals rely on accurate and timely clinical documentation. This is important to stay on top of, but is becoming more and more of a chore for clinicians. They often spend around 12 hours per week on paperwork alone.

Voice recognition and conversational AI promises to help with this burden. We speak three times faster than we type. Therefore, using speech recognition to write up admission notes, discharge summaries, or outpatient letters can dramatically cut down on the time clinicians spend on documentation.

Thanks to recent advances in technology, these AI have dramatically improved word recognition and require very little correction. When the right LLM is used, one trained on a comprehensive medical dictionary, a clinician can speak their notes without having to take time adjusting and correcting the output.

The Potential of Conversational AI

Ultimately, speaking and listening is the most fundamental form of human communication. As a result, being able to integrate voice technologies into AI tools and systems unlocks a natural and intuitive way for users to interact with machines. This is where conversational AI comes into its own.

Devices like smartphones, smart speakers, and home automation systems often come equipped with voice-activated assistants (e.g., Amazon's Alexa, Apple's Siri, Google Assistant). Users can issue voice commands to set reminders, play music, or control smart home devices. The conversational AI component of these systems understands the intent behind the user's words and responds accordingly.

Voice technologies powered by conversational AI are making significant impacts in areas like customer service automation, healthcare (e.g., voice-assisted patient care), automotive (voice-activated controls), and many more, by providing more accessible, efficient, and often hands-free ways to interact with technology.

A good example of this is Uniphore. I spoke with their CEO, Umesh Sachdev, for the podcast.[8] He explained how he started the company in 2008 with the goal of building a speech recognition engine that could understand multiple languages, along with associated natural language understanding programs. Over time, this transformed Uniphore into a company focused on conversational AI across voice, video, and text.

Umesh highlighted customer care and contact centres as a key use case for conversational AI. In contact centres, Uniphore's technology acts as a "co-pilot" for agents, understanding customer issues and finding quick answers even before the agent has to put the customer on hold. This improves the customer experience by shortening call times and resolving issues faster. It also improves agent efficiency by automating routine inquiries.

Uniphore has seen large-scale adoption of its conversational AI in contact centres. For example, there are 65,000 agents at one financial services customer and 26,000 agents at a major telecom company using it to enhance customer service interactions.

By understanding customers and automating routine inquiries in real time, conversational AI can significantly improve customer and agent experiences when interacting via phone calls or other communication channels in customer care departments. The technology works on both voice and text, reviewing the transcript of a call and the notes written by the agent at the end of the call.

This solution should negate the need for a customer to wait on hold while the agent "reads the notes" from a previous call, instead presenting them with a summary of the past interactions and a possible resolution as the customer is connected to a particular agent. I, for one, welcome this, as the friction experienced with call centres after frequent calls and speaking to a new person with no history of the issue will likely be removed with solutions such as these.

Despite their advancements, voice technologies face several challenges. Privacy and security concerns top the list, as voice-activated devices often process sensitive personal information. Ensuring the security of this information and gaining user trust is paramount for the continued adoption of voice technology.

The message at the start of a customer service call, which says "your call may be recorded for training and quality purposes", takes on a whole new meaning, as what we say is likely to be transcribed and analysed by an AI system in this scenario.

Another challenge is improved context understanding and emotional intelligence in voice assistants. Current systems can misinterpret user intent or fail to recognise the user's emotional state, leading to unsatisfactory interactions.

A more nuanced understanding of language and user context will help enhance the functionality and usefulness of these voice interfaces.

Curious Five

Try the following to stay digitally curious about voice-enabled devices and systems.

1. If you don't already have a voice-enabled device, purchase one or enable the voice recognition features on your smartphone from Apple's Siri and Google's Assistant.

2. Try out voice transcription services such as Otter.ai, which are also powered by AI. These services allow you to interrogate the transcript and find out who contributed most and least to a meeting.

3. Investigate areas in your company where voice-enabled systems could help your staff and customers, especially when linked to GenAI tools.

4. Look at how voice interfaces could be used in your current workflows, from simple interfaces to meeting summaries and action items.

5. If you run a customer contact centre, consider how conversational AI could improve the overall customer experience.

CHAPTER 8
CLOUD COMPUTING

In 2018, when I started mentioning the concept of becoming digitally curious, I used the example of a typical board meeting where a cloud migration project costing $10M was being considered. I mused that digitally curious board members would ask questions such as:

- Where is the data being stored?

- Who is the provider?

- What is their disaster recovery strategy?

- What type of encryption is used?

- What level of access will we have to the servers?

A less digitally curious board might just look at the price tag and say: "That looks about right." One of the reasons that I wrote this book was to ensure that people making large technology decisions are better informed about what they are being asked to approve. I want them to have a raised level of understanding about technology, or at the very least, the hunger to be more curious and ask better questions.

I currently sit on the Board of a Charity in London. In Australia, I was a member of three different boards, including the Duke of Edinburgh's Award and the Rotary Club of Sydney. Due to my experience, I was (and still am) the most technically skilled person on these boards, but it troubled me that everyone left the technical analysis of proposals to me. My view is that you need two or more digitally curious members on any board to demystify new technologies.

What is Cloud Computing and What Does it Mean for My Business?

I don't blame less digitally curious boards for focusing on the price tag of course. Having the resources and facilities in place to meet your enterprise's computing needs is a complicated job in itself and it can quickly get expensive.

There is a fine line to walk between underinvesting and overinvesting in cloud computing. An organisation needs to have the digital infrastructure and capacity to meet consumer needs and demand. Those who have tried to buy popular items in a Black Friday sale, or tickets to a Taylor Swift concert, will have experienced the frustration of the "server busy" error that happens when a company's digital resources just can't keep up.

This means that for organisations that run their own computing facilities, preparing for a big event would mean buying and installing additional servers, bandwidth, and storage capacity, only to have these lie idle during periods of lower demand. Not only are these idle times wasted investment, but managing servers gets costly. Power, connection, security, cooling, and maintenance is an additional expense for each server.

Cloud computing is a more modern answer to this problem. This model enables users to rent access to computing resources as needed, rather than investing heavily in physical hardware and software. This allows on-demand access to data storage and computing power, without direct or active management by the user. Not only this, but the typical pay-as-you-go model used by cloud providers dramatically reduces expenses compared to running "on-premises" servers.

My first experience with cloud-like services was in 2000 when I worked for Telstra in Sydney. They were developing a range of products that would allow customers to "rent" time and space on Telstra-owned servers, which were configured to accommodate peaks in demand due to a specific event.

There are significant benefits to a cloud computing approach: cost reduction, scalability, improved performance, to name a few. However, it has its drawbacks too. With this outsourced ownership, companies are ceding risk and control to a third party. Therefore, some applications and industries in regulated markets need to maintain their own servers and infrastructure. It is for this reason that the questions I asked at the start of the chapter are so important.

Security and Privacy Considerations

While cloud computing offers many benefits, it also raises concerns about security and privacy. Data breaches and unauthorised access to sensitive information are potential risks. However, reputable cloud providers invest heavily in security measures, including encryption and multi-factor authentication, to protect user data. By being aware of the potential risks of hosting your data in the cloud, you can make a better decision about the risks.

Cloud Computing Providers

While cloud computing is not new, many readers may not realise that they use cloud services almost exclusively all day, every day, for work and in their personal lives. At the time of writing, the top 10 cloud providers ranked by Dgtlinfra are:[1]

1. Amazon Web Services (AWS)

2. Microsoft Azure

3. Google Cloud Platform (GCP)

4. Alibaba Cloud

5. Oracle Cloud

6. IBM Cloud (Kyndryl)

7. Tencent Cloud

8. OVHcloud

9. DigitalOcean

10. Linode (Akamai)

Digital curiosity and a will to embrace future technologies plays a major part in Amazon's power as a company today. Before 2023, when audiences were hungry for information on a broad range of technologies, other than AI, I would play a video of an interview with Warren Buffett and Becky Quick aired on CNBC in 2017.[2] In this interview, he talked about how Jeff Bezos, the founder of Amazon, had a "7-year head start" on his competitors regarding cloud services.

He was describing Amazon's transition from an online bookseller to the world's largest cloud computing provider, Amazon Web Services (AWS). The story is a simple one. Bezos realised that he had surplus computing capacity after optimising his own IT infrastructure for his book and merchant business. In 2002, he allowed developers to "rent" time on these servers for their own applications.

One obvious omission from the top ten list of cloud computing providers is Apple. While they do own and operate their own data centres for things like iCloud storage, they do not make it commercially available for others to purchase. (We'll talk more about the difference between public and private clouds in a second.)

Understanding Where Your Data Is in the Cloud

Those with an iPhone full of family photos will be familiar with the nagging "storage full" warning when you exhaust the free 5GB tier and need to purchase more storage to keep syncing your photos. In this example, your data may be stored on Apple's own servers in one of eight Apple-owned data centres operating in the US, Europe, and China. It may also be stored on AWS and Google Cloud servers.[3]

This is the magic of the cloud. As an end user, I don't know where my data is stored, and most users probably don't care until something happens and they are not able to access their data. Similarly, cloud computing has been one of the drivers of new web services and social media networks. Undoubtedly, the social media service you interacted with before reading this chapter will run the application and store your data on a cloud computing platform.

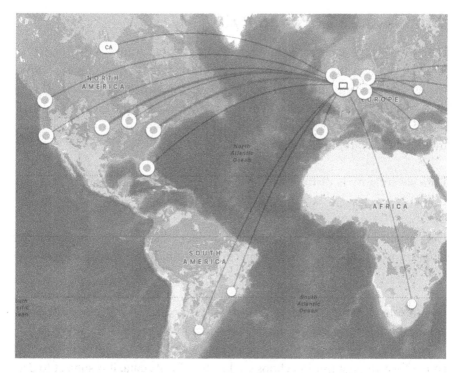

Figure 8.1 A typical set of connections from my MacBook Pro to servers around the world. Credit: Objective Development Software

Being digitally curious, I wanted to better understand where my data went. I found a program for my Apple Mac called Little Snitch[4] that plots every server connected to my laptop on a world map. You can download it from curious.click/snitch, and there are equivalents for PC, such as Netlimiter.[5]

What surprised me was the number of connections made to and from my computer. On a typical day, I see around 80 programs accessing over 650 servers. When you realise this is happening, you may want to turn straight to Part IV: Curious About . . . Your Data to understand how to protect yourself online.

Most of these programs are ones I expect to see. However, it surprised me that they stayed permanently connected, and that my data is being moved worldwide. This may be an issue if you operate in a highly regulated industry or country, where the concept of "data sovereignty" is key and your personal or corporate data is not allowed to leave a particular country.

What is Data Sovereignty?

Data sovereignty refers to the laws applicable to data because of the country in which it is physically located. The legal rights of data subjects (any individual whose personal information is being gathered, retained, or processed), and data protection requirements, depend on the location in which their data is stored. Accordingly, organisations will have different responsibilities for data in different geographical locations.

Data sovereignty is distinct from the concepts of data localisation and data residency.

Data localisation refers to a governmental policy that prohibits organisations from transferring data outside a specific location. It is a special case of data sovereignty.

Data residency is a decision by a business to store data in a specific geographical location. Organisations might store data in a specific location to satisfy legal requirements, take advantage of tax regimes, or for performance reasons. Once an organisation chooses a location for its data, it is subject to data sovereignty – the laws applicable in that region.[6]

The Impact of Cloud Computing

Cloud computing's flexibility and efficiency have transformed business operations, enabling small startups and large enterprises to adapt more quickly to market changes and customer needs.

Cloud platforms support various applications, from basic email and cloud storage to complex data analysis and AI functions, all accessible via the internet.

The companion website for this book – digitallycurious.ai, where you can find up-to-date information on issues raised in this book – is hosted on a cloud platform. These days most websites are. More specifically, it is hosted on a Virtual Private Server (VPS) at a co-location data centre in Nottingham, around 170 km north of London. However, imagine trying to access this website from the other side of the world – it would introduce unacceptable delays, and my readers might become impatient.

As I expect to have readers access this website from around the world, I employ a Content Delivery Network (CDN),[7] which hosts a copy of this website much closer to where it is needed. For a very reasonable price, based on how much data is consumed, my website "appears" as if it is hosted in any one of 84 locations from Stockholm to Sydney. This leads to a much faster loading time than if the website was only serving the pages from the UK.

This would be impossible without cloud computing, as I am not likely to want to build my own data centre in 84 cities. Another model that follows the same concept is Virtual Private Network (VPN) services, which allow you to connect to sites securely as if you were in that location. An example of such a service is the one I use, Surfshark.[8] These and other business models only existed after cloud computing became widespread and affordable.

This increased connectivity and flexibility is what allowed many firms to continue to function during the COVID-19 pandemic, while their staff were sent home. This made possible the rapid rise of Zoom and other collaborative tools during this time. In Chapter 22, where we discuss XaaS (Everything as a Service), it will become evident that these new types of services would never have existed without the cloud.

Companies of all sizes can leverage cloud services to deploy and scale applications rapidly, analyse big data for insights, and deliver enhanced customer experiences. Moreover, it levels the playing field, allowing small startups to access the same resources as large corporations. Companies can also use software hosted in the cloud to run their entire business and connect to other platforms and services.

Cloud computing also plays a critical role in data security and disaster recovery, providing businesses with robust backup solutions and ensuring data integrity and availability.

In February 2022, the Ukrainian government made the decision to migrate terabytes of critical government data, property records, and information to the

AWS cloud. Their hope was to preserve integral digital services for its citizens with the threat of Russian forces invading becoming imminent. This strategic decision meant that this data was stored "off country" on AWS servers worldwide, reducing the impact of a strike in critical banking and other financial and government services. The Ukraine Tech Chief, Mykhailo Federov, said: "Cloud migration saved the Ukrainian government and economy."[9]

AWS delivered three of its Snowball devices[10] to Ukraine through Poland during the early days of Russia's invasion. Each Snowball, an edge-computing device designed to transport data into and out of the cloud, is capable of storing up to 80 terabytes of data offline, ready to be uploaded to the cloud.

Public vs Private Clouds

The security of the data and information being moved around in the cloud means that services like AWS, Google Cloud Platform (GCP), or Microsoft Azure might not always be the best option. Public clouds like these are available to operate with any and all customers using the same infrastructure and resources, though their data and applications remain isolated.

An alternative is a private cloud – a cloud that is dedicated to the exclusive use of one specific business that could be maintained and hosted on-premises by the organisation or by a third party.

Private clouds appeal to businesses with stringent data security, regulatory compliance, and customisation requirements.

By keeping data in a private infrastructure, organisations can ensure that sensitive information is not shared with other entities, as it might be in a public cloud scenario. Moreover, private clouds offer more flexibility according to specific organisational needs. This can include customising storage, networking, and computing resources to optimise performance and efficiency.

Despite the higher initial investment and ongoing management costs compared to public cloud services, the private cloud model is favoured by industries such as finance, healthcare, and government, where data privacy and regulatory compliance are paramount.

Hybrid Cloud

A hybrid cloud is an integrated cloud service utilising both private and public clouds to perform distinct functions within the same organisation. This model combines the best of both worlds: the public cloud's scalability and flexibility with a private cloud's control and security.

By allowing data and applications to move between private and public clouds, a hybrid cloud gives businesses greater flexibility and deployment options. For instance, a company can use the public cloud for high-volume, lower-security needs, such as web-based email. Meanwhile, sensitive, business-critical operations like financial reporting can run on a private cloud.

The hybrid cloud model is particularly beneficial for businesses with dynamic or highly changeable workloads. It also works well for organisations with big data-processing requirements. In this instance, the sensitive data can be processed in the private cloud, while the public cloud can be used to run analytics on the processed data.

Moreover, it provides a cost-effective way for businesses to scale their operations without compromising on security or performance, enabling them to quickly adapt to market demands and technological advancements. The flexibility of the hybrid cloud allows organisations to innovate faster by leveraging the public cloud's resources while keeping core systems secure within a private cloud. Therefore, it offers a balanced solution for digital transformation.

Multi-Cloud

Multi-cloud refers to using cloud services from multiple cloud computing providers in a single heterogeneous architecture. This strategy allows businesses to distribute their cloud assets, applications, software, and more across several cloud environments, leveraging the specific advantages of each service provider.

By adopting a multi-cloud approach, organisations can optimise their cloud solutions for cost efficiency, performance, and redundancy, while avoiding dependence on a single cloud provider and reducing the risk of vendor lock-in. Multi-cloud environments can include any combination of public, private, and hybrid clouds. This enables companies to achieve more flexible and resilient IT infrastructures tailored to their specific operational requirements and strategic goals.

What is the difference between hybrid cloud and multi-cloud?

Hybrid and multi-clouds have a fundamental difference – their architecture. A hybrid cloud environment comprises a mixture of private and public cloud services, while a multi-cloud model includes two or more public cloud services.

The key difference is that hybrid cloud users own and manage a private cloud resource as part of their cloud infrastructure. This is usually hosted in-house, in on-premises data centres, or on dedicated servers in third-party data centres. The private aspect then syncs with public cloud workloads to create an overall business solution. Multi-cloud systems use only public cloud services.[11]

Common Hybrid Cloud Use Cases

A hybrid cloud, or hybrid multi-cloud, strategy allows organisations to customise solutions to meet their specific technical demands and business needs. Here are some typical use cases that may exist in your organisation.

1. *Digital transformation*: When the COVID-19 pandemic hit, businesses needed to modernise their IT infrastructure and create a more resilient business. A hybrid cloud solution allows organisations to migrate sensitive data to their private on-premises servers while making key applications and services on the public cloud accessible to any employee in any location.

   For financial institutions that are heavily regulated and still rely on legacy systems such as mainframes, a hybrid cloud solution is ideal. It provides a way to isolate this data by hosting applications on industry-compliant public clouds and storing sensitive information on-premises in their private cloud.

2. *Disaster recovery (DR)*: DR solutions prevent or minimise data loss and business disruption resulting from catastrophic events such as natural disasters or a targeted cyberattack. They also allow organisations to store data in a private cloud and back up that infrastructure on a public cloud. If a disaster strikes, the organisation can quickly and smoothly move workloads to the public cloud with minimal disruption and continue running business applications.

3. *Cloud bursting during peak periods*: Many companies need to deal with dynamic workloads prone to rapid spikes in resource demands, such as a Black Friday sale or major concert ticket launch. When a private cloud has reached 100% capacity, external workloads that would otherwise overwhelm an organisation's private servers "burst" to external third-party cloud services. In doing so, they avoid interruption to business applications during sudden workload surges.

4. *Hybrid cloud and AI*: A hybrid cloud environment forms a critical foundation for AI capabilities, including GenAI. This is due to the large additional amounts of computing power demanded by LLMs associated with GenAI in an environment that supports security and rapid scalability.

Edge Computing: Extending the Cloud

Data goes to work in challenging and unlikely places, such as the International Space Station, connected vehicles, factory floors, ships at sea, and the neighbourhood pharmacy. While data might have traditionally belonged in a data centre or in the cloud, many important decisions need to happen out in the field and at the edge of a network.

I spoke with Mark Simpson from RedHat, an open-source software provider now owned by IBM, about this relatively new branch of cloud computing that promises to deliver insights and experiences at the moment they are needed, right where they're needed.[12]

He explained on the podcast that while cloud computing offers numerous benefits, the rise of IoT devices (we'll talk about this in Chapter 9) and applications requiring real-time processing has highlighted its limitations in latency and bandwidth. This means we need an approach that lets us process data from anywhere more flexibly.

Edge computing has emerged as a complementary solution, processing data closer to its source – the edge of the network – rather than relying solely on centralised data centres. This proximity reduces latency, improves response times, and conserves bandwidth. This is essential for applications like autonomous vehicles, smart cities, and real-time analytics.

Edge computing does not replace cloud computing. Instead, it offers an opportunity to create a more distributed computing architecture where cloud services are extended closer to the data source. This hybrid approach combines the broad reach and scalability of the cloud with the speed and efficiency of edge computing, enabling businesses to leverage the best of both worlds.

Case Study: Aurrigo Autonomous Vehicles, AWS, and Vodafone in the UK

Aurrigo CEO David Keene spoke with me on a podcast about how Aurrigo is collaborating with AWS and Vodafone on edge computing and 5G to enable remote supervision of autonomous vehicles.[13] AWS servers have been located directly at 5G masts in Cambridge, bringing latency down to around 20 ms.

This is the first practical example of AWS edge computing outside the US. It allows Aurrigo to potentially remove safety supervisors from their autonomous shuttles connected via Vodafone's 5G network. This is made possible because the low latency of the 5G network connected to an edge server means that there can be a much quicker response time. This removes the need for a human to supervise the vehicle in person. This collaboration helps pave the way for fully autonomous, remotely monitored vehicles.

So, Where is the "Edge" in Edge Computing?

Edge has become a very widely used term, but it refers to the edge of a network. If you're talking to a car manufacturer, they would consider the edge to be a server embedded in the car.

In the Aurrigo case, the edge refers to the server at the base of a cellular tower. We can also consider your smartphone an edge device. When you unlock your phone with a fingerprint or face scan, the processing is done locally and securely on the phone – at the edge – without ever needing to send highly sensitive biometric data to the cloud.

Steve Young from Dell Technologies predicts that 80% of the world's data will be created at the edge in the next 5 years.[14] On the podcast, he said: "Edge is just an extension. It's a mini data centre, which is closer to your customers or your source of data. People want to make real-time data decisions where the data exists. And that's why we believe 80% of the world's data will be created at the edge."

The cloud is everywhere. Modern applications and networks would not exist without it. We all use it, and most organisations are using private, hybrid, and multi-cloud without their employees or customers realising it. While the cloud promises a range of benefits, it is not without risks. Redundancy from having data spread across multiple cloud facilities and data centres is critical for disaster recovery.

Cloud computing has revolutionised how businesses and individuals operate by offering scalable, flexible, and efficient computing solutions. As I've already explained, one of the primary benefits is its scalability.

Furthermore, cloud computing promotes collaboration by enabling data and applications to be accessed from anywhere in the world. Teams can work on projects simultaneously without the need for physical infrastructure or file transfers, enhancing productivity and accelerating project timelines. This global accessibility also supports remote work. Allowing employees to access their work environment from any location fosters a more flexible and satisfied workforce.

Another significant advantage is the reduction in IT costs. Cloud services eliminate the need for large upfront investments in hardware and software. Maintenance and upgrade responsibilities shift to the cloud provider, reducing the burden on in-house IT staff and lowering overall operational costs. Additionally, cloud computing offers robust security features, protecting data against cyber threats with advanced encryption, firewalls, and security protocols.

Lastly, cloud computing ensures reliability and disaster recovery. Data is mirrored across multiple redundant sites on the cloud provider's network, which means businesses can rely on data backup, recovery, and continuity of operations even in the event of hardware failure, natural disasters, or other disruptions.

By offering scalability, collaboration, cost savings, enhanced security, and reliability, cloud computing continues to be a pivotal technology in driving operational efficiency and innovation in today's digital landscape.

You should build your own cloud application as part of your digitally curious journey. This is called "spinning up an app" and refers to quickly provisioning and deploying an application on a cloud infrastructure. This term originates from rapidly starting or "spinning up" virtual servers or containers to host the application.

Curious Five

How can I start to act on the opportunities for cloud?

1. Create your own cloud service. Sign up to AWS free via curious.click/aws-free and follow the tutorials to create a simple solution in the cloud such as a VPS.

2. Sign up for a cloud service and understand what happens to your data and where it is stored by reading the documentation related to where the "data buckets" are physically located.

3. Enable a network monitoring tool such as Little Snitch or Netlimiter to see where in the cloud your data is being sent.

4. Understand what cloud services you already use. What control do you have over the data, and do you have the ability to recover the data if your cloud provider ceases to operate?

5. Explore the opportunities to move more of your in-house (on-premises)-hosted applications to the cloud and find out what your organisation's plans are to move more of your data into the cloud.

CHAPTER 9
THE INTERNET OF EVERYTHING

With the proliferation of affordable computer chips and the always-on internet, billions of devices can now communicate. This connectivity allows everyday objects – from fridges and dishwashers to cars and industrial machines – to transmit data and respond with intelligent insights to users via small sensors.

This interconnected network of devices, known as the "Internet of Things" (IoT), is not a technology often visible to consumers, but we use IoT devices every day.

Examples include:

- Temperature sensors such as Google's Nest.[1]
- Internet-enabled security cameras from companies such as Arlo.[2]
- Wearables like Google's Fitbit[3] and the Apple Watch.[4]

The concept of the IoT is not new; engineers have been integrating sensors and processors into everyday items since the 1990s. Initially, radio frequency identification (RFID) tags were utilised to track valuable equipment, but their size and cost were restrictive. As technology advanced, these tags became smaller, faster, and more efficient. Today, they are widely used in items such as ID badges and are expected to be incorporated into clothing in the near future,[5] something we examined in Chapter 6.

The unique properties of smart objects are that they can transmit data to and from the internet at low data rates and can be battery powered, which is crucial for sensors placed in hard-to-reach areas such as buildings or factories. Cloud computing has also meant that the "heavy lifting" of computer processing can be done away from the device, lowering the cost to integrate processors into small objects.

What Technologies Have Made the IoT Possible?

While the idea of the IoT has existed for a long time, recent advances in several different technologies have made it practical.

- *Low-cost, low-power sensors*: Affordable and reliable sensors enable IoT technology to be available to more manufacturers. Small "lick-and-stick" sensors can be attached to anything to transmit data about that object, something I discussed with Ron Rock, CEO of IoT company Microshare, on the podcast.[6]

- *Mobile connectivity*: Various network protocols facilitate the efficient transfer of data between sensors, the cloud, and other devices. Specific mobile technologies developed for the IoT, such as long-term evolution for machines (LTE-M) and narrowband IoT (NB-IoT), help to optimise mobile networks for IoT applications.[7]

- *Cloud computing*: As we covered in Chapter 8, the availability of cloud platforms allows businesses and consumers to scale up their infrastructure almost immediately without the need to deploy their own equipment.

- *Artificial intelligence*: AI significantly enhances the capabilities of the IoT by enabling devices to analyse vast amounts of data and make intelligent decisions in real time. In smart homes, AI can learn user behaviours and preferences to automate climate control, lighting, and security systems more effectively. In industrial settings, AI can predict equipment failures and schedule maintenance, reducing downtime and improving efficiency.

- *Conversational AI*: Natural language processing (NLP) advancements are making digital assistants such as Amazon's Alexa, Google Assistant, and Apple's Siri more useful, and powering the concept of home automation for every household, something we explored in Chapter 7.

According to PwC Partner Darshan Chandarana: "We could do lots with IoT and IoT has been around for a while. Now you've got AI and IoT, and the way you can interrogate that data has changed, you'll see a resurgence of IoT, a resurgence of blockchain, and a resurgence of some of the other technologies around the edges. And then you'll see a few new technologies popping up that couldn't have worked without AI."[8]

How Does the IoT Work?

Amazon Web Services has an excellent overview of how IoT systems work.[9] They explain that a typical IoT system collects and exchanges data in real time and consists of three main components.

1. *Smart devices*: These devices have computing and networking capabilities, such as motion detectors, security cameras, or exercise equipment, and collect data from their environment, user inputs, or usage patterns.

2. *An IoT application*: These are collections of services and software that integrate data from various devices, analyse it using machine learning or AI, and make informed decisions communicated to the devices.

3. *Graphical user interface (GUI)*: This allows users to manage IoT devices through a mobile app or website "dashboard" providing a summary of all connected devices and their performance.

Why is the IoT So Important?

The IoT has become critically important today because it transforms how we interact with the world around us. By connecting everyday objects to the internet, the IoT enables real-time data collection and analysis, leading to smarter decision-making and automation.

This technology improves efficiency, reduces costs, and enhances convenience in various sectors such as healthcare, manufacturing, transportation, and home management. With the ability to monitor and control devices remotely, the IoT enhances safety, optimises resource use, and provides new opportunities for innovation.

As IoT devices become more common, the idea of the "Internet of Everything" is turning into a reality. It's not just about connecting individual items or "things", it's about connecting every aspect of our daily lives with tangible benefits.

Connected Devices Could Change Your Entire Morning Routine

Imagine if your alarm clock could automatically start the toaster and adjust the thermostat when you hit the snooze button. Your pantry could detect when supplies are running low and order them for delivery. Your fitness tracker could schedule workout reminders, and your electric bike's GPS could automatically plan the best route to avoid traffic. The possibilities in an IoT world are now limitless.

Examples of IoT systems in use today include the following.

Connected Cars

Many modern vehicles are already enabled to collect data from various sensors to monitor driver performance and vehicle health, delivered via an embedded SIM card. Applications include fleet monitoring for rental companies, tracking driving behaviour, alerting friends and family in case of a crash, and predicting when the vehicle is due for maintenance.

The Connected Home

Smart home devices, such as connected thermostats, lighting systems, and security cameras, allow homeowners to control and monitor their environment remotely through mobile apps or voice assistants. These devices can learn user preferences and habits, optimising energy usage and enhancing security by providing real-time alerts and automated responses to potential threats.

Smart appliances like refrigerators, washing machines, and ovens can communicate with each other, with homeowners, and with the manufacturer, streamlining daily tasks and even managing inventory by ordering groceries or supplies when they run low.

I recently experienced a fascinating example of the IoT in action. While my friend was at a party, they remotely turned on their Wi-Fi-enabled Smeg oven,[10] ensuring the pizza was cooked to perfection just in time for the babysitter's arrival to feed their children.

Smart Cities

Smart cities leverage IoT technology to enhance urban living by creating more efficient, sustainable, and responsive environments. Using interconnected sensors and devices, cities can monitor and manage infrastructure, utilities, and services in real time. Smart traffic lights can adjust themselves based on traffic flow data, reducing congestion and improving commute times.

Thanks to IoT sensors embedded into rubbish bins, waste management systems can optimise collection routes based on how full a bin is, and smart grids can balance energy distribution to minimise outages and improve efficiency.

IoT-enabled environmental sensors monitor air quality, noise levels, and water conditions, providing critical data for public health and safety initiatives. Smart lighting systems adjust street lighting based on pedestrian activity, saving energy and reducing costs.

Smart Buildings

The integration of IoT devices into smart buildings represents a significant advancement in modern architecture and urban planning. By embedding sensors and interconnected devices throughout a building, the IoT enables real-time monitoring and control of various systems such as heating, ventilation, air conditioning (HVAC), lighting, and security.

Predictive cleaning of bathrooms can be undertaken by understanding how often people enter the facility. Climate sensors can detect and manage CO_2 levels in offices – the higher the level of CO_2, the more likely people are to fall asleep, something important to know in an office environment!

This seamless connectivity not only enhances the efficiency of building operations, but also significantly reduces energy consumption and operational costs. For instance, the IoT can automate lighting based on occupancy, adjust HVAC settings for optimal comfort and efficiency, and provide predictive maintenance for equipment, thereby preventing costly breakdowns.

As Microshare CEO Ron Rock points out: "You can't reduce your carbon footprint if you don't have the data in the first place of how your building is behaving, living and breathing."

What Industries Can Benefit from the IoT?

The organisations best suited to benefit from the IoT are those that can use sensor insights to enhance their business processes. When we discussed this on the podcast, Ron Rock pointed out that the power of these sensors and data lies in predicting and preventing accidents – avoiding unnecessary costs.

Manufacturing

The manufacturing industry stands to gain significantly from the integration of IoT technology. By embedding sensors and connectivity in machinery and equipment, manufacturers can achieve real-time monitoring and analysis of production processes. Data collected from IoT devices can be analysed to improve product quality and customise manufacturing processes, catering to specific market demands.

Automotive

The automotive industry can reap substantial benefits from IoT technology by leveraging it for both manufacturing and vehicle maintenance. In production, IoT sensors enable real-time monitoring of equipment and processes, ensuring that potential issues are identified and addressed promptly to prevent costly downtime.

For vehicles already on the road, IoT applications provide invaluable data that can detect impending equipment failures, allowing for timely alerts and recommendations to drivers. This not only enhances vehicle safety and reliability, but also improves the overall driving experience by keeping car owners informed about their vehicle's condition.

How is the IoT Changing the World? Take a Look at Connected Cars

One example of how the IoT is transforming the automotive industry is through the advent of connected cars. With IoT technology, car owners can remotely control their vehicles, such as preheating the car before entering it or summoning it via a smartphone. The seamless device-to-device communication facilitated by the IoT enables cars to autonomously book service appointments when necessary.

Connected cars also redefine the car ownership model, allowing manufacturers and dealers to maintain a continuous relationship with customers, instead of a one-time transaction. This shift paves the way for "Transportation-as-a-Service", where users pay for usage rather than ownership, and enables continuous software upgrades, significantly improving the vehicle's performance and value over time. We will look at the concept of "Everything-as-a-Service" in Chapter 22.

Transportation and Logistics

The transportation and logistics industry can significantly benefit from IoT technology through enhanced fleet management and real-time tracking capabilities. Temperature-sensitive goods like food, flowers, and pharmaceuticals can be equipped with sensors to monitor conditions and send alerts if any parameter threatens the product quality.

IoT applications provide comprehensive visibility into the supply chain, allowing for better resource allocation, reduced operational costs, and improved customer satisfaction through accurate, real-time updates.

Retail

Smart shelves equipped with weight sensors and RFID technology can automatically monitor stock levels and trigger alerts when items run low, ensuring timely restocking and preventing out-of-stock situations. This enhanced efficiency and customer-centric approach not only boosts sales and customer loyalty, but also provides retailers with valuable data to refine their strategies and store operations.

Public Sector

Government-owned utilities, such as water, power, and sewer services, can use IoT applications to monitor infrastructure in real time, quickly identifying and addressing issues like leaks or outages. IoT sensors can be deployed in public spaces to monitor environmental conditions, traffic flow, and public safety, allowing for data-driven decisions that improve urban planning and deal with emergencies, leading to faster response times and reduced downtime, ultimately providing more reliable services to citizens.

Healthcare

IoT sensors can be used to track the location and status of critical medical equipment in hospitals, such as wheelchairs and defibrillators, ensuring they are readily available when needed. Wearable IoT devices can monitor patients' vital signs in real time, allowing for continuous health monitoring and early detection of potential issues. This facilitates timely medical interventions and enables remote patient monitoring, reducing the need for hospital visits.

If this data could be collected ethically and anonymously, recording and collecting information like body temperature changes across a whole nation, doctors could make better medical predictions and potentially catch future pandemics much earlier.

General Safety Across All Industries

IoT technology can significantly enhance worker safety across all industries by providing real-time monitoring and rapid response capabilities. In hazardous environments such as mines, oil and gas fields, and chemical plants, IoT sensors can detect dangerous conditions like gas leaks, temperature fluctuations, and equipment malfunctions, alerting workers and management immediately to prevent accidents.

Wearable IoT devices can monitor workers' health indicators, such as heart rate and body temperature, ensuring timely intervention if any abnormal signs are detected. Additionally, IoT-enabled systems can track the location of workers, ensuring they are accounted for and safe, especially in emergencies.

Curious Five

Here are five things to make you more curious about the IoT.

1. Look at the internet-enabled devices you have in your home and realise how many IoT devices you're already using – for example, if you own a voice-enabled device like Alexa.

   - Is there an app or platform that allows all your devices to be connected to give you a broader picture?

   - Can you use your IoT devices to automate things in your home – such as heating, lighting, and cooling?

   - Can you see the state of your IoT devices away from home?

2. If you're not already using the IoT at home, consider getting a simple kit that allows you, for example, to understand the temperature at home when you're away.

3. Take a similar look at the internet-enabled devices in your work environment.

   - What "things" at work are already instrumented?

   - Are they connected to a single platform to make informed decisions about the data?

   - Can AI be employed to leverage the insights from the sensors better?

4. What other "things" could you connect at work to gain better insights and make more informed business decisions?

5. Look at future uses of the IoT at home and in the office.

- Where would better insights about your environment help you?

- What simple devices could you deploy tomorrow?

- How are you using the devices you already own – can you connect them all to one platform to gain better insights?

PART III
CURIOUS ABOUT ...
THE INTERNET

Why Am I Curious About the Internet?

When it comes to more recent technologies such as the metaverse, block-chain, the Internet of Things (IoT), and Non-Fungible Tokens (NFTs), you've probably heard them mentioned, but you may well be less familiar with what they do, and how they can help us in our lives and at work.

The internet to some seems to work as if like magic. It's always available to us on any device. When it stops working, we get annoyed and want it working again as soon as possible.

My curiosity about the internet was piqued back in 1993 when I was using a dial-up modem to connect to a Bulletin Board Service (BBS). When I was working as an executive at Telstra, I had an Integrated Services Digital Network (ISDN) 128kB/s (kilobits/second) line installed at my home. This was a precursor to consumer Asymmetric Digital Subscriber Line (ADSL) connections that were able to connect at around 1.5MB/s (megabits/second). I spoke about ADSL on my "Visions for the Future" webinar[1] mentioned in the Introduction, and predicted that these speeds would only get faster.

Today in west London where I live, fibre-optic internet subscriptions are available for consumers from companies such as Community Fibre[2] that can deliver speeds of up to 3GB/s (gigabits/second). These speeds were unheard of in a home environment, let alone the office even a few years ago.

Other topics that were in the news before the AI news avalanche, such as the metaverse, are still worth discussing, even though the focus of the media and tech publications has moved firmly towards GenAI.

The metaverse has promise, but the benefits have not been well explained. In 2021, Facebook created unrealistic hype around this technology, even changing their name to "Meta". Similarly, Bitcoin has weathered a hype cycle from 2017, and this is something that my audiences still say they don't know much about – which should automatically make you curious to know more.

One way that I stay curious is to look at the Gartner Hype Cycle[3] for emerging technologies to see which technologies they predict are coming next. Looking at the latest 2023 hype cycle, as expected, GenAI is at "peak hype". Meanwhile, post-quantum cryptography is an innovation trigger.

Apart from Bitcoin, one of the most hyped technologies in recent years were NFTs. In the same way I was curious about the variability in the value of Bitcoin, buying some at peak hype to understand the hype better, I looked at creating my own NFT. I wanted to see how the process worked, and get a better understanding of what it might mean for me and my business.

Of course, the IoT (as discussed in Chapter 9) could not function without the internet. And as with the internet, many of us use the IoT daily. Naturally, my fascination with the internet made IoT particularly intriguing to me. I have installed temperature sensors in my home, and as I write this in France, I can see the temperature of the different rooms in my home in London. All of this is thanks to IoT technology.

Why Should You Be Curious About the Internet?

The evolution of the internet has had, and will continue to have, a profound impact on the business world. It has progressed from being a platform where we are allowed to read, to one where we can read and write. It has now evolved into one where we can read, write, and *own*. Until Web 3.0, consumers and smaller companies were at the mercy of "big tech" who own most of the components linked to popular internet tools and products. With this next phase of the internet, we will now be able to monetise what we make, from the smallest creator to the largest multinational. This sentence alone should make you curious about what's next for the internet.

The following chapters will examine the evolution of the web from version 1.0 through to version 3.0, where we expect to have more control on what we read, write, and own online, and what that means for you and your company.

CHAPTER 10
THE NEW INTERNET

Over the last few decades, the internet has radically changed how we connect, communicate, and conduct commerce with each other. The technology behind it was initially conceived of in the late 1960s as a military and research network that allowed computers to share information.

In the years since Sir Tim Berners-Lee developed the World Wide Web (WWW) in 1989,[1] the internet has undergone three profound transformations: Web 1.0, Web 2.0, and now Web 3.0. Each has opened up further opportunities and potential that redefined how we interact and do business.

Let's examine these transformations in more detail.

Web 1.0 – Read-Only Data

At its core, Web 1.0 was a content delivery network that allowed for straightforward information sharing across university and research centres. It was predominantly read-only – meaning you could only view information but not change it. It offered no interactive content or user-generated features. The design of these web pages was basic, largely text-based, and driven by the limitations of early browser technologies and slow connection speeds.

As time went by, the internet became more user-friendly and expanded beyond academic and military institutions. Browsers like Netscape Navigator and Internet Explorer allowed websites to become more visually engaging. As internet use became more widespread, the dot.com boom signalled a period of speculating, investment, and entrepreneurship.

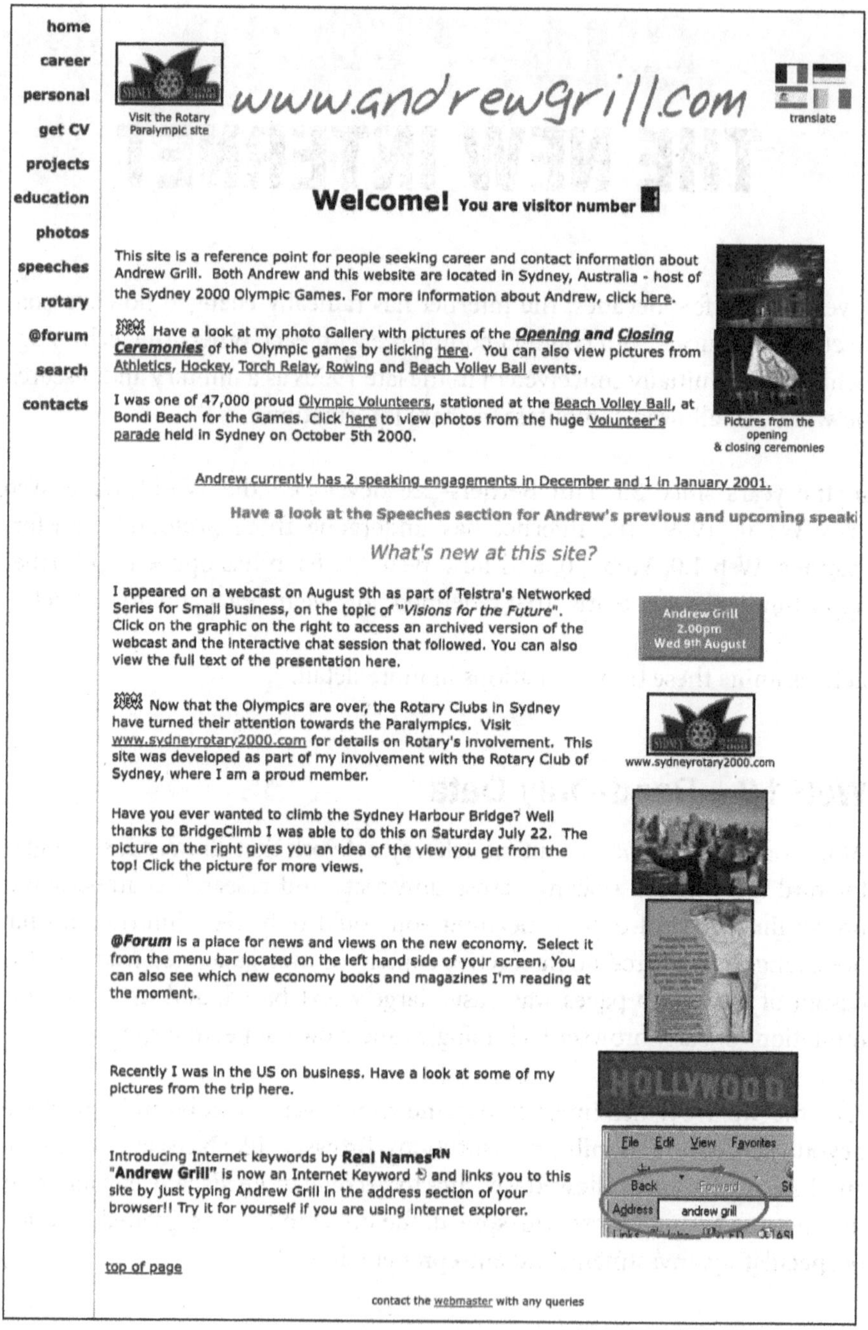

Figure 10.1 A screenshot of my website, andrewgrill.com, from 18 October 2000. Credit: Internet Archive

Look Back in Time

A useful resource for seeing how old websites looked is archive.org, also called "The Wayback Machine". It takes snapshots of a website at a certain point in time. You can even see what Google looked like as far back as 11 November 1998. Using this tool, I found a copy of what my website looked like on 18 October 2000.[2]

Web 2.0 – An Interactive Internet

Unlike its predecessor, Web 2.0 was characterised by its dynamism and interactivity. Instead of being limited to reading a webpage, we could now write on them as well. Users were no longer just consumers of content; they became creators. This new era was marked by the rise of social media, blogging, and e-commerce platforms.

Most of the websites we use today fall into the Web 2.0 category, such as Facebook, YouTube, or Wikipedia. These websites let you contribute, allowing you to read stories as well as publish content. This revolutionised how information was created, shared, and consumed. Web 2.0 democratised content production. Anyone with internet access could contribute to the global conversation.

The issue with Web 1.0 and Web 2.0 sites is that many are owned by large tech companies, also called "Big Tech". If we want to put something on Facebook, we must agree to Facebook's terms and conditions. In doing so, we agree that the content we produce belongs to Facebook forever.

Facebook provides a platform for us to share our content and experiences at no cost. However, if our content is unique or valuable, we cannot monetise it while it is hosted on Facebook.

Web 2.0 also ushered in the era of the "platform". The data generated by user interactions became a valuable commodity, leading to the rise of targeted advertising and data analytics as powerful business tools. Tech giants like

Google, Amazon, and Apple have built ecosystems that leverage the network effect to grow at unprecedented speed and scale.

Despite the many advancements, Web 2.0 has also faced criticism for its centralisation of power. A few platforms began controlling vast amounts of user data, raising privacy concerns and prompting debates over data ownership.

Web 3.0 – Owning Our Data

Web 3.0 is the answer to that centralisation of power and ownership. If we want to create and monetise our own content and have more control over how and where the content is used, we need a way of proving that we own and have rights to this content. In response to these challenges, visionaries and developers began conceptualising Web 3.0, the "semantic web" or "read–write–execute" web. This emerging phase of the internet aims to address the issues of data ownership and privacy.

With a focus on decentralisation, Web 3.0 seeks to return control to the users through blockchain technology and peer-to-peer networking. These technologies promise to create a more secure, transparent, and equitable internet, where network-generated value is shared more broadly among its participants.

In a Web 3.0 world, we can create and share valuable content, prove ownership, and make it available for sale. An early example of this is Non-Fungible Tokens (NFTs), which we will cover more in Chapter 13.

Web 3.0 is still in its infancy, but its potential to usher in a new era of the internet, a more democratic and decentralised network, is profound. The principles of interoperability, user sovereignty, and open standards will be key to realising the promise of a futureproof internet.

What are the Core Components of Web 3.0?

The goal of Web 3.0 is to create an internet that lets us interact with each other securely and openly, and reinstates the internet's original ethos of open, free, and secure information exchange while protecting a user's right to privacy. This means that it is based on several core principles:

- Decentralisation
- Ownership of your personal data
- Interoperability

Let's examine each of these in more detail.

Decentralisation

Decentralisation emerged as a response to these concerns that the existing internet was under the control of Big Tech. Rather than data being stored and managed on servers owned by single entities, it is spread across multiple nodes in a network, reducing reliance on central points that can be compromised or censored. This approach aligns with the original ethos of the internet – to be a free and open space for all.

Blockchain technology is instrumental to this decentralisation. We will explore this in more detail in Chapter 12. However, what is important here is that it's a method of recording information that makes it difficult or impossible to change, hack, or cheat the system. This offers a new architecture for the internet itself, where users can interact without intermediaries and retain control of their data.

Ownership of Your Personal Information

With increased data breaches and misuse in the Web 2.0 era, one of the promises of Web 3.0 is the ability for users to have better control over their personal information. Encryption, anonymising technologies, and secure protocols are inherent to the design of decentralised networks. This security-first approach aims to protect data integrity and confidentiality, mitigating the risks with centralised servers of the current internet.

In an interview on The Digitally Curious Podcast with Anton Christodoulou, Co-Founder of the Digital Privacy Advocacy Group, Trust 3.0, he notes that this alone will have an immense impact on our ability to control our own identities, something I will talk about more in Chapter 21.

> "There's real benefits to having a completely decentralised identity. And I would go further as to say, having an anonymised, decentralised identity, so that you can essentially prove who you are, and that you have the ability to pay for a service, or to consume the service safely, without necessarily the service knowing exactly who you are."
> —Anton Christodoulou, Co-Founder, Trust 3.0[3]

Interoperability

Interoperability is another key tenet of Web 3.0. It refers to the ability of different systems, devices, applications, and services to work together within and across organisational boundaries to meet diverse user needs. For the internet, this means seamless experiences where information and services can be accessed and used in diverse and dynamic environments, irrespective of the platform or technology.

The semantic web takes this further by enabling data to be shared and reused across application, enterprise, and community boundaries. It is a collaborative movement led by the World Wide Web Consortium (W3C) that promotes common data formats and exchange protocols on the web.

The idea is to tag information in a way that allows computers to process the meaning of words rather than just the pattern of characters. Creating a web of data that machines can process – semantics – enables greater connection and integration between systems.

Web 3.0 has the potential to rebalance the internet's power dynamics, favouring the user over the platform. As these technologies mature and integrate, the next generation of the internet could mark a significant leap towards a more democratic, user-empowered global network.

The Future of the New Internet with Web 3.0

We can expect a more symbiotic relationship between AI and human input, creating an internet that's more responsive to our needs and more protective of our digital autonomy. One of the pivotal changes will be the shift from Big Tech-dominated platforms to decentralised ecosystems, where individuals have control over their data and privacy.

This promises to dismantle current data silos and redistribute power away from corporate behemoths to the individual user, potentially rebalancing the digital economy. The decentralisation aspect of Web 3.0, facilitated by block-chain, will allow for the creation of digital identities that users solely control, potentially reducing the risks of identity theft and privacy breaches.

In the financial realm, Web 3.0 may revolutionise not just how we conduct transactions but the very essence of financial interactions. With the growth of DeFi (Decentralised Finance), we're likely to see a surge in peer-to-peer lending, borrowing, and trading conducted securely and transparently on the blockchain. Individuals will have more autonomy over their financial transactions and reduce transaction costs.

The implications for businesses are that the transparency and security provided by blockchain could result in more trustworthy and robust systems for supply chain management. This will allow for the real-time tracking of products from manufacturer to end consumer, ensuring authenticity and quality. The ability to execute smart contracts automatically on blockchain networks will likely lead to more efficient business operations, cutting down on bureaucracy and the potential for human error.

Web 3.0 will also revolutionise the creative industries. Content creators will have the power to monetise their work directly through blockchain, bypassing intermediaries that often take a significant share of the revenue. Artists can sell music, art, or literature directly to consumers using NFTs, ensuring they retain a fair portion of the profits.

On a societal level, the semantic web component of Web 3.0 promises to make information more accessible and useful. Machine learning and AI will enable new services that can understand and leverage vast online data, providing more personalised and efficient user experiences. This will lead to advancements in healthcare, where patient data could be analysed to provide tailored medical advice or treatment plans.

The continuous collaboration between technologists, regulators, and the wider community will define how swiftly and smoothly this future unfolds.

The Challenges of Web 3.0

The optimism surrounding Web 3.0 is tempered by significant challenges and criticisms that pose questions about its feasibility and desirability. One primary challenge is accessibility; Web 3.0 operations, particularly those involving blockchain and cryptocurrencies, can require substantial computational power and expertise. This creates a barrier for widespread adoption, potentially excluding those without the technical knowledge or financial resources to participate.

Moreover, while decentralisation is touted as a benefit of Web 3.0, it also raises concerns about regulation and governance. The lack of centralised control means there is no single authority to manage fraudulent activities, enforce legal compliance, or protect consumer rights. This could result in an environment where illegal activities can thrive and where users have little recourse in the event of fraud or theft.

Global standards and governance models will be required to ensure that the benefits of Web 3.0 are realised ethically and equitably. Without the creation and adoption of effective regulatory frameworks, adoption might end up lagging far behind the actual developments.

The user experience of Web 3.0 also presents challenges. Current interfaces and systems can be complex and non-intuitive, making it difficult for non-expert users to navigate and understand them. Without significant improvements in user interfaces and educational resources, adopting Web 3.0 technologies might be slow and limited to a tech-savvy minority.

While Web 3.0 promises enhanced privacy and security, it also risks creating a persistent digital footprint that is immutable and publicly accessible on the blockchain. Data permanence raises serious concerns about privacy and the right to be forgotten, as mistakes or outdated information cannot be easily erased.

The environmental impact of blockchain technology, which is central to many Web 3.0 concepts, is also a growing concern. The massive energy consumption required for cryptocurrency mining and transaction processing has raised alarms about the sustainability of these technologies, sparking debates about their long-term viability in light of global climate change.

As Web 3.0's ecosystem continues to develop, addressing these challenges will be crucial for its success. Only through a concerted effort to improve accessibility, governance, user experience, privacy protection, and environmental sustainability can Web 3.0 hope to achieve its full potential and wide acceptance.

How Can You Embrace the New Internet?

Katie Burke, Global Thought Leadership Lead at Accenture Song sees great potential in Web 3.0 and believes it will have a significant impact.[4] Community is at the heart of Web 3.0, and it opens up opportunities to shift the relationship between brands and customers in a positive way. Brands could give power and control to select parts of their communities in new ways. However, the ultimate experience is what will drive mass adoption.

For this to happen, the technology needs to fade into the background for widespread use. Overall, Katie sees great potential for Web 3.0 to empower communities and enable deeper, more collaborative relationships between brands and their customers, if the experience is designed properly around human needs and behaviours.

Curiosity about Web 3.0 is warranted because it represents a potential paradigm shift in how the internet functions, with profound implications for users and creators. Being informed about Web 3.0 empowers individuals in several ways:

- *Ownership and control*: Web 3.0's decentralisation gives users ownership and control over their data. Unlike Web 2.0, where large corporations could exploit user data, Web 3.0's use of blockchain technology could help safeguard personal information, allowing users to choose how and where their data is used.

- *Financial opportunities*: Web 3.0 technologies like blockchain and cryptocurrency open up new avenues for investment and entrepreneurship. For example, DeFi offers financial services without the need for traditional banks.

- *Enhanced security*: With cyber threats rising, Web 3.0's emphasis on privacy and security is more critical than ever. Its encryption and decentralisation can protect against data breaches and hacking.

- *New career pathways*: As Web 3.0 infrastructure grows, so does the demand for professionals skilled in blockchain, smart contract development, and cybersecurity. Being informed can help individuals prepare for and adapt to these emerging roles.

- *Democratic participation*: The decentralised nature of Web 3.0 allows for more democratic governance models in digital spaces, like DAOs (Decentralised Autonomous Organisations), where stakeholders make decisions collectively.

Web 3.0 also presents numerous opportunities for enterprise-level applications. Here are five significant opportunities it brings.

1. *DeFi integration*: Web 3.0 enables enterprises to integrate DeFi applications. In doing so they can streamline financial transactions, reduce processing times, and lower costs associated with traditional financial services. This integration can revolutionise how companies manage capital, access liquidity, and conduct transactions with enhanced security and transparency.

2. *Supply chain management*: By leveraging blockchain technology, enterprises can create transparent, immutable ledgers for supply chain tracking. This visibility can significantly reduce fraud, ensure authenticity, improve compliance, and enhance efficiency by providing real-time, trustable data on the movement and origin of goods.

3. *Decentralised data storage and management*: Web 3.0 offers enterprises the opportunity to store data across a decentralised network, improving security and data sovereignty. This method of data storage mitigates

the risks of centralised data breaches and ensures data integrity. This is because information is stored in multiple locations and can be accessed without depending on a single provider.

4. *Smart contracts for automated business processes*: Enterprises can use smart contracts to automate and enforce agreements without the need for intermediaries. This automation can streamline business operations, reduce the potential for disputes, and ensure the execution of contracts is both transparent and efficient. Smart contracts can revolutionise contract management, from vendor agreements to employment contracts.

5. *Enhanced customer privacy and data ownership*: Web 3.0 empowers users with control over their personal data. This also enables enterprises to build trust by offering services that prioritise customer privacy and data ownership. Companies can innovate new business models around user-centric data usage and privacy, providing a competitive edge in markets increasingly concerned with data ethics.

We'll cover sovereign identity and the ability for users to own their own data in Chapter 21.

These opportunities illustrate how Web 3.0 can redefine traditional business models, offering enterprises new avenues for growth, innovation, and efficiency. By adopting Web 3.0 technologies, companies can not only improve their operational processes but also position themselves as leaders in the digital economy's next phase.

Curious Five

What can you do to ensure you're aware of the latest developments in Web 3.0?

1. Familiarise yourself with the foundational concepts and terms of Web 3.0, such as blockchain, decentralisation, smart contracts, and tokenisation. Resources like IP With Ease's comprehensive guide to Web 3.0[5] can provide a solid foundation on the subject and help you understand the key characteristics that differentiate Web 3.0 from its predecessors.

2. Interacting with Web 3.0 applications is a great way to grasp their potential and functionality. Try out decentralised applications (DApps), explore NFTs, or participate in a DAO to see firsthand how these work.

3. Taking a structured course or accessing educational material can provide a guided pathway to understanding Web 3.0. Platforms like AWS offer explanations of the principles and technologies of Web 3.0. Moreover, ethereum.org[6] emphasises the importance of education for understanding the new paradigms introduced by Web 3.0.

4. Consider buying a small amount of cryptocurrency ($20) from a reputable crypto exchange to better understand the buying, holding, and selling crypto experience.

5. Join online communities and networks. Become part of online forums, social media groups, or platforms like Creative Tim's blog that discuss Web 3.0.[7] Such communities are good sources for staying updated on the latest developments.

Each of these steps can contribute to a comprehensive understanding of Web 3.0, enabling you to appreciate its potential better, prepare for its implications, and navigate its complexities confidently.

CHAPTER 11
THE METAVERSE

I'm sure we all remember how in October 2021, Mark Zuckerberg bravely rebranded Facebook to "Meta" to try and capture some share of the hype and messaging around the metaverse, reportedly pumping tens of billions into this part of the business.[1] In 2021 and 2022, I was regularly speaking on the metaverse and Web 3.0 – it looked certain that this would be the next big thing.

This only illustrates the challenge futurists face. ChatGPT's arrival on the world stage in late 2022 changed everyone's focus. Since then, interest in the metaverse has waned in favour of AI. However, it is still valuable to talk about the metaverse for two reasons:

- It has the potential to show us how the internet may evolve as Web 3.0 and technology advances.

- It serves as a warning to be careful of the difference between the hype behind a technology and how things might unfold. During peak metaverse hype, some companies created entire "Metaverse divisions" and hired metaverse experts. Looking at the profiles on LinkedIn of people in these teams in 2024, I see many of them have removed the word "metaverse" from their job title.

Where Did the Concept of the Metaverse Come From?

The idea of the metaverse might seem a little sci-fi and for good reason. The word "metaverse" came from science fiction in the first place. Back in 1992, Neal Stevenson[2] wrote a book called *Snow Crash* where he coined the term "Metaverse" while describing his main character.

"Hiro's not actually here at all. He's in a computer-generated universe that his computer is drawing onto his goggles and pumping into his earphones. In the lingo, **this imaginary place is known as the Metaverse.**"

The point being made is that Hiro is not experiencing reality – instead, he's living in a virtual universe being fed into his senses by a computer. Does this sound familiar?

So, the terminology has been around for a long time. The trouble with the metaverse is that the term is actually quite overused. Many describe existing Virtual Reality (VR) applications – including those available through Meta's Oculus headsets – as manifestations of the metaverse. But is a VR interface enough to count as a virtual universe?

My favourite definition of the metaverse comes from Sam Gilbert of the University of Cambridge, who describes it as:

"The open, persistent, real-time, interoperable, virtual world that could be built using Web 3.0 technologies. NFTs, blockchain, smart contracts, and cryptocurrencies are said to provide the payments and legal infrastructure needed to complement virtual reality (VR) capabilities, meaning that the vision presented in *Snow Crash* – or more optimistically, the movie *Ready Player One* – can finally be realised."
— Sam Gilbert, University of Cambridge[3]

This gives us several criteria for something to be considered a manifestation of the metaverse:

- Open

- Persistent

- Real-time

- Interoperable

- Virtual

Testing existing metaverse applications against Sam Gilbert's definition, we see that they are neither persistent – because they reset when users quit them, nor interoperable – because there are many competing *metaverses* and it is currently not possible to seamlessly move between them.

It is therefore more realistic to talk about the metaverse in terms of its potential.

How Has the Metaverse Evolved?

So, how has the metaverse evolved since Neal Stevenson's book in 1992? Many readers may remember a website called Second Life from 2003.[4] It's still there, with about 300,000 people that use it every day. It was the first attempt at virtual worlds and at the time, companies such as IBM developed a presence there.

The impact of the metaverse concept is that there is now a whole new generation who are entirely comfortable existing in a virtual world. I've often tried to get my own head around why you would want to live in a world that is not reality, but I have to stop myself and realise that this is a world that a very different generation is growing up in, and is entirely comfortable with.

The way I started to understand the concept of the metaverse is by observing the gaming community. While I played computer games as a child, I didn't really continue my interest with gaming into adult life. I recall buying a PlayStation as an adult, thinking I might become immersed in the world of gaming, but I returned it after just a week, as it wasn't something that I could get into.

Despite my inability to get into gaming, there are many for whom game worlds are just as important as those in real life. People build entire lives for their characters, and make friends with others in these virtual worlds. When you look at how gamers use the virtual worlds in the likes of World of Warcraft to interact with one another, the way in which the metaverse could work becomes clearer.

I was very digitally curious about the metaverse in 2022, but am less interested in 2024. However, it was this gaming analogy that helped me better understand it.

The metaverse started its life in the gaming world. Gamers want to win something. They are always looking to gamify things. Perhaps they want to change character, buy a new sword, or buy a new horse within their game's world. Some people will pay "real" money for these in-game purchases, which can help you to see how the metaverse might evolve. By thinking about the metaverse from a gaming point of view, and the way people like to play games and compete in real life, you can begin to explore how to extend the concept of the metaverse from the gaming world into recruitment, finance, or logistics.

However, not being deeply into computer games myself, I struggled to find where the metaverse might fit in a corporate world. To be honest, a couple of years on I'm still struggling. Interestingly, companies that set up dedicated metaverse groups pre-ChatGPT seem to have quietly realigned these divisions into looking at broader emerging technologies, or pivoted over to GenAI.

Let's look at the Facebook/Meta virtual world called Horizon Worlds. When it was released in 2022, many compared the initial, very simple graphics to those from Second Life in 2003. Meta has reportedly spent $10 billion a year developing it. Back in 2022, Meta expected to spend about $70 billion over the life of their metaverse project.[5]

If we put this into context, to develop the Apple iPhone cost about $3.2 billion, and they've sold about 2.3 billion iPhones.[6] This is a huge investment with a large upside. In 2023, Meta decided to pivot and invest in AI, stating that it would be the company's biggest investment area in 2024. This led to an increase in revenue, and the metaverse is a topic that seems to have disappeared from Mark Zuckerberg's lips lately.

Today, the metaverse is still a concept and a vision for the future rather than a fully realised, singular entity. However, elements of the metaverse, such as VR experiences, online social platforms, and immersive gaming environments, do exist.

Companies are actively working on creating more interconnected and immersive digital spaces that could eventually resemble the concept of the metaverse. So, while the complete metaverse as envisioned in science fiction may not exist yet, the groundwork is being laid for its development.

The problem with the metaverse today is that some pundits – and I'm one of them – agree that it doesn't actually exist as a homogenous thing. It is fair to say that there are lots of "metaverses" and there is a lot of metaversal activity, but no one metaverse.

An Interoperable Metaverse

The issue with having multiple metaverses is that this holds back user adoption. One of the conveniences of mobile phone networks is their interoperability. You can leave London, go to Paris, and still use your phone without needing to contract with a local French network. Over the years, standards have been developed to ensure that your phone will work no matter where you've travelled from.

This means you can enjoy the benefits of the technology without having to go through the inconvenience of working across multiple networks or systems. In addition, less interoperability means people stick to one system and the user base fragments.

I believe that technologies like Web 3.0, blockchain, and tokenisation are what will help realise the metaverse's potential. These technologies will evolve to provide smart contracts on a blockchain and cryptocurrencies will provide the payments and legal infrastructure needed to complement these virtual reality aspirations.

NFTs in the Metaverse

In an interview with Nick Abrahams, Global Co-leader, Digital Transformation Practice at Norton Rose Fulbright Australia, we discussed the potential of the metaverse.[7] Nick made the good point that a potential avenue of exploration for the metaverse is through embracing its gaming roots and NFTs. In the gaming world, people already are willing to pay a lot to collect exclusive art and appearances for their characters. This could be a valuable way for a brand to build and monetise a community around them and their products.

"I think probably the better way to think of this is to think of NFTs first and then think about the metaverse. The first to embrace NFTs were fashion labels or sports brands like Dolce & Gabbana or Nike. They've got a very big proposition in the metaverse. You can buy a whole range of digital assets to dress up your avatar.

We're also starting to see beverage companies playing here. Miller Lite has a big land where you can go and drink in a metaverse bar. McDonald's launched a world which would allow you, as you cruise through the metaverse, to order your McDonald's, and then that would actually be delivered to you in real life."

— *Nick Abrahams, Global Co-leader, Digital Transformation Practice, Norton Rose Fulbright Australia*

As things are, any in-game collectables are limited to the system or app you earnt them in. This limits their value. The power of an interoperable metaverse means that these NFTs could be traded anywhere or for anything.

The key to remember is that the gaming world is what younger demographics are used to. As time goes by, the real and gaming worlds are starting to collide more. For example, Nick believes that one motive for Meta to embrace the metaverse was the growing realisation that gamers tend to do social networking in-gaming. Over time, this might mean our social media experience will be replaced by a metaverse social media experience.

Use Cases for the Metaverse

In an interview with Thomas Bedenk, Vice President Extended Reality at Endava, we discussed other possible uses of the metaverse and virtual reality technology.[8]

"Endava's strapline is 'we are reimagining the relationship between people and technology,' which lends itself very well to what we're doing in the (eXtended Reality) XR space. It's important to understand people and then how technology is actually helping people in solving their problems."

— *Thomas Bedenk, Vice President Extended Reality, Endava*

If you look at VR, Jeremy Bailenson, founding director of Stanford University's Virtual Human Interaction Lab, has developed a framework called "DICE".[9] This concludes that VR is most useful for experiences that would be "Dangerous", "Impossible", "Counterproductive", or "Expensive" in the real world.

Activities like training firefighters, rehabilitating stroke victims, studying art history through sculpture museums, and exploring time travel for a better understanding of climate change are all experiences that align with the DICE framework. Conversely, tasks such as checking emails, watching movies, or general office work were deemed unsuitable for VR.

"During the pandemic, I was able to put DICE to the test at Stanford", says Bailenson. The university bought 200 Oculus Quest 2s for my Virtual People class, which I've taught since 2003. In four separate courses over a 2-year period, more than 500 students learned about VR in VR, across various platforms.

"We logged hundreds of thousands of minutes in-headset together. It was an incredible endeavour, and exciting to finally get to use VR at scale. We spent more than a year planning the course, and quickly realised our biggest challenge wasn't hardware or software."

In the history of VR research and coursework, no one had ever put hundreds of people in VR for extended periods like this. During the course, the lab found that the DICE framework effectively kept participants engaged for long hours. To fill the many hours, the lab incorporated activities such as floating on yoga mats into space, learning paced breathing from a meditation expert while gazing at Earth, and building entire cities block by block in an empty virtual world.

"We experienced life in other bodies, practising empathy while wearing avatars of different skin colours or genders", says Bailenson. "We experienced a corner kick from the goalie's perspective in a German national football team training session to learn body position and posture. We time-travelled by visiting past recordings of our own avatars and walking around like ghosts inside a rendering of our recent social past."

In contrast, activities such as "knowledge work", which mainly involved talking in meetings, working on shared documents, and watching videos, were ineffective in VR. The lab found that these activities had very little value in the virtual world, as laptops could perform them just as well, if not better. VR headsets were more of a hindrance.

> "One of the best use cases I have ever seen in VR is Penumbra's REAL System, a full-body tracking system used by thousands of patients in hospitals and clinics across the country for rehabilitation for stroke, orthopaedic injuries, and other conditions", says Bailenson.

Gaming and Gen Alpha

I spoke with Zoe Scaman, founder of strategy studio Bodacious, about a groundbreaking study she conducted in partnership with the Walton Family Foundation and Dubit, entitled "The Creation Generation – How creating gaming is revolutionising educational engagement for generation Alpha".[10] The research focused on the use patterns and perspectives among Generation Alpha, those born between 2010 and 2025, on creation gaming platforms Roblox and Minecraft.

The report surveyed over 2500 children under the age of 13. Some key findings from the research included:

- Children from lower-income households were struggling more with creation tools due to issues like latency and lack of devices/internet access, putting them at a disadvantage.

- Children from more affluent households and schools with better connectivity were developing important cognitive, social, and 21st-century skills through creation gaming.

- Creation gaming was found to be fundamentally reshaping education and how children approach learning.

The report noted there was a growing "chasm" between the "haves and have nots" in terms of access to these creative opportunities due to connectivity and device inequality.

When I spoke with Zoe about the report, I had my own "ah-ha!" moment. Gaming can actually aid education among young children, as it encourages creativity, and also exercises skills such as buying, selling, and creating contracts.

The Evolution of Extended Reality Headsets

The launch of Apple's Vision Pro[11] XR headset in February 2024 changes the game. In my view, it starts to remove the friction of engaging with VR content by seamlessly blending digital content with your physical space.

Gamers I've spoken to tell me that the issue with previous headsets is that because you cannot "see" what is in front of you, after 2 hours of usage they experience motion sickness and have to remove them.

While Apple's first-generation headset is still quite bulky, their approach presents the content in a very different and innovative way. The Vision Pro is more than Apple's latest offering; it's a preview of the future of mixed reality.

A feature called EyeSight[12] allows the display on the outside of the headset to be personalised with your own eyes. When using an app or in an interactive experience, EyeSight shows an animation to let others know you may not be able to see them. This helps to solve some of the problems experienced with Google Glass, which was released in 2013.[13]

Concerns at the time from the public were that wearers were able to record conversations without other participants' knowledge, leading to some establishments banning their use.[14]

Always the futurist, I discovered a photograph taken at the 1999 CeBit Exhibition in Hannover, Germany where I was wearing a prototype developed by IBM of a computer display that could be worn like glasses.

I expect that the next versions of all XR headsets will integrate features like EyeSight in some way.

Figure 11.1   My experiments with early iterations of VR. Credit: Andrew Grill

Eventually, I see a time when thin-film technology will evolve to allow a wearer to fit a contact-lens-style device onto their retinas, and have the same experience as today's Vision Pro.

Like any technology, if you introduce friction between the user and the tech, adoption will be much more difficult.

Curious Five

Understanding the business benefits of the metaverse involves recognising its potential to transform industries, enhance customer experiences, and open new revenue streams.

Here are five actionable items for you to investigate.

1. Educate yourself on the fundamentals: Start by learning the basics of the metaverse, including its technology (like VR and AR), platforms, and how it's currently being used by other businesses. This foundation will help you understand the broader implications and opportunities the metaverse presents.

2. Buy, or rent a VR headset, and try out a game like golf together with your friend or colleagues in a different physical location. This will help you understand what the social interaction feels like in that space. This will lead you to a lot of ideas for your own organisation. If you're not ready for this, head into the closest Apple store and ask to try out the Vision Pro headset.

3. Review the DICE analogy – is there an activity in your organisation that is "dangerous", "impossible", "counterproductive", or "expensive" that could be replicated in the metaverse?

4. Participate and experiment: There's no substitute for firsthand experience. Participate in the metaverse through existing platforms like Decentraland or Roblox to understand user interaction, engagement mechanics, and the potential for brand visibility. If possible, consider experimenting with creating your own metaverse content or experiences, even on a small scale, to learn about the development process, costs, and potential ROI.

5. Connect with experts and communities: The metaverse is a rapidly evolving space, with many enthusiastic experts and communities discussing its trends, technologies, and business opportunities. Engage with these communities through social media, forums, or professional networks. Attend webinars, conferences, and listen to podcasts focused on the metaverse.

CHAPTER 12
BITCOIN AND BLOCKCHAIN

One of the ways to get a sense of what exciting up-and-coming technologies there are is as simple as tracking what people are talking about. In Chapter 2, I talked about the Starbucks test and how ChatGPT and AI are all anyone is talking about these days. This chapter is going to look at something from the before-times: Bitcoin and blockchain.

Back in 2017, Bitcoin was all over the papers because it had grown from a thing that "techies" played with, to an important financial instrument that was making people wealthy overnight, with little or no effort. Though AI has since stolen some of its thunder, the technology behind Bitcoin and blockchain still promises to reshape the internet and how we interact with each other online.

When you are operating online, there is a lot of trust involved. When you are trading anything of value, there comes a point where too much trust is a bad idea. This is where some sort of central authority, like a government or bank, comes in and provides security. However, as the internet becomes more decentralised, this becomes less practical.

Bitcoin as a concept was introduced in a 2008 whitepaper entitled "Bitcoin: A Peer-to-Peer Electronic Cash System" by an unknown person or group under the pseudonym "Satoshi Nakamoto".[1] It was intended to be an alternative to the banking system, a "bank buster", and create a decentralised digital currency that operated without the need for a central authority.

This electronic cash system was designed to send online payments directly from one party to another without going through a financial institution. Instead of traditional methods for securing transactions, it creates security using cryptographic encryption and a technology called blockchain. This is a type of Distributed Ledger Technology (DLT) that acts as a record of any and all transactions or interactions between all users on the blockchain network.

It is important to note that Bitcoin and blockchain technology are intrinsically linked, as blockchain is the foundational technology upon which Bitcoin is built.

When explaining this concept to audiences, I show a picture of an accounting ledger from 1926 which records debits and credits in written form. When my mother, Rhonda, ran the accounts for our family electronics company in Adelaide, Australia, she would carefully enter all of the transactions in the ledger. This created an honest and accurate record of the financial position of the company. It could then be audited or shown to others as needed.

That changed in the early 1980s when their first computer was installed – a Wang VS system – to manage finance, payroll, accounts, stock inventory, and order management.

Figure 12.1   An accounting ledger. Credit: Chris Pastrick / Pixabay

When a ledger is a physical item, transactions have to be centralised by their nature. There is only one copy of the ledger, so it can only be updated or checked by one person, in one location, at a time. Maintaining multiple ledgers in multiple places risks introducing errors into the accounting. What happens if multiple different transactions are recorded in both books before they are synchronised?

Making a digital version, for example as a spreadsheet in Microsoft Excel, makes this a little easier, but the same problem still exists. How can you trust that this particular version of the file is the latest, and has not been changed incorrectly? You need a method by which you can only update the ledger if your version is the most accurate and up-to-date.

How Blockchain Works

Using a distributed ledger, one version of the truth is available to everyone who is provided access to the ledger. Blockchain technology ensures that this one version of the truth is irrefutable.

Blockchain works by creating a chain of "blocks". Each block in the chain contains many transactions, and once completed, a new block is generated and linked to the previous one. Through cryptographic techniques, each block is securely linked to its predecessor, creating a chain that is nearly impossible to alter. New transactions can only be recorded if the network has consensus on every transaction that came before it, preventing the record being changed.

This immutability provides trust in the system, as users can be confident that once a transaction is recorded on the blockchain, it cannot be changed or reversed fraudulently.

Creating Consensus

As mentioned earlier, the central principle of blockchain is to ensure the integrity of every transaction. If I promise to give you a dollar over the phone, you need to know that the dollar has left my account and is in yours. With a centralised banking system, I can instantly pay someone via my bank app and see it leave my account. Because my bank is regulated, I trust that my dollar is now safely in the other person's account.

In a decentralised world, you must work harder to prove this transaction has occurred. One other tenet of the Bitcoin whitepaper was to allow people to transact with each other without a trusted relationship.

Unlike traditional banking systems that rely on central authorities, Bitcoin operates on a decentralised network of computers called nodes. Every single node has its own complete ledger. Each ledger is verified through cryptography with each transaction and then the node adds to a block in the block-chain. Once this happens, every node uses a process called "consensus" to agree that they have identical and accurate records.

This ensures that no single entity has total control over the Bitcoin network – keeping the system decentralised. It also means every Bitcoin transaction is recorded and publicly available, providing transparency and security.

There are two different mechanisms by which a blockchain network confirms transactions and reaches consensus before adding new blocks to the block-chain: Proof of Work (PoW) and Proof of Stake (PoS). Each has its unique approach and principles for achieving consensus and ensuring the security and integrity of the blockchain for every transaction.

Proof of Work

PoW is a consensus mechanism that requires participants (called miners) to solve complex mathematical puzzles to validate transactions and create new blocks. These problems require significant computational resources to solve. The first one to solve the puzzle wins the right to add the next block to the blockchain, as well as being rewarded with some Bitcoin for their work. (This form of earning Bitcoin is also where the term "Bitcoin mining" comes from).

The effort and cost of solving the puzzle ensures the network's security by making it prohibitively expensive and time-consuming to attempt malicious actions, such as double-spending or attacking the network. However, this does mean PoW is criticised for its high energy consumption as miners require powerful hardware and consume a lot of electricity to perform computationally intensive calculations.

Proof of Stake

PoS is generally more energy-efficient than PoW, as it does not require extensive computational work. Instead of solving complex puzzles, PoS involves validators being chosen based on their "stake". This secures the network through economic incentives, where validators have a financial stake in maintaining the network's integrity.

Another popular blockchain, Ethereum, is more suited to enterprise applications primarily due to its flexibility, robust smart contract functionality, and active ecosystem. Initially, they also used PoW, but on 15 September 2022, Ethereum 2.0 adopted a PoS consensus mechanism. Analysts estimate that PoS has reduced the energy consumption of creating consensus by 99.98% compared to PoW.[2]

Experimenting with Bitcoin

Being digitally curious, when media interest intensified, I started to ask more questions about Bitcoin and blockchain. In 2017, I did two key things when Bitcoin experienced peaks of around $20,000 in value. Firstly, I bought some Bitcoin – £20 worth. Not enough to get rich, but enough to see what the experience was to buy, hold, and then sell Bitcoin.

The buying experience was complex, and holding the currency was a wild ride. Looking at the Coinbase app on my phone that I used to purchase the cryptocurrency, £20 became £23. When I refreshed the app a few minutes later, it was £26, then £22. I thought to myself, I'm sitting here refreshing, and the value is going up and down with no inherent action on my behalf.

When I wanted to understand what it was like to turn Bitcoin back into fiat – that is, currency issued by a government (in this case, the Bank of England) – it took me two banks and four weeks, including depositing €1 in an Estonian bank so that my bank could send the proceeds of the sale to me.

At this point I realised that it wasn't ready for mainstream adoption. Later the same year, I was fortunate to be sat next to someone at a Christmas party who was a proclaimed "Bitcoin expert". I remember that my opening sentence to him was: "This is your lucky day, I have so many questions about Bitcoin."

Over the ensuing hours, I learned several things about Bitcoin. Did you know the global transaction speed for the cryptocurrency is just SEVEN transactions per second?[3] I asked my dinner guest if this was a mistake. He explained that it wasn't. PoW, the primary consensus mechanism at the time, was designed to be time and energy intensive. This meant that seven transactions per second was the maximum throughput.

When you compare that against Visa, which can process 24,000 transactions per second, you quickly realise that Bitcoin was never designed to be a global currency. The intent was in the right place. However, if designed in 2024, it most likely would have used an architecture that was far more efficient.

The Power of Blockchain

While using cryptocurrency itself is not necessarily quite there yet, remember that blockchain and Bitcoin are different things – be wary of confusing blockchain with the applications running on those blockchains. Blockchain technology is already being used in multiple industries.

There are many situations in which having a decentralised, tamper-proof record of every transaction and interaction can be invaluable. An example of this is in supply chain management, where it enhances transparency, efficiency, and security throughout the process.

By utilising a decentralised and immutable ledger, blockchain can provide a tamper-proof record of every transaction and movement of goods, from raw materials to final delivery. This ensures traceability and accountability at every step, allowing companies to verify the authenticity of products, reduce counterfeits, and ensure compliance with regulations.

This increased visibility helps manage inventories more effectively, reduce costs, and improve the overall reliability of the supply chain. Furthermore, blockchain's ability to provide a single source of truth improves collaboration among all stakeholders, including suppliers, manufacturers, distributors, and retailers, leading to more transparent and efficient supply chain networks. A good example of using a blockchain is from Australian company Everledger, where they help track provenance history around diamonds.[4]

Walmart, IBM, and the Food Trust Blockchain

A notable real-world example of blockchain used in supply chain management is Walmart's collaboration with IBM on the Food Trust blockchain.[5]

This initiative aims to increase the transparency, efficiency, and safety of food supply chains. By leveraging blockchain technology, Walmart has been able to track the origin of over 25 products from five different suppliers. This system enables them to trace the journey of food items from farm to store shelves in a matter of seconds, significantly reducing the time it takes to trace the source of food products in case of a health scare or contamination issue.

In a pilot project, Walmart demonstrated that it could reduce the time to trace the source of sliced mangoes from 7 days to just 2.2 seconds. This dramatic improvement in traceability not only enhances food safety for consumers by quickly identifying and addressing contamination issues, but also increases the efficiency of the supply chain by reducing waste and ensuring the freshness of products.

Ethereum and Smart Contracts

Ethereum is a blockchain platform that enables the creation of smart contracts and decentralised applications (DApps). Smart contracts are self-executing contracts with the terms directly written into code, which run on the block-chain and automatically enforce agreements without intermediaries.

With blockchain, every aspect of an employee contract, including amendments and updates, can be recorded in a transparent, immutable ledger. This ensures a clear, indisputable history of the terms and conditions agreed upon by both parties, potentially reducing disputes and increasing trust.

These contracts can also be set up to be self-executing. They function as programs with the terms of the agreements written into the code. Enterprises use smart contracts to automate and enforce contractual agreements. In doing so they reduce the need for intermediaries and increase the efficiency of business processes such as payments, settlements, and compliance. This reduces administrative overhead and eliminates the need for intermediaries.

Decentralised Autonomous Organisations

By issuing identity tokens, blockchain can provide a secure and unforgeable method of managing digital identities. This is particularly useful for enterprises in ensuring secure access to information and resources, improving privacy controls, and reducing the risk of identity theft and fraud. It can also be used to provide alternative and more demographic structures for an organisation in the form of a Decentralised Autonomous Organisation (DAO).

Some people describe this as the company of the future. Conceptually, it's more like a partnership with people who are members of it and who have voting rights in relation to what it's going to achieve. If you've got a certain number of governance tokens, you get a certain number of votes and every decision has to be voted on.

I don't think that's going to work in the way it was initially designed because of human behaviours. Anyone who's ever been involved in a partnership will know that everyone voting on everything is a very poor way of organising any complex business. However, the concept of DAOs is very strong in the crypto community and it will continue to grow.

L'Oreal was one of the very first beauty brands to create a DAO, called NYX. This allows them to involve their community more in product creation and in governance. They are allowing their community and followers who have joined the DAO to govern the future of virtual makeup and virtual looks. Each member gets to vote on the designers who are going to be creating these actual designs. This example can be extrapolated into any business that has fans, and a community. If you are brave enough to allow decisions about a product or service to rest with your community, then a DAO might be worth investigating. It will allow your customers to have a direct say in the evolution of your product and potentially your brand as well.

This said, while DAOs hold a lot of potential, security is still important. In 2016, "The DAO", the first DAO on the internet, suffered a catastrophic loss of $60m after the network was hacked. This early disaster proved to the crypto community the importance of proper security and protection – the weaknesses that allowed this to happen were quickly patched up.[6]

However, the lesson to learn is the importance of having an active security strategy to protect your digital assets online.

Curious Five

Taking the lead from my curiosity in 2017, I suggest you look at these five actionable things.

1. Buy some Bitcoin – a small amount. Understand the onboarding and holding process and wait a few weeks, then see how easy it is to convert back to fiat currency.

2. Investigate blockchain projects in your industry and look at what issues they have solved.

3. Look at how companies are using smart contracts for transactions.

4. Understand if your company is currently using blockchain technologies.

5. Understand what central banks are doing to regulate cryptocurrencies. A good start is a whitepaper from Nuvei: "The Future of Crypto Payments".[7]

CHAPTER 13
TOKENISATION AND NFTs

After discussing Bitcoin and blockchain in Chapter 12, we now turn to two more members of the Web 3.0 family: tokenisation and Non-Fungible Tokens (NFTs).

Blockchain's transparency, security, and immutability means that we can now trade and exchange things online directly – without needing to go through a centralised authority. However, we don't need to limit ourselves to just currency.

Think about it: is a bank note something that actually holds value, or is it a representation that you have the right to that amount of money? Humans have been using physical representations, or tokens, of their valuable assets for most of human history. Through a process called "tokenisation", it is possible to do the same thing digitally.

Tokenisation refers to the process of converting rights to an asset into a digital token on a blockchain. This can include assets such as real estate, art, financial instruments, or individual products and services. Once something has been tokenised, it can then be transferred or exchanged securely and efficiently using the blockchain.

Non-Fungible Tokens

Just as with Bitcoin in 2017, the media started to pick up on NFTs in 2021 when several high-profile sales of NFTs – including digital art, sports collectables, and other digital media – captured public attention. But what exactly is an NFT?

If you use a token to represent currency – whether a physical coin or a Bitcoin online – each token is functionally identical. It is possible for you to directly exchange your token for another one of the same value, and it is otherwise identical. They are "fungible".

A *non*-fungible token is something unique with its own distinct value that can't be exchanged on an equal basis with another token just like it. They are typically used to tokenise digital art, collectables, game items, and other digital goods, allowing creators to monetise their digital creations directly. The sale of digital artist Beeple's collage *Everydays: The First 5000 Days* for over $69 million at Christie's auction house in March 2021 marked a significant milestone in NFT media coverage.[1]

By leveraging blockchain technology's transparency, security, and immutability, NFTs ensure the authenticity, provenance, and exclusive ownership of digital assets. This enables a new economy for digital content in various industries, from art and entertainment to gaming and beyond. Just like Bitcoin, they have been controversial and often misunderstood because real money is involved.

The Potential of NFTs

Counting myself as an NFT sceptic, I was among many who questioned the value, utility, and future of digital ownership and art in the digital age, and this only made me curious to find out more. Nick Abrahams is an Australian lawyer and Global Leader in Technology & Innovation for the law firm Norton Rose Fulbright, who sees a positive future for NFTs. I spoke with him about Web 3.0, cryptocurrency, NFTs, and tokenisation on The Digitally Curious Podcast.[2]

"Web 3.0 brings about the ability for people to own digital things. With Web 1.0 and Web 2.0, we've seen the democratisation of content. We can have a million digital image files, and they can be transported around the world at no additional cost; however, we are unable to establish ownership of any of those files."
—*Nick Abrahams, Global Leader in Technology & Innovation, Norton Rose Fulbright*

Case Study: Ticketing

Tickets are a good example of a way to benefit from tokenising physical items. Ticketing is a great use case for NFTs. It solves two problems: proving that you've got the correct ticket and the fact that people love to collect tickets to significant events.

I've been to many concerts in London and I've always dealt with the authorised ticket outlet. Still, several secondary ticket-selling services have fallen foul of the regulators because they charge very high prices. I saw one example of an NFT ticketing company on a London Underground billboard called SeatLabNFT.[3]

They describe themselves as: "An NFT event ticketing marketplace helping artists foster closer connections with fans, eliminating fraud and reducing the impact of scalping." They are selling tickets to events that are also collectable. This is one way to potentially disrupt the secondary and illegal "ticket tout" market that drives up ticket prices for fans to see the bands and performers they love.

Their vision for the future of ticketing is one where "genuine fans are able to get their hands on the tickets they deserve". This is a good example of where NFTs break out of gaming into the real world and solve real-world problems like ticket touting. Coachella Music Festival did their ticketing by NFT in 2022, and the 2022 Super Bowl did the same.[4]

Nick categorised NFTs into six categories:

1. **Flex club** NFTs are limited edition, usually around 10,000, that provide additional benefits like future NFT drops or access to VIP events. They allow owners to show off their wealth in the digital world. A good example is the "Bored Apes" NFTs, with one selling for nearly $3.4 million.[5]

2. **Art** NFTs are one-of-a-kind digital artworks that sell for millions, like traditional contemporary art. While some question the value, art is subjective, and some are willing to pay huge sums.

3. **Collectible** NFTs include things like digitised sports trading cards. The NBA's Top Shot collected over $700 million in sales, and all major sports leagues are entering the NFT game for collectables.

4. **Twin** NFTs provide a digital twin of a real-world luxury purchase, which is popular in fashion. An example is Dolce & Gabbana, which sells digital twins of suits for millions.

5. **Gaming** NFTs allow ownership of in-game assets like skins and swords that can be traded. They are a big driver of the play-to-earn economy.

6. **Brand** NFTs allow major brands to build communities through exclusive NFT drops that benefit holders. Over 100 top brands have minted their NFTs. An example I will explore shortly is the Starbucks Odyssey NFT project.

An early example of this NFT craze was in 2019 when the Italian artist Maurizio Cattelan duct-taped a banana from a local supermarket to a gallery wall at Miami's Art Basel festival. He called it Comedian and sold it for $120,000. The actual banana wasn't included in the purchase. The purchaser bought a certificate of authenticity, which included instructions on the correct angle and height at which to affix the fruit to a wall.[6]

I'm the wrong target market for this artwork. If you Google "Bored Apes NFT" you might agree with me. Paying millions for a link to a .jpg file doesn't seem like a great investment. My hypothesis is that during the early phases of new technologies that intersect with the ability to quickly make large sums of money, this type of behaviour is expected.

Humans can become greedy, and there is always someone who will take advantage of this. The phrase "a fool and his money are easily parted", first coined by Dr John Bridges' *Defence of the Government of the Church of England* in 1587, came to mind at the peak of the NFT frenzy. Somewhat proving my analogy, since the heady days of NFTs in 2021, the market has normalised. At the time of writing, Bored Apes NFTs are now selling for an average price of $71,800. It would be interesting to see the average price when you are reading this chapter via curious.click/price.

Brand NFTs – A Next-Generation Loyalty Programme

A good example of a brand NFT in action is the Starbucks Odyssey NFT project.[7] This was launched as an extension of the Starbucks Rewards loyalty programme. It aims to offer its customers a unique experience by leveraging NFTs to create a series of digital collectables and experiences, ensuring authenticity and exclusivity for participants by using blockchain to secure transactions and ownership records.

Participants in the Starbucks Odyssey programme can earn and purchase NFTs, which Starbucks refers to as "Journey Stamps", by engaging in various activities, challenges, and experiences related to the brand. These digital stamps serve as collectable items and unlock access to exclusive rewards, experiences, and perks, such as special merchandise, unique events, and even trips.

Loyal customers and fans often crave something more significant to acknowledge their fidelity, something more exclusive and distinctive. Before the advent of Starbucks Odyssey, the conventional rewards for accumulating points through coffee purchases were not much more than a digital version of the original "coffee card stamp", consisting of discounts and free coffee.

This new style of NFT loyalty programme plays well into fandom, providing activities and rewards to your most loyal and engaged fans. This is a sensible extension of an existing loyalty programme and something that existing members would see as beneficial. While the programme hasn't been launched in the UK, I have signed up to join once it is available.

The MetaBirkin

One excellent example of how new technologies such as NFTs are challenging existing regulations and norms is the "MetaBirkin" controversy.[8] In this scandal, virtual art met the law in 2023 when a jury returned a verdict against artist Mason Rothschild on claims of trademark

(continued)

(*continued*)

infringement, dilution, and cybersquatting, and ordered him to pay $133,000 in damages.

Rothschild created digital versions of the iconic Birkin bags covered in colourful fur. Luxury fashion house Hermès objected to Rothschild's use of the Birkin name and design, arguing that it infringed their trademark rights and could confuse consumers about the origin and association of the digital bags with the Hermès brand.

The artist claimed his freedom of artistic expression by drawing parallels with Andy Warhol's famous artworks, which transformed everyday objects into art, permitting him to create these NFTs.

Hermès' legal action against Rothschild sparked a debate on intellectual property rights, the boundaries of artistic expression, and the commercial use of trademarks in the emerging digital and NFT landscape. The dispute raised important questions about how existing laws apply to digital assets and the extent to which artists can draw inspiration from and reinterpret branded goods in their work.

The legal ramifications of this case, and the intersection of NFTs, Web 3.0, and digital art, are worth exploring further. Law firm Baker McKenzie analysed the deeper legal issues of the Birkin case in their article "Power of the Purse – Hermès Prevails in NFT Trademark Trial".[9]

The jury's verdict confirms that brands can still enjoy robust protection over their intellectual property assets in digital space. The case also highlights the delicate balance that courts must strike in preventing consumer confusion while protecting artistic expressions in worlds both real and virtual.

The MetaBirkin verdict reinforces the notion that the incorporation of a trademark into an NFT could constitute infringement. But because NFTs openly straddle the line between commerce and artistic expression, the outcome of similar cases will continue to turn on fact-intensive questions of artistic expression and the likelihood of marketplace confusion.

While the hype around NFTs has subsided somewhat, you should ensure that your legal teams are briefed on the law around virtual goods and ensure that existing and future trademarks include this additional category.

Applying Tokenisation and NFTs in the Workplace

While collectable NFT artwork can be an interesting avenue to explore, tokenisation will drive this concept deeper into the enterprise. We have already discussed one interesting application in the previous chapter regarding smart contracts, which leverage blockchain technology to innovate how work agreements, compensation, and benefits are managed and executed.

Tokenised contracts can support more flexible, dynamic compensation models. For instance, they can automate the distribution of profit shares, stock options, or performance-based bonuses in real time, providing employees with immediate rewards tied directly to their contributions or company performance.

Nick Abrahams believes tokens could provide a more liquid and valuable form of compensation compared to traditional equity in private companies by giving employees tokens that can immediately be sold on decentralised exchanges upon vesting, providing liquidity that traditional equity lacks.

In 2022, Nick pioneered one of the first employee token option plans in Australia. He feels that tokenisation also allows companies to attract and retain talent through compensation that employees can realise value from much sooner.[10]

A final benefit of tokenisation is that it can facilitate secure, blockchain-based employee credentials and portable and easily verifiable achievements. This could revolutionise hiring and onboarding processes, allowing employees to carry a tamper-proof record of their employment history, skills, and qualifications. Chapter 21 – Sovereign Identity covers this in detail.

What is Tokenomics?

Tokenomics, the blending of "token" and "economics", embodies the intricate economic models that underpin the functionalities of digital tokens within blockchain networks and DApps. It delves into the intricacies of how tokens are created, distributed, valued, and utilised, aiming to establish a balanced ecosystem that incentivises participation while ensuring the platform's sustainability and growth. At its heart, tokenomics is about crafting a system that aligns the interests of all stakeholders – developers, investors, users, and validators – to foster a thriving and secure network.

The foundational pillars of tokenomics include token supply, distribution methods, utility, and incentive mechanisms. Supply dynamics play a pivotal role, where a token can have a fixed cap, mirroring scarcity as seen with Bitcoin, or an inflationary model to support ongoing rewards for network participants. The distribution strategy is equally vital. This determines how tokens are initially allocated through mechanisms like public sales, airdrops (distributing cryptocurrency tokens to a large number of wallet addresses, often for free), or earning via platform engagement.

Utility defines the token's purpose within its ecosystem. It could serve as a medium of exchange, a tool for governance, a means to access specific functionalities, or a combination. This utility not only adds value to the token but also enhances user engagement and retention by providing tangible benefits for holding and using the token within the ecosystem.

Incentive models are the linchpin in tokenomics. They are designed to encourage behaviours that secure the network, provide liquidity, and drive governance participation. Mechanisms such as staking rewards, transaction fee sharing, and voting rights incentivise users to contribute positively to the ecosystem, enhancing its overall health and resilience.

Moreover, tokenomics addresses the economic sustainability of a project, outlining how funds are raised, allocated, and managed to support development, marketing, and operational needs. A well-structured tokenomic model is transparent, ensuring participants understand how their contributions and participation impact the ecosystem.

Effective tokenomics requires a delicate balance, carefully calibrated to prevent excessive inflation, ensure fair distribution, and mitigate centralisation risks, all while fostering innovation and participation. As blockchain technology and decentralised platforms evolve, so too will the complexities of tokenomics, challenging creators to innovate in creating sustainable, equitable, and thriving digital economies.

Understanding tokenomics is crucial for companies engaging with NFTs for several reasons. Firstly, it assists in evaluating the value and potential of an NFT project. By examining the supply mechanisms, distribution plans, and utility of the token, stakeholders can make informed decisions about investing in or participating in the ecosystem.

Secondly, tokenomics structures incentives for all parties involved. Well-designed tokenomics can encourage behaviours that support the sustainability and growth of the platform, such as content creation, community engagement, and network security.

As the NFT market continues to evolve, regulatory and compliance aspects become increasingly significant. Knowledge of tokenomics allows creators and businesses to navigate legal frameworks, ensuring their projects comply with financial regulations and intellectual property laws.

An understanding of tokenomics is also essential for innovation and competitive advantage. By utilising token-based models, businesses can unlock new revenue streams, customer engagement strategies, and forms of digital ownership, positioning themselves at the forefront of digital transformation.

Tokenomics is also linked to cryptocurrency as it outlines the rules for creating and distributing tokens, directly influencing the supply of a particular cryptocurrency. These rules can include mechanisms for mining or staking, Initial Coin Offerings (ICOs), and token burns (the process by which a given amount of a crypto asset is permanently removed from the circulating supply in order to decrease the overall supply of that particular crypto asset). All of these things affect a cryptocurrency's value and scarcity.

Curious Five

While the concept of NFTs can be initially difficult to grasp, adopting a collector mindset can help enterprises realise their possibilities.

Here are five actionable things you can do to understand NFTs and tokenisation better.

1. Understand your business objectives before jumping into an NFT project. Now the initial hype around NFTs has died down, companies need to understand what type of NFT (Flex Club, Art, Collectible, Twin, Gaming, Brand) makes commercial sense.

2. Experiment with creating an NFT and posting it for sale on an NFT marketplace, involving your legal teams.

3. Buy your own (low-cost) NFT collectable to understand better how NFTs and tokenomics work in practice.

4. Think about how you could better engage your loyal fans with an NFT programme that leverages any existing loyalty programmes.

5. Examine the legal implications of virtual goods ownership, IP, and trademark laws. Do you have your legal team across your NFT project?

Above all, with any digital currency or collectable, just because you can doesn't mean you should. Don't always believe the hype. Be curious, but be cautious as well.

PART IV
CURIOUS ABOUT ...
YOUR DATA

Why Am I Curious About My Data?

There are so many reasons why I'm curious about my own data. Everything from how I appear online to potential clients and keeping my data protected, to what happens to my data when I die, and how regulators are working to keep my data safe. All of these things have alerted my curiosity over the last 30 years.

When I define "my data" I refer to everything from what I publish on my own website and on my LinkedIn page, to more personal information such as my date of birth, home address, bank account details, and even passwords. I would like to think I have some level of control over where, how, and when this information is made available, but in an increasingly digital world, this is becoming much harder to track and maintain.

From my talks and interactions with audiences over the years, it appears that many don't share my curiosity about data. We don't think about how we "show up" online and what our digital first impression might look like. We're unaware about how to keep our data safe online, and I'm sure (as I was before speaking to a digital legacy expert) we have little consideration for what happens to our data when we die, and who might have access to it.

Why Should You Be Curious About Your Data?

For the same reasons, you should personally care about your own data, but it now goes further and will impact your business. Your digital first impression can help you land that new client or role you've been chasing. By being curious about how your data is being kept safe and deploying a few simple tricks and tools, you can ensure you're less likely to be the source of a data breach, potentially costing your company millions in fines and lost revenue, not to mention a loss of reputation.

What I've learned about digital legacy will make you equally curious to know what happens when you die; and knowing more about the regulations to protect your data and data privacy is an important step for anyone in business.

CHAPTER 14
YOUR DIGITAL FIRST IMPRESSION

When you meet someone for the first time, what is the first thing you do?

Apart from a handshake or other formal greeting, you most probably look them in the eye, perhaps at what they are wearing and notice whether they are smiling or not.

In many cases, we arrive at our first impressions about someone new in the first 90 seconds. In this initial period, the other person has an opportunity to leave a lasting impression on you. Do you continue to speak with them, or make excuses and find someone else to talk to?

We take great care to form a great first impression in real life, but do we also consider our digital first impression when we meet online?

In many ways, this is more important as people can "meet you" digitally before you meet in person. As the world continues on a path of hybrid and remote working post-pandemic, we can expect many of our "first impressions" to be formed online.

Analogue Networking

I've been networking at events all my adult life, and before that I watched my father do this at events we went to. When I provide career advice to students at universities and schools, I speak about how much easier it is to network today, and how I and others had to do it the old-fashioned, "analogue" way before LinkedIn and Twitter were invented.

Now people can form a first impression about you before you even meet in person.

I am fortunate to meet many senior business leaders from around the world, and I often ask them a probing question when we first meet: "What was the first thing you did when you saw my name listed for this meeting?"

"I Googled you", is the most frequent reply. Some add that they also looked me up on LinkedIn.

So, I know first-hand that my digital first impression is exactly that – the very first impression they have of me. I also know that I have just 90 online seconds to make that impression count – and so do you.

What Happens When a Client "Googles" You?

Try it yourself, but make sure you use "incognito mode" on Google Chrome, also known as "private browsing" on Safari and Firefox, to see what they will see, otherwise your recent searches will skew the results.

On the next page you will see what happened when I Googled my name in April 2024.

You can see that I "own" the front page of Google for a search on my own name. I am not the only Andrew Grill in the world. I know of 18 other "Andrew Grills", so this has been no mean feat. In fact, I've been working on it since I set up andrewgrill.com in 1999 and started to care about my digital footprint.

I am also lucky that my name is fairly unique, and hence if I can produce content that has my name in it, then search engines do the heavy lifting for me and make it easy to find me and my content.

Let's do a quick audit on what that first page tells the world about me, and how you can have this work for you also and enhance your digital first impression.

The first result is my own website, then LinkedIn – meaning you absolutely have to be on this site and have a decent profile. The third result is the bio

Figure 14.1 A screenshot of the results Google returns to a search of my name. Credit: Google Search April 2024. Google is a trademark of Google LLC.

from my site, followed by X (formerly Twitter), and Instagram. The fact that two of my "owned" properties are in the top five results is important, as I have full control over what is displayed here. I own my domain name, and I host my own website on my own server. In this instance, this is the site I want clients to see first, as it shows off my business credentials and lists what I do and my achievements.

Instagram being in the top 10 is also interesting, and I also have a strong presence there. As this is a very visually focused site, I ensure that this content shows off my speaking events, and also the places I travel to.

This highlights that you need to think about your digital first impression across ALL platforms, not just the more business-related ones.

Your Online Strategy Drives Your Digital First Impression

Having a broad content strategy, across multiple owned and public platforms, means that my digital first impression is hopefully one that can secure me a meeting with a potential or existing client. They research my background and make that first in-person meeting much more rewarding.

Anyone can use this same strategy, but you need something credible to say, and you need to say it across as many platforms as makes sense. People won't always go directly to your own website, unless you encourage them to do so on your business card or email signature. Therefore, you need to make sure your name is associated with what you want to be known for, and your areas of expertise.

One thing that I've been an advocate of is having your own domain name and email address. In 1999, I registered andrewgrill.com. I then connected an email platform to this domain, so that emails sent to contact@andrewgrill .com would come directly to me.

I see many vehicles driving around London that have a gmail or, worse still, a hotmail email address displayed *on the side*. Call me a purist, but these email addresses promote Google and Microsoft brands, not yours. If you decide to set up your own domain name and custom email address, you can then set email from your existing provider to forward to your new address. This will ensure that you create an excellent digital first impression when a potential client receives an email from your new @myname.com email address.

The next task will then be to set up a presence on your new domain name, as the most likely thing your recipient will do is see what is at the myname.com address. This brings me to my final point on digital first impressions – the balance between your "public" and "private" online personas.

Public vs Private

Recently I gave a career talk at a high school in London as part of my involvement in the charity Speakers for Schools.[1] This is a UK charity launched in 2010 helping government schools inspire their students and broaden horizons through access to the insights, experiences, and expertise of the UK's leading figures through free talks and more – at no cost to the school.

In front of more than 100 Sixth Formers (16-year-olds in one of their final years of high school), I explained that as a potential employer, I would not hire someone if I searched their name and all I could see was them drinking at parties on Facebook.

I had a number of questions about this from students in the room. A couple of students also quizzed me via email and Twitter direct message after the talk. They could not see the link between what they did "in private" affecting their suitability for a job.

The bombshell I dropped was that when you share what you do in your own private time online (even with tight security settings), it is no longer private. You have published it for all to see, including a potential client.

Just as the audit of my Google name search proved, most of my social networks – even Facebook – appeared linked to my name. When I was at IBM, I was aware of the graduate recruitment team researching social media profiles as part of their reference checks – as an indication of a candidate's suitability for a role.

If you are reading this and have pictures that you would not want an employer to see, then it may be time to hit the delete button. Perhaps store them on an external drive that you own, not one owned by Facebook.

When I mention the need to be careful about what you post online to Gen Y and Gen Z audiences, I always get the pushback that there is "nothing wrong" with posting pictures of yourself at a party, or having fun with friends. I always agree with these statements – there is nothing wrong at all. But you need to also consider if these pictures contribute to that 90-second digital first impression.

The impression you present online can have ramifications beyond your own personal brand.

Let me amplify why the concept of your digital first impression can be important, and perhaps even have a monetary value ascribed to it.

Imagine the following scenario: I've just pitched for a large piece of consulting work and I've named all of the consultants we're planning to deploy, along with sharing their CVs so the client is aware of their skills and experience. Naturally, the client puts the names of the consultants into Google. Within the first few results are pictures of one of the consultants out partying and behaving in a way not fitting for the brand. The client becomes concerned about the calibre of the consultants that have been put forward and decides not to proceed. A few silly photos on the internet cost the company millions, thanks to a bad digital first impression.

On the other side, having a sound digital first impression can drive revenue. While I was at IBM, I was able to influence a number of companies to do business with the consulting arm, earning $100 million in incremental revenue as a result. This was linked to my online presence (directly linked to my digital first impression) and eminence in the space in which clients required my experience and expertise. When clients were searching for me online, or asking their staff about recommendations, my digital first impression was building confidence. In this case my digital first impression was worth millions.

If I can see a picture of you drunk at a party via a Google search, then my client, by putting your name into Google, will see the same when they are checking out the A-list team I have put together to work on their top-secret project. If they get a bad first impression from this digital "first meeting", then they will think poorly of my judgement in putting your name forward, and of my firm. Publishing photos online is just that – publishing for all to see.

This is why it is imperative that you audit and evaluate what digital first impression you are sending to the world. Now more than ever, your digital first impression matters.

Which brings me to the next point related to your digital first impression. How do you "sell" a product online, when the product can be your own services, or those provided by the company where you are an employee?

As I've already outlined, in this digital always-on age, buyers can make a decision in the first 90 seconds. Recalling a recent buyer journey of a prospective client emphasised how important that digital first impression is.

As a public speaker, my "product" is time on stage in front of an audience, so what I am "selling" is a mix of domain expertise, stage presence, and over 30 years of business experience. Typically, in the professional speaking industry, a prospective client will contact a speaker bureau such as Speakers Corner, JLA, Champions Speakers, or London Speaker Bureau, to name a few.

In my case, the client will have asked for a "Futurist" or an "AI speaker". These are some of the hottest segments at the moment, so there are a large number of different speakers to choose from.

In this particular instance, I was one of four futurists put forward to the client. At this stage, I still had no opportunity to influence the client personally. What normally happens next is that the speaker bureau will send the biographies of each speaker along with their short video showreel to the client as their recommendations.

My video showreel[2] is a 2-minute opportunity to show potential clients exactly what I do. So, what happened when this client watched my showreel?

He told me when we met in person that he sent all four showreels provided by the speaker bureau to the three most cynical people he could think of in his office and asked them which one they would like to see perform at their event. The feedback was unanimous. Apparently, my energy and passion for the subject came through instantly on the video.

The first 90 seconds in front of a prospective client are critical – so make them count!

How to Manage Your Online Presence

Managing and monitoring your digital identity effectively involves several strategies and tools aimed at maintaining a positive online presence and ensuring your personal information is secure. Here are various methods and tools you can use to manage and watch over your digital identity:

1. *Google Alerts*: To monitor the web for new content about you. Head to google.com/alerts[3] and set up alerts for your name (or any variations of it) in "quotes" to receive notifications whenever new content, like articles or mentions, is published online.

2. *Social media settings and privacy check-ups*: To control who sees what you post and to manage your online presence. You should regularly review and adjust your privacy settings on platforms like Facebook, X, LinkedIn, and Instagram to control your visibility and the information you share.

3. *Virtual Private Networks (VPNs)*: To secure your internet connection and protect your privacy online. When on public, unsecured, or unfamiliar Wi-Fi networks, you should use a VPN service to encrypt your internet connection, to prevent others from intercepting your data. The VPN I use and recommend is Surfshark.[4]

4. *Regular online searches*: To see what others see when they search for you on Google and LinkedIn, you should regularly conduct searches on your name to see what information about you is publicly accessible.

5. *Identity theft protection services*: To monitor your personal information for signs of identity theft. Services like LifeLock[5] or Experian[6] can alert you to potentially fraudulent use of your personal information, helping you to act quickly.

6. *Digital footprint clean-up services*: To remove old or unwanted information about you from the internet. Services like DeleteMe[7] or Reputation-Defender[8] can remove your personal information from the internet and reduce your online footprint.

7. *Educate yourself on phishing scams*: To avoid falling victim to scams that could compromise your digital identity, as part of your digital hygiene regime, you should stay informed about common phishing tactics and always be sceptical of unsolicited emails or messages asking for personal information.

8. *Regular software updates*: To protect against vulnerabilities and hacks, you should keep your operating system, applications, and security software up-to-date on all your devices. When you see that annoying indication that there is a software update available, see it as a chance to get one step closer to being safer online.

Curious Five

Here are five activities to help you leverage your digital first impression.

1. Try "Googling" yourself using a private or incognito browser window. What you see is your client's digital first impression of you.

2. Audit your LinkedIn profile – does it show off your unique set of skills and experience?

3. Review the headshot you use across social media profiles. Make sure it is professional and consistent.

4. Consider buying your own domain name and adding an email address that contains your own brand. Namecheap[9] is a good place to find a domain, and Fastmail[10] allows you to have your own personalised email address connected to your domain.

5. Consider setting up a presence with your own custom domain name – as an "online business card". Sites such as About.me[11] allow you to set up a one-page website for free using your new domain name, and domain companies such as Namecheap allow you to set up a simple website for a low monthly fee.[12]

CHAPTER 15
STAYING SAFE IN THE AGE OF AI

As the resident tech expert among my friends, I'm always being asked for technical advice. If I was to rank the types of issues I'm asked to help with, number one would be creating, managing, and remembering passwords.

A few of my friends have a physical book of passwords and write them all down. Sadly, possibly like most of my readers, the passwords you use across multiple websites are the same or similar, because it is becoming so hard to remember them all.

Like many of you, I started my digital life with a simple password. I recall it was "huxley" created back in 1986 when I was studying a science degree at Flinders University in Adelaide, Australia, and the "green screen" university computer terminal asked me to "choose a password". This password was, of course, named after Aldous Huxley, author of *Brave New World*, mentioned in the Introduction.

Some years later, when I was entering what I thought was this brilliant password into a new system, it had the nerve to tell me that this password was too simple! It was time to understand how password management would become key in my digital career.

Those who are fans of British comic Michael McIntyre may have seen his Netflix special where he talks about passwords.[1] In his show he reveals that many of us are guilty of creating a password with a 1 and a $ at the end when told that "Password" is not strong enough and we need to add numbers and "special characters".

I used to have just three passwords for all of the sites I used:

- A short1

- A LonGer0ne

- A muchLong3RandH4der2guessone

To be clear, these were not the actual passwords! I used the short one on websites I visited infrequently, the longer one on more important sites, and the much longer one on sites where my personal information needed to be kept secure such as banking sites.

The Best Password is One So Long and Complex You Can't Remember It

It was nearly 20 years ago that I decided to get serious about my passwords. I've used a variety of password managers over the years, starting off with Sticky Password in 2007 and in 2019, I changed from LastPass to 1Password.

Cyberattacks, hacks, and data leaks are on the rise, and it is quite probable that your prized password is already out in the open.

One site that can be used to check this was launched by Australian security researcher Troy Hunt in December 2013, named Have I Been Pwned.[2] At the time of writing, the site has around 13 billion password breaches that can be searched by email address, telephone number, or the actual password.

Troy provides this as a public service and also licences the database to governments and password managers such as 1Password.[3] This is why I now use this manager, as it ensures that I don't use or create passwords that have already been breached.

I've been talking about this service for years now in each and every one of my talks, and it is the one thing that is consistently mentioned in the coffee breaks after I've spoken. Some of the most senior executives from companies you use every day suddenly discover that their email address and password have been the subject of a breach. It serves as a wakeup call (as I hope this chapter will for you) that they need to take password hygiene seriously.

Inside the 1Password app there is a feature called "watchtower", which runs an audit of your password hygiene. When I first ran mine, the results shocked me. Even though I had been using a password manager for many years, my password hygiene was poor. I had hundreds of reused passwords on multiple sites, weak passwords, and 438 that were included in the Have I Been Pwned website.

Regardless of which password manager you use – be it a scrapbook with passwords written down, one of the services I've mentioned, or the password manager that is built into Google Chrome, Safari, or your Apple or Android device, you should be using one.

More importantly, here is why you need one. As password requirements become more complex, it is unlikely that we will be able to remember each and every password we create. If you only have a handful of passwords that you use across multiple sites then I'd like to explain why this needs to change, today.

If you've used the same password on multiple sites, and it has been compromised, then every one of those sites is now likely to be at risk also. One other trait I've noticed among my friends is that they use the same @gmail.com or @yahoo.com email address as the username across every site. This means that a cybercriminal can set a process in place to try and log in to all the main websites with the same username and the compromised password.

If you haven't been diligent in changing your password across all the sites you use, then you've likely already been compromised.

So, Why Should You Use a Password Manager?

Using a password manager means that EVERY site can have a unique and LONG password assigned to it – one that I could never remember, such as #s=JA=i%:Pyxg+8DT.^. Yes, that is an example of a strong password that 1Password can generate for you instantly.

The role of a password manager is to keep track of all the passwords and then I need to just remember one master password (hence the name 1Password) to access the password vault.

You can use a password manager like 1Password on all of your devices. On your desktop, when a password or login screen appears, the job of 1Password is to automatically fill in the fields so you can log in without having to remember the password.

The passwords are securely synced so you can also use the app on your phone and tablet. Both LastPass and 1Password allow me to use an additional level of security – two-factor authentication (2FA) so that my master password is useless if breached without my phone and the 2FA code. It goes without saying that all the passwords are encrypted. 1Password have published their security methodology and also have a whitepaper outlining what they do to keep your passwords safe. This is the sort of transparency that allows me to trust one app with all my digital secrets.

A neat feature of 1Password is that it also provides an "Emergency Kit". This allows you to print out the way to access your password vault in case of emergency. I have provided this for safekeeping with someone I trust so they have access to all my sites in case something happens to me, or my equipment is stolen.

I am sure that you don't want your personal information, or your company's secrets, splashed all over the internet. Therefore, it is up to you personally to be part of the security solution, and not rely on what your company or school provides in terms of firewalls or gateways.

If you hold a high-profile or senior role at a well-known company, then you should be even more concerned that you will be personally targeted by cybercriminals. This type of attack can be quite subtle, and is called "spear phishing".[4] Let me paint a picture of how cybercriminals operate.

They decide on you as a target. They quickly find that you have a Gmail account and guess the password using a "brute force" approach of trying passwords until they are successful. If you don't have an additional layer of protection, such as 2FA, then your email account will be much easier to hack.

What they do next may surprise you. Rather than logging into your Gmail account and wreaking havoc, they log in and wait. You won't detect that they are in your account each and every day, learning the names of your children, your parents, your parents-in-law, places you like to go on vacation, and the names of your pets.

They need this information to build up a profile of what someone who knows you well might say to you in an email. Now with GenAI voice cloning being available they might clone your voice, or the voice of someone close to you, and call you in a panic asking for money, knowing things about you that only a close friend or family member would know.

Having this exclusive access to your life, undetected and unobserved, leaves you, your friends and family, and importantly your company, completely vulnerable to cyberattacks and potential extortion.

If the last few paragraphs have unsettled you, then I'm glad. The public service announcement I've been delivering for the last 17 years has not been in vain.

The Power of Multi-Factor Authentication

Having a strong password is one thing, but in the age of AI and deep fakes, this is simply not enough. I am sure that your bank has issued you with a physical "token" or "dongle" that generates a code before you can access your accounts. Just as your bank needs you to stay secure, you need to take the same approach to all of the sites you use.

We will see the rise of "passkeys", which will ultimately replace passwords, and make it much harder for criminals to gain access to our information using a compromised password.

Passwords vs Passkeys

Passkeys and passwordless access are two modern approaches to authentication that seek to enhance security and user experience by moving away from traditional password-based methods.

Passkeys are a form of passwordless authentication that rely on cryptographic key pairs to securely authenticate a user to a service.

Unlike traditional passwords, passkeys do not require the user to remember or enter any information during the login process; instead, authentication is achieved through a device that the user has with them, such as a smartphone, which stores the passkey and confirms the user's identity through biometrics or a PIN.

Passwordless access can encompass a broader range of methods, including passkeys, but also others like biometric verification (fingerprint or facial recognition), one-time codes sent via SMS or email, or authentication apps. Both approaches aim to eliminate the vulnerabilities associated with passwords, such as phishing attacks and password reuse. However, passkeys specifically leverage cryptographic principles to provide a seamless and highly secure authentication experience.

Modern password managers such as 1Password also allow the generation, storage, and presentation of passkeys for all of your sites – so we may soon see the end of having to remember multiple passwords.

1Password surveyed their users[5] and found the following:

- People are desperate to simplify their digital lives. Nearly two in three people (65%) say they're open to using any new technology that makes life simpler.

- Passkeys aren't going mainstream overnight. Only one in four people say they've heard the term "passwordless".

- People are open to passkeys once they understand what they are and how they work. Three in four people (75%) indicate they'd be open to using passkeys, when shown a description and example.

- Phishing isn't going away any time soon. 67% of respondents personally received phishing attack messages in the past year, while 100% either received phishing messages or know someone who did.

Why is This Important in Business?

The preceding information was all related to your own ability to stay safe online. You therefore might be thinking that there is a lot to do to stay safe, such as reviewing passwords and turning on two-factor authentication, so focusing on this within your organisation might not be a high priority as there are already a number of security protocols and systems in place.

Your employees are your last line of defence in any organisation.

I cannot stress enough the link between company data breaches and your own approach to online security. According to an IBM security report,[6] the global average cost of a data breach in 2023 was $4.45 million, a 15% increase over three years.

Ponemon Institute analysed data from 553 organisations affected by data breaches worldwide. The report revealed that the top five vulnerable industries that experience the costliest data breaches are healthcare, financial, pharmaceutical, energy, and industrial organisations.

Three of the most common types of data breaches are caused by the following.

- *Social engineering*: This type of malicious activity is aimed at obtaining user credentials or other sensitive information without hacking. It often involves impersonating trusted parties to trick people into giving up sensitive information or taking harmful actions. Common forms of social engineering include phishing, email compromise, phone calls, and pretexting – a social engineering tactic where an attacker fabricates a scenario to deceive someone into divulging confidential information.

- *Human error*: People within organisations may send emails to the wrong recipients, upload sensitive data to public cloud storage, or misuse their privileges. The average annual cost to remediate incidents caused by negligent insiders is \$7.2 million. This is according to the 2023 Cost of Insider Risks Global Report by Ponemon Institute.[7]

- *Insider attacks*: This type of attack is caused by a user with legitimate access to sensitive data: a disgruntled employee, a third-party vendor, or a malicious inside agent. Insiders are usually more dangerous than external threat actors since they know exactly what data they can obtain and they already have access to the network.

With the fines for data breaches in many jurisdictions becoming linked to global revenues, the question remains, can you afford not to take your personal and your organisation's data security seriously?

Of all the chapters in this book, this is the one you now need to reflect on and do some homework. As with all of the previous chapters, here are five things that you need to do as soon as you have finished this chapter.

Curious Five

Here are five very simple things you can do to protect your data online.

1. Head to HaveIBeenPwned.com to scare and surprise yourself about how many of the sites you use every day have been hacked, and how many of the passwords you thought were safe are already compromised.

2. Agree that you need to involve a password hygiene strategy and sign up for a password manager such as 1Password. If available, purchase a family plan and have the rest of your family take this step with you.

3. Start a process of adding sites you use regularly to the password manager and change the password for each of these sites, storing the new, randomly generated one in the password manager. This may take weeks, or even months as you come across sites that you use less frequently. Become friendly with the "change my password" button.

4. For each of the sites where you are upgrading and storing your new password, if they offer 2FA then turn this on. These 2FA codes can also be generated by a reputable password manager to make the process of entering them seamless.

5. Instigate a "family password" – a word or phrase that you could ask for in an email or on the telephone if someone contacts you claiming to be someone close to you. An attacker would not know your family password and you can simply say that you're just checking that they know the "family password".

CHAPTER 16
CREATING YOUR DIGITAL LEGACY

Leading cyberpsychologist and counselling psychologist Dr Elaine Kasket[1] is an expert on how digital choices shape our humanity and relationships. She tells stories about the impact of the digital age on how we live and die, and is the author of a fascinating book *All the Ghosts in the Machine: The Digital Afterlife of Your Personal Data.*[2]

Elaine specialises in preserving your digital legacy. Or, to put it another way, what happens to our data when we die. This may seem like a morbid subject to address. Still, after interviewing Elaine for The Digitally Curious Podcast[3] and reading her book, she provided some actionable advice you can put in place today. Until we connected, I hadn't considered what happens to our digital self when we die and, more importantly, how you can start planning for your digital legacy.

Facebook has allowed you to "memorialise" an account for some years now, but most people I speak with are completely unaware that this function exists. I've had the experience of a former colleague in Australia passing away, and no one is looking after his account. Each year, people are wishing him a happy birthday, blissfully unaware that he has passed away.

Elaine explained that as a psychologist, she was fascinated to see the kinds of behaviours that were occurring on her Facebook groups where people were memorialising people who had passed away. As our relationships with big technology companies have changed, we're conditioned to ask questions such as who owns our data, controls it, and has the right to it.

My discussion with Elaine was a wake-up call for me to look at my own data settings and investigate how we can get these issues out in front of the broader public – because it's not just about what happens to our data when we die. It is about who owns you and who owns your digital identity.

Questions include whether their ownership and control over that decrease or increase when you're not there anymore. And whether big tech has more of a say over what happens to your digital remains after you die than the next of kin, your family, or other important people in your life.

This is a complex subject that requires a sensitive and thoughtful approach.

In reading Elaine's book, I was struck by the opening chapter. Here she talks about how she found out more about her grandmother's love for her grandfather through the love letters they wrote to each other while he was at war. This didn't come across in person, but was made real by Elaine's reading of these letters.

Elaine's discovery was via a chance conversation with her mother, who was relating the discovery of a box of letters. They discussed what they'd forgotten about, and all the different facets of a person's life that they don't necessarily show you, or they don't necessarily remember, and how that all comes to light again on reading such letters. In many ways this is a parallel for what happens with all of the data that persists online.

One of the challenges that confronted Elaine following the discovery of the letters was how different family members thought about exposing these memories to other family members, essentially without the author's permission – a tricky area for physical or digital assets. Elaine explained that everybody in her family had a different idea about the privacy level of these artefacts and who could access them.

However, we are thrown into sharper relief by the digital age. This kind of cache of letters – a very coherent, chronologically arranged set of communication over many years – is becoming an increasingly rare phenomenon. Digital remains don't present themselves to us like that. It's much more comprehensive in many ways, but also a much more fragmented set of objects.

Many of us will have digital memories stored on our laptops, portable storage drives, or securely backed up in the cloud. When we pass away, the ability for people to access these memories may depend on the physical access required or access to these online services.

One actionable tip – and also a public service announcement that I provide at all of my talks – is to ensure you have all of your passwords stored safely in a password manager and securely document how to access all these passwords when you're no longer around.

In the previous chapter, I recommended the password manager app 1Password.[4] It has an "Emergency Kit" where you can print out the details required for someone to access all of your passwords. This can be stored in a safe, alongside a physical will, to become part of your "digital will". You should think about doing this today. But even if we have the "keys" to someone's digital legacy, then the question becomes, what do we do with it?

Who Owns Your Digital Content?

My personal experience is worth mentioning here. I've kept a regular digital journal since 2011. It has taken several forms and now resides on the Day One app,[5] which I use to share my daily thoughts and feelings with just myself. I don't expect anyone to read it when I pass away, so it is a personal account of my daily musings. In many ways, this has become a very chronological, searchable way of looking back on my life since 2011.

However, because it is digital, it is not exactly something a relative could find on my shelf once I am gone. In my discussions with Elaine, I kept asking myself: "Who owns our content when we die?"

Many people assume that when their loved ones die, they will have the same right to digital content as they would have to a box of photographs, an album of pictures, or a box of letters – something that's physical. It is surprising then to find that when a big technology company controls that data, it has a different idea about who owns those things.

The rationale presented by some big tech companies like Facebook for not giving next of kin access to all this material is that it would be betraying the deceased entity's privacy. However, historically, the deceased has not had a right to privacy. That's a human right. Human rights belong to people with legal personalities, and legal personalities belong to the living. Regulations and laws haven't yet caught up with the digitally deceased.

The argument from tech companies is that the data that a deceased person created also includes data created by a living person (and is therefore subject to existing laws). For example, the people the deceased person traded messages with. This is why, the tech companies argue, providing a dead person's data becomes very tricky because the users with whom the deceased person has interacted will have an expectation of privacy about the data they created.

Some organisations have thought about these issues. One example is the Digital Legacy Association, which created a worksheet[6] to help navigate this issue. The challenge is that no matter how much you make your wishes known before you die, and in whatever format, there will always be limits to your control of your digital data until we have the right to say: "This is my information." We are currently unable to grant our digital data to another person in a way in which it's enshrined in law in most jurisdictions.

In the future, Facebook may perform the role of our digital undertaker. A legacy contact on Facebook allows you to "memorialise" a person's account. However, this role is much more complicated and long-lived than a traditional will executor.

The ability to set a legacy contact on Facebook[7] may be something you had not heard of until you read this chapter. So, tech companies still have a way to go to promote this feature. However, their main business is selling ads, not memorialising accounts, so this may be something that privacy campaigners take up to raise awareness.

One feature that Google already has is the ability to delete the data they hold on you after a certain period with their Inactive Account Manager.[8] You can share everything, like your Gmail, Google Photos, and more, with up to 10 people. You can also tell Google to automatically delete all your private information after a preset amount of inactivity.

I have mine set to try and contact me if I haven't used any Google services for 3 months. As I practically live on Google Search and Google Maps, any lack of activity after 3 months would be a pretty good indication I've gone to meet my digital maker.

Doing this may be one of the most actionable things from this book, so I suggest you set aside 30 minutes once you have finished this chapter to do the basics to develop your digital legacy on Facebook, Google, and Apple if you have an iPhone.

Some companies like Yahoo have a "delete on death" policy. An example of this was the case of Justin Ellsworth and his father trying to get his emails from Yahoo.[9] He was killed in Iraq, and his father wanted access to his content. It took a court order for the company to release Justin's emails to his father. However, the most challenging part of this process might be demonstrating and proving that a person is dead to the department handling it, or the means to verify it.

When I spoke to Elaine, she had a 9-year-old daughter and I asked her how she was educating her daughter about her digital legacy. This opened up another interesting line of discussion – namely, how we can affect our children's digital legacies through what we share online. Elaine explained that she didn't initially realise how much influence she had on her daughter's ultimate digital legacy, and going beyond that, on the formation and development of her personality through posting about her online.

After all, posting photos of our children or other family members on social media is a very different proposition to showing someone a physical photo album. Yet many of us don't stop to think that we are impacting someone else's digital legacy before they are even old enough to understand what social media is.

What Steps Have You Taken to Protect Your Professional Digital Legacy?

If you or one of your team was to suddenly pass away, how would you be able to recover the data related to current and future projects? Your "professional" digital legacy strategy should extend for other reasons too. For example, ensuring your employees' data is not lost if they quit, are unavailable, or sadly die in service.

Many of the digital legacy issues discussed here also have relevance in the enterprise, and if you manage staff, you should ask your HR department what their guidelines and policies are in this area.

Curious Five

Here are some things you can do to prepare your digital legacy.

1. Consider creating a digital will.

2. Decide what you want to do with your data when you die.

3. Request copies of all data held on you by Google, Facebook, etc.

4. Set up your Google Inactive Account Manager.

5. Select a legacy contact on your phone and for Facebook.

CHAPTER 17
DATA PRIVACY AND REGULATION

In an era when information is as vital as currency, protecting personal data has become a crusade in its own right. The genesis of data privacy as a social and legal concept has transformed dramatically with the advent of the digital age. From the early days of simple password protection to today's complex landscape of encryption and cybersecurity, the value and vulnerability of data have never been more important.

The 2016 Cambridge Analytica scandal brought the issue of data privacy and the rights of the individual to the front page of every UK newspaper and reverberated around the world.[1] Years on, though, and I wonder if consumers truly care about their own data or place a value on it.

Anton Christodoulu from Imagination discussed data privacy with me on The Digitally Curious Podcast.[2] During our conversation, he explained how so much of the data being collected on you is "implicit" data – information collected on you and your behaviour that you might not be aware of.

> "Even before the current advances in AI, they can pretty much work out what you want or will do, even though you may not have done that before. They have so much data on you that they can predict you're going to order a coffee in 20 minutes from the Starbucks on the high street in Sheffield for example."
>
> —Anton Christodoulu, Imagination

This might not identify you specifically, and it has its advantages. In Anton's example, I could have a coffee waiting for me and a table outside ready for me to sit in the sun while I work on my book. The issue is how long they would be keeping that data on me, how it's used, who uses it, and the transparency with which they use it.

In Australia, the second-largest telecommunication company, and my former employer, Optus suffered a large data breach in 2022.[3] A hacker breached their systems and was able to steal both current and former customers' personal information, including customer names, dates of birth, phone numbers, and email addresses, with a smaller subset of customers having their street addresses, driving licence details, and passport numbers leaked. This led to large lines forming outside government offices in Sydney and Melbourne, where people urgently attempted to get new driving licences. It also emerged that some customer Medicare details – government identification numbers that could provide access to medical records – had also been stolen.

While there is a need to collect passport and licence numbers for identification purposes during customer signup, the decision to keep this data for longer than needed put Optus and their customers' data at a much higher risk.

This sort of breach raises the issue of data privacy on the front pages of newspapers. With new GenAI systems being developed, there will be a need for greater regulation by governments worldwide.

Data Privacy as a Human Right

Human rights lawyer Susie Alegre spoke with me on the podcast about data privacy actually being a human right.[4]

> "Data Privacy is so important, it's actually a fundamental human right, enshrined in the Universal Declaration of Human Rights. It underpins human dignity and other key values such as freedom of association and freedom of speech. In the context of data, privacy translates to the right to have control over how one's personal information is collected, used, and shared."
>
> —Susie Alegre, human rights lawyer

Susie is an international expert on AI, neurotechnology, and other emerging technologies through the lens of human rights. She brings a background in law and philosophy to address the key ethical questions of our time.

She has appeared on the podcast twice, and each time has forced me to rethink how I view privacy and regulation, through the lens of our enshrined human rights. Your data reveals a huge amount of deeply personal information about who you are and how you might behave.

Data protection is not just a technological issue but a comprehensive approach encompassing legal, ethical, and communicative measures. Data protection principles form the backbone of this approach, outlining the essence of data privacy laws worldwide.

Consent is the cornerstone of many data protection laws. It is how individuals can exercise control over their personal data. However, in a world where our digital footprint constantly expands, the notion of consent becomes increasingly complex.

Unregulated use of our personal data without our consent could transform how we live our lives. Imagine a data profile being built out of your digital behaviours and being used without you even knowing about it, to influence the options you have in life. What if data assigned to you resulted in an AI assigning you higher insurance premiums? What if it prevented you crossing a border?

What if something had gone wrong with the system? What if the wrong people had access to this data?

An example Susie gave in one interview was the ability to control people's voting behaviours. It is possible to gather enough information on certain demographics to predict how they might react to certain situations. You could then present information in a way that might encourage one demographic to vote while discouraging others. This was the issue behind the Cambridge Analytica data scandal mentioned previously.

Implementing data privacy is a multifaceted task that demands vigilance and adaptability. From corporate policies to everyday digital hygiene, practical steps towards data privacy are necessary at institutional and individual levels.

The entwining of emerging technologies with data privacy presents a dual-edged sword – offering both solutions and new challenges. Blockchain technology, for instance, offers immutable records but also raises questions regarding the right to erasure. GenAI brings in new issues around the data source, some of it personally used to create new content.

At the heart of data privacy is consumer empowerment. Educating the public on their rights and the tools at their disposal is crucial in ensuring that privacy is not relegated to the backdrop of the digital stage.

Ultimately, I believe that consumers need greater control of their own data. Part of the puzzle is self-sovereign identity, covered in Chapter 21. Organisations such as Trust 3.0 – covered on the podcast with Anton Christodoulou[5] – will play a key role in consumer education.

The field of data privacy and regulation will experience continuous evolution. It is a narrative full of tension between innovation and the imperative to safeguard personal data, while balancing the commercial interests of companies that need or want our data.

Regulating Data Privacy

Globally, data protection has a colourful quilt of regulatory frameworks, each with its own unique approach. The European Union (EU)'s General Data Protection Regulation (GDPR) stands out as a rigorous and comprehensive model that has inspired legislation in other jurisdictions. GDPR has been in place since 2016 and has provided a good model for other countries and jurisdictions to evaluate.

The dynamism of technology poses significant challenges in data regulation. Emerging tech trends such as the IoT and AI constantly reshape the boundaries and definitions of personal data, and regulators are scrambling to keep up. A good example is the recently negotiated EU Artificial Intelligence Act.[6]

This Act is a pioneering regulatory framework designed to govern the development, deployment, and use of AI technologies within the EU. It marks a significant step towards establishing legal boundaries to ensure AI applications are developed and used in a manner that is safe, transparent, and respects the fundamental rights of individuals.

The primary goal of the Act is to mitigate the risks associated with AI systems and foster trust in this rapidly evolving technology. Doing this requires balancing promoting AI innovation with protecting public welfare, consumer rights, and fundamental freedoms.

The Act categorises AI systems based on the risk they pose to rights and safety, tailoring regulatory requirements accordingly. Risks are broken down into four levels.

- *Unacceptable risk*: AI systems that are considered a clear threat to people's safety, livelihoods, and rights are banned. This includes AI that manipulates human behaviour to circumvent users' free will (e.g., exploitative AI systems targeting children) and systems that allow "social scoring" by governments.

- *High risk*: AI applications in critical sectors like healthcare, policing, and transport, as well as those that could significantly affect individuals' rights or safety, must adhere to strict compliance requirements before being deployed.

- *Limited risk*: AI systems requiring specific transparency obligations, such as chatbots, must inform users that they are interacting with an AI. This ensures users are aware of the artificial nature of their interaction.

- *Minimal or no risk*: Most AI systems fall into this category and can be developed and used freely. The regulation encourages innovation in AI applications that pose little to no risk to public safety or rights.

AI systems must be secure, reliable, resilient against errors or manipulation, and function accurately under all conditions for which they were designed. The Act emphasises the need for human oversight to minimise risks, particularly for high-risk AI systems. Decisions made by AI should be overseeable and reversible by humans, ensuring that AI acts as an aid rather than a replacement for human decision-making.

The EU will have a comprehensive market surveillance framework to monitor and ensure compliance with the Act. National authorities will enforce the regulations, and non-compliance can result in hefty fines, up to 6% of an organisation's annual global turnover.

Ethical Data Use

One of the most interesting aspects of the EU Artificial Intelligence Act is the emphasis on the importance of responsible development, particularly focusing on the ethical use of data and respect for intellectual property rights.

AI technologies often rely on vast datasets, including text, images, videos, and music, to learn and make decisions. The Act mandates that developers must ensure that the data used to train AI systems does not infringe copyright laws. This requirement is pivotal in encouraging the development of AI systems that are not only innovative but also ethically and legally compliant.

The Act demands that AI systems be transparent and have accurate data governance mechanisms to ensure data privacy and security. High-risk AI applications must include detailed documentation to facilitate traceability and accountability. It also stresses the need for high-quality, accurate, and relevant data to train AI systems, particularly high-risk ones.

The Act calls for meticulous documentation of data sources, ensuring that data collection processes are transparent and comply with data protection regulations, such as the GDPR. This means that AI developers in the EU will have to label the data sources used to train these AI systems, and have the ability to reverse-engineer answers generated by AI systems.

An example from my experience was when I asked ChatGPT if I had written any books. It confidently told me I had written a particular book in 2015 with a co-author I had never met. Under the EU Artificial Intelligence Act, Chat-GPT would have to identify the sources that created this answer and, under GDPR laws, allow me to correct this inaccuracy.

A Global Change

The EU Artificial Intelligence Act represents a significant move towards regulating digital and AI technologies at a time when such innovations are rapidly transforming societies and economies. While the Act is an EU regulation, its impact is expected to be global. Non-EU companies offering AI systems in the EU market must also comply with the Act's requirements.

This could lead to a de facto global standard, pushing companies worldwide to adhere to these regulations to access the lucrative EU market. While the Act sets a high standard for AI regulation, it also poses challenges. These include potential impacts on innovation and the need for ongoing adaptation to technological advancements.

There are concerns about the potential for excessive regulation to stifle innovation, the burden of compliance on startups and small businesses, and the practicality of enforcing such comprehensive regulations across diverse AI applications. Moreover, the dynamic nature of AI technology means that the regulatory framework must be adaptable to future developments.

As the Act moves towards full implementation, its success will depend on the ability of regulators, developers, and users to navigate its complexities. The aim for all parties is ensuring that AI serves the public good while fostering technological advancement.

Technology regulation is only going to get more complex, and complicated, as legislators grapple with the fine balance of allowing technology innovations such as GenAI to flourish to benefit their citizens, and the need to protect the intellectual property and human rights of these same citizens.

Curious Five

How can you stay ahead in the age of enhanced AI and data regulation?

1. Have a look at the work of the Digital Privacy Advocacy Group.[7]

2. Ensure that your risk and legal teams are involved in all AI projects, because, as we have seen, regulation is becoming more specific and existing regulations (IP law, human rights, GDPR) still apply. Yet many AI systems today are accidentally or deliberately breaching these laws.

3. Review the current EU Artificial Intelligence Act,[8] as this is likely to become a blueprint for legislation in other regions.

4. If you are in an industry association, leverage the power of your members to lobby legislators to think broadly about how they apply technology regulation in your sector.

5. Audit the current way you handle and process data, to ensure not only that you are being compliant with the relevant laws, but that you are also using the data you hold on your customers in the best possible way to create a true value exchange.

Also, read Suzie Alegre's book[9] and listen to her views on freedom to think on The Digitally Curious Podcast.[10]

PART V
CURIOUS ABOUT ...
THE FUTURE

Why Am I Curious About the Future?

I've made a career out of being digitally curious, and the next stage in my curious journey is this book to share the wisdom and tips I've picked up over the last 30+ years.

Ever since I wrote my final-year essay on the future, I've been fascinated to learn, and predict, what's coming next. Subjects that I'm particularly curious about are the future of AI and, in particular, where we go beyond GenAI. Namely, the move towards Artificial General Intelligence (AGI) and how the world of work is being impacted in the age of AI.

New topics that I'd heard about but not really understood around quantum computing, sovereign identity, and "everything as a service" were brought to life by a number of experts on the podcast over the last few seasons. In researching the interviews ahead of recording these episodes, I became more fascinated about where these technologies are now, and where they are likely to be in the next 5–10 years.

And you should be just as curious about these technologies as I am.

Why Should You Be Curious About the Future?

Technology is already impacting your job – both positively to help improve productivity, but also negatively as decisions and tasks are being taken away from us and given to AI tools and platforms. What will this mean for your current and next role? Will you need to retrain and upskill? I'm confident that this book will set you on the right path to better assess where you are on your digital maturity journey, and what you need to do next.

It's more than likely that all of the topics mentioned in the preceding sections have been mentioned in your workplace at some point. Increasingly, boards are being asked to approve investments in AI, while redistributing other technology projects to pay for it. Is this a good strategy? A digitally curious board (especially the ones I advise) will already have the answers to these, thanks to their own investigations. However, what if your manager or CEO comes to you and asks: "What are we doing about AI?" A broad question, but how would you answer this? What questions would you ask of the business? What resources would you suggest? Are you the person that your manager turns to first?

If you're digitally curious like me, you will be the go-to person when it comes to better understanding new technologies. Therefore, the more knowledge you can gather about future technologies, the stronger your position will be, and the more valuable you will be to your current organisation and your next.

CHAPTER 18
THE FUTURE OF AI

GenAI burst onto the scene at the end of 2022 with ChatGPT 3.5, and ever since everyone has been trying to predict what's next for AI. You can stay up-to-date with the latest thinking around this chapter and the rest of the book at curious.click/latest.

Thankfully, some of the topics and predictions here will still be in development by the time this book is in your hands. But with the pace of change from companies such as OpenAI – examples being the release of their text-to-video tool, Sora, in February 2024, and then ChatGPT 4o in May 2024 – who knows where AI will be as you are reading this in late 2024 and beyond.

Undoubtedly, the future of AI will be in the field of Artificial General Intelligence (AGI).

What is AGI?

In Chapter 3, I explained that modern AIs are "narrow" – they are designed to perform specific tasks, such as recognising speech, playing chess, or driving a car, with human-like efficiency or better. These narrow AIs are optimised and focused to excel at their one specific task. They tend to struggle when they encounter tasks or situations that they have not been designed to do or trained on.

Designing and building these AI tools requires human input in some form or another. A human programmer or data scientist is required to help provide and train it for that specific task.

When I described this process in Chapter 3, I talked about the concept of "deep learning" – the subset of machine learning which can help an AI to train itself on data through simulating how human brains work. AGI is taking this process further.

An AGI can generalise its intelligence across a wider range of tasks, adapting its reasoning and problem-solving capabilities to new challenges without needing to be specifically programmed for them. In theory, AGI can learn how to solve different problems and adapt to new circumstances on their own, similar to how humans learn and think.

What characterises an AGI is its ability to copy and simulate how the human brain works. As a result, an AGI system could perform any intellectual task that a human being can, learning and adapting its knowledge to new and unforeseen situations. This can overcome some weaknesses of modern AI and allow them the capacity for abstract thought, solving complex problems, making decisions in an uncertain environment, and learning from experience in a generalisable way.

The development of AGI is a major goal of AI research. However, it remains a theoretical concept at this point, with many technical and ethical challenges yet to be overcome. Achieving AGI would mark a significant milestone in the field of AI, potentially leading to revolutionary advances in technology, science, and society.

In 2023, Microsoft researchers published a detailed evaluation of GPT 4.[1] They concluded:

> "Given the breadth and depth of GPT 4's capabilities, we believe that it could reasonably be viewed as an early (yet still incomplete) version of an artificial general intelligence (AGI) system. This feels like progress given the view of AI experts of the likelihood we will reach AGI within 10 years."

Sam Altman and AGI

OpenAI's CEO Sam Altman published his views on AGI in a blog post in February 2024.[2]

Saying in part: "If AGI is successfully created, this technology could help us elevate humanity by increasing abundance, turbocharging the global economy, and aiding in the discovery of new scientific knowledge that changes the limits of possibility."

He articulated three focus areas for AGI:

1. We want AGI to empower humanity to maximally flourish in the universe. We don't expect the future to be an unqualified utopia, but we want to maximise the good and minimise the bad, and for AGI to be an amplifier of humanity.

2. We want the benefits of, access to, and governance of AGI to be widely and fairly shared.

3. We want to successfully navigate massive risks. In confronting these risks, we acknowledge that what seems right in theory often plays out more strangely than expected in practice. We believe we have to continuously learn and adapt by deploying less powerful versions of the technology in order to minimise "one shot to get it right" scenarios.

The future of AI is a vast and multifaceted topic, encompassing an array of predictions, possibilities, and ethical considerations. In addition to AGI, one of the most significant developments on the horizon is the improvement of AI algorithms through quantum computing. This could unlock new capabilities in AI, making current machine learning tasks more efficient and enabling the processing of complex datasets that are currently unfeasible to analyse.

These could make AI more capable in many areas, including the following.

Natural Language Processing

NLP technologies are what gives an AI the ability to understand and generate human language. With AGI, this is expected to become more sophisticated, allowing for more natural and intuitive human–computer interactions.

Autonomous Systems

Autonomous systems are also set to advance significantly. Self-driving cars are the most commonly cited example, but we can anticipate developments in autonomous drones for delivery and logistics, robotic assistants for the elderly and disabled, and autonomous systems in agriculture to optimise food production.

Expert Predictions on AGI

People used to say low-skill, repetitive tasks would be the only ones replaced. Now we're seeing slightly more complex things like customer service agents getting replaced. Other categories like management consultants, financial modellers, and investment banks are starting to be replaced because the AI are getting better at what they do.

Every job category might eventually be at risk. However, the jobs that are the most resistant to being replaced are service jobs which interface between people, for example restaurant servers, healthcare workers who change bedpans and give sponge baths, or primary care physicians.

As part of my research for this chapter, I drew on a range of discussions with leaders in this space on the podcast, including one with David Shrier, Professor of Practice, AI & Innovation with Imperial College Business School.[3]

Those who work with AI and technology might also be safe according to David – which might cover a wider range than just mathematicians or software engineers.

> "Interestingly enough, a good friend of mine, Tommy Meredith, who was the original CFO at Dell, now invests in a lot of strong AI companies. He told me, the best AI programmers they can hire out of University of Texas, Austin, are philosophy majors. These are people who understand formal logic, and can hold multiple ideas in their head at the same time, which helps you understand Bayesian math. A lot of machine learning systems are built around this probabilistic maths."
>
> —David Shier, Imperial College

Similarly, if we develop AGI and end up with a machine that thinks like a human being, it might develop a personality that needs to be nurtured. We would need AI ethicists and psychiatrists to support this. Imagine if the AI running your transport network got depressed?

According to David, preparing for AGI and other advances in AI means we need to be ready to rescale and upskill so we can stay ahead of any changes and disruption. Luckily, the better we understand how the human brain works, the more we understand what makes it unique and how to embrace these strengths.

While an AGI would be able to grow and train itself, the human brain is plastic and malleable. Leaning into this quality is a powerful way to stay ahead of any future disruption. The issue is that we often misunderstand what we need to learn and grow.

> "People like doing intensive short courses over a weekend because they think it's efficient. That's the worst way to learn. If you do interval training, it's like lifting weights at the gym. You can't build muscle with one 8-hour intensive session. But if you do 1 hour a week, over 8 weeks, or 1 hour a day, over 8 days, you'll make more progress than if you just try and do it all at once."

We need to design our lives to embrace what humans are best at. David explained in our interview how AI tools have helped leading universities create cognitive AI learning platforms that allow users to learn more effectively by providing chances to practise what they are learning. Without practising something new, half of it will be gone within an hour of learning it. We need time to reflect on and internalise it.

Similarly, we are social and creative animals. Interacting with others and discussing things lets us learn from each other and collaborate, which is why the Oxbridge tutorial[4] is one of the most effective ways to learn.

Bret Greenstein, PwC Partner and Generative AI Leader agrees that a potential benefit of AGI is better understanding ourselves as people.[5] As we learn more and more about how AI learns and develops, we understand more about how we think and communicate as humans. This, combined with conversational AI, could potentially transform how we interact with future generations.

> "I've talked to many researchers recently who've been wanting to kind of capture themselves so that their children and grandchildren can interact with them in the future. Also, there's a new AI system that will animate a still image. I took a picture of my grandfather, who passed away quite some time ago, holding me as a baby and animated it using that AI. When I shared it with my mom, I wasn't sure how she would react. It was beautiful because it brought to life an image we could share and look at."

AGI is Firmly on the Agenda

I also drew upon an interview with OpenAI CEO, Sam Altman, and Satya Nadella, CEO of Microsoft, conducted at the WEF in Davos by Zanny Minton Beddoes, the Editor-in-Chief of *The Economist*.[6]

As Sam Altman put it, AI can't do jobs yet, but it is very good at tasks.

> "One way to measure this is what percent of tasks in the total workforce could GPT do for you, not what percent of jobs it could replace. Imagine it could replace 20 percent of tasks we do today? What would the resulting improvement look like when people are able to use it for productivity in their workflow in so many ways? It could become a new way to learn things or work with knowledge."

The trigger for AGI is around the corner. The blog post from Sam Altman referenced above points to the fact that they are firmly investing time, effort, and money into the areas of AGI. As Altman pointed out, reaching AGI might be a gradual process, where every year we get closer and closer. We might only realise we have an AGI when we look back.

> "If you have an iPhone from 2007 in one hand, and an iPhone 15 in the other, they are, like, unbelievably different. You might look at the older model and think 'this was so bad, the newer version is a revolution'. But I never remember any one year in there where I was like the phone went from 'so bad' to 'so great'. Yet when I get to see the whole thing start to finish. It's amazing."

It's not just OpenAI either. When they fired their first public salvo on 30 November 2022 with the public launch of their ChatGPT 3.5 model, I believe they lit a fire under all the other AGI contenders. Soon after OpenAI's launch, Google released their Bard offering (later renamed Gemini), Amazon made a significant investment in Anthropic,[7] and Facebook seems to have pivoted from the metaverse to AI.

Peter Voss, CEO of Aigo.ai, and one of the first people to use the phrase "Artificial General Intelligence",[8] seemingly saw this coming. My interview with Peter was in September 2020, well before anyone was really talking about OpenAI or GenAI.

His view then was that an AGI solution "was likely to come from some startup company in the same way that who would have ever thought that little startup Google could dominate the search space, or little startup Amazon would later dominate online retail".

Peter was right. No-one really expected the advances we have seen in GenAI to come from a little-known startup, OpenAI. However, he also pointed out that one of the major hurdles to overcome before we achieve AGI has nothing to do with engineering.

In my talks, I share some of the resources I use in my own quest to be more digitally curious. One such resource is from Stephen Wolfram. Through Wolfram Alpha and his work on computational knowledge, Stephen aims to make the world's knowledge computationally accessible and interpretable, allowing both professionals and the general public to leverage complex computations for everyday questions and tasks.

I read an excellent paper by Stephen entitled "What is ChatGPT Doing ... and Why Does it Work?"[9] This paper for the main part helps to describe how ChatGPT works. As I explained in Chapter 3, it essentially predicts the next word in a sentence. His explanation of how neural networks are used in GenAI platforms such as ChatGPT allowed me to reflect on how incredibly complex the human brain is.

In short, neural networks are computational models inspired by the human brain's architecture, designed to recognise patterns and solve problems. They consist of layers of interconnected nodes or "neurons", each layer processing an aspect of the input data. This process allows neural networks to learn complex relationships and make predictions, making them powerful tools for tasks like image recognition, language processing, and more, in various AI applications.

The goal of an AGI is to create a more human-like intelligence. This means that the logical starting point is not a logical or mathematical one, it's cognitive psychology. We need to understand what intelligence is – how does human intelligence help us learn or identify problems and solutions? – before we can build a machine with those same capabilities.

Most of those working in the field are mathematicians, software engineers, statisticians, or similar. These are valuable, but we also need those with cognitive psychology skills who understand how the human brain thinks. It has taken the world's greatest minds over the last 70 years to be able to mimic conversational speech within an AI.

For this reason, I can understand why AGI is still some way off, and requires a more scientific and physiological approach rather than a truly mathematical route.

Technology Required

The race to AGI will also be powered by access to the fastest chips that power Graphics Processing Units (GPUs). Until recently, GPUs were the domain of gamers who needed faster video processing to render their games consoles with realistic graphics.

Nvidia is one of the leading providers of GPUs suitable for AI projects, and their share price has skyrocketed as a result.[10] Amazon also mentioned in their Anthropic announcement that they will use their own AWS Trainium and Inferentia chips.[11] This is important to companies, because there is already a danger that the GenAI race will come down to who has the fastest chips.

Just as there was a post-pandemic shortage of cars due to high demand, there is now a shortage of GPUs to train AI models. The result is that enterprises will need to wait longer, which may impact their ability to run larger workloads, and scale their GenAI offerings.

In early 2023, tech website The Information reported[12] that Microsoft was rationing AI servers to internal teams, to be able to offer Copilot to its broader customer base.

Part of the GPU supply chain issue centres around Nvidia, which has an estimated 80–95% share of the market for GPU chips that train AI models.[13]

AWS, Microsoft, and Google have showcased launches of their own GPU chips, allowing them to reduce their reliance on externally sourced devices from companies such as Nvidia. This area is constantly changing, so keeping up-to-date requires a very curious mindset.

Curious Five

Here are five things you can do to help you better understand the future of AI.

1. Learn about deep learning and neural networks. Since AGI and modern AI technologies like ChatGPT rely heavily on deep learning and neural networks, taking online courses or reading up on these subjects can provide a solid foundation. Websites like Coursera,[14] edX,[15] and Khan Academy[16] offer courses in machine learning, deep learning, and cognitive psychology, which are crucial to understanding how AI develops and learns.

2. Listen to my AI-focused podcasts from a range of experts on the future of AI.[17]

3. Read or subscribe to *MIT Technology Review*.[18] This publication covers the latest in technology, including AI. Its articles explore current trends, future predictions, and the societal impact of AI. Their content is accessible for both technical and non-technical audiences, making it a great resource for staying informed about the future of AI.

4. Read and subscribe to the blogs of the organisations leading the discussion on AGI, such as OpenAI,[19] Google,[20] Microsoft,[21] and Anthropic.[22]

5. Watch TED talks on AI. They offer accessible and thought-provoking presentations by experts in the field of AI, covering a broad range of topics from the potential of AI in various industries to ethical considerations and the future of humanity in an AI-driven world. These talks are great for getting inspired and informed about the broader implications of AI.[23]

CHAPTER 19
THE FUTURE OF WORK

For much of the pandemic, I was presenting virtually from my home studio in London, and the most requested talk at that time was about the future of work.[1] In the 2020–2022 timeframe, the focus for companies was how they could get their employees back in the office on a more regular basis.

Now that we are through this period, the focus has shifted to the impact of GenAI on a range of jobs. When I survey my audience on the number of people who have tried ChatGPT as an example versus those who use it every day, the result is regularly less than 5%. While we may feel the threat from GenAI, we are still some way off on the real impacts.

In this chapter, I will look at the issues around remote and distributed work, the different generations and how they approach work, and the likely impacts from AI on the workplace. I'll also discuss what you can do now to prepare for this new world, and become resilient.

Post-pandemic discussions continue around the right balance of in-office and remote working. Some companies are now demanding employees come back to the office 5 days per week, and they are being met with resistance. Employees got used to the freedom of working from home and the savings in transport fees.

Companies have tried 4-day working weeks, with mixed success. Magyar Telekom in Hungary is returning to a standard work schedule after a 4-day working week didn't meet expectations in a pilot project.[2] Regular operations will return after an 18-month trial period, during which 300 of its almost 5000 employees worked only 4 days a week for the same pay, the Hungarian unit of Deutsche Telekom AG said.

While the setup has been found to have benefits on work–life balance in some studies in other countries, the pilot at Magyar Telekom failed to provide sufficient grounds for a switch. The company said it was difficult to synchronise the work of all staff during the project, which included customer service, technical, and sales support.

Pre-Pandemic – The View from Dom Price

In 2018, I interviewed Work Futurist Dom Price from Australian tech unicorn Atlassian. He was in London during Tech Week and I interviewed him live at Australia House.[3] Now we're the other side of the pandemic, his insights still are very relevant.

He believes that the future of work will involve a balance of place, technology, practices, and people. New technologies like AI can automate undesirable tasks but also require unlearning old habits to fully realise their benefits.

Large organisations can undergo successful agile transformations through clear vision setting, involving employees in the change process, and being open about successes and failures along the way. Attracting and retaining top talent requires a focus on company culture, shared values, and meaningful work, rather than just perks. Scaling globally necessitates flexibility in sourcing talent wherever skilled individuals exist.

The exercise he recommends to help with unlearning old habits and becoming more focused on building a better culture he calls his "four 'Ls'". Every quarter, he recommends reflecting on the tasks that were loved, longed for, and loathed, as well as the lessons learned.

This lets you identify the areas in which your organisation or team has improved, as well as identifying the areas which would be best suited for implementation of an AI tool. The tasks that were loathed should be automated, while you should find opportunities to optimise your workflows and make what you do more effective and enjoyable.

"It's about how we enable them to do the best work of their life every day, that is the secret sauce to being effective."
—*Dom Price, Work Futurist at Atlassian*

For a broader view of the nature of work, I spoke with social researcher Mark McCrindle, who is based in Australia. A key point in future-proofing organisations, according to Mark, is understanding generational differences.

As I put it in our interview: "The new generations, when they're going from learning to earning, they're not afraid to play with new technologies. They are naturally digitally curious." While older generations need encouragement to experiment with technology, the younger generations are far more comfortable with it and can adapt it in new ways.

The key is making sure that the work being done is meaningful and impactful. After all, nobody likes spending time doing something that feels pointless.

"A life where technology does all the work and humans don't have to is not what the human psyche looks for. We are designed to create, to contribute, to add value, to make a difference. We are designed to work and we want to. We want, hopefully, to not work in areas of drudgery and instead work where we can see those impacts."
—*Mark McCrindle, social researcher*

Speaking to Darshan Chandarana and Julia Howes from PwC, we zeroed in on the impacts that AI is likely to have on the workforce of the future.[4] Organisations need to embrace constant evolution and change as the pace of technology increases, with periodic "revolutions" in operating models.

AI can help eliminate non-value-adding work, allowing professionals to focus more on tasks that add real value. This includes reducing internal processes and meetings. It may unlock time for employees to be more creative and focus on applying critical thinking skills, rather than spending time on basic tasks. Productivity could be redefined more broadly as freeing up time for reflection and creativity, not just headcount reductions.

As a result, remote and flexible work may become more common as AI makes remote collaboration and productivity easier. Human connection and in-person interaction will still be important for creativity and innovation, and as a result, offices may transform into "creative hubs".

Workers Displaced by AI

The automation of routine tasks, while boosting efficiency, raises the issue of what happens to workers displaced by AI. While new jobs will undoubtedly be created, they may require skills that those displaced workers do not have. This highlights the need for significant investments in education and training to prepare the workforce for the jobs of the future.

Helsinki University launched an AI education programme aimed at educating its citizens about AI and its applications, called the Elements of AI.[5] This initiative, part of the country's broader aim to become a leader in AI knowledge and use, is designed to demystify AI and empower citizens with the knowledge to navigate the digital future.

AI could also lead to the creation of entirely new industries. Just as the internet gave rise to e-commerce, social media, and online entertainment, AI is expected to create new sectors that we can scarcely imagine today. These could include personalised medicine, AI-driven content creation, and advanced simulation technologies for research and development.

While some fear mass unemployment as a result of automation, others see a future where AI complements human workers, enhancing their productivity and allowing them to focus on creative and strategic tasks rather than routine ones. We will likely see the rise of digital agents, or co-pilots, to supplement our daily tasks.

Education and lifelong learning will become increasingly important in an AI-driven world. As the demand for skills shifts, workers will need to continuously update their knowledge and abilities. This could lead to a reimagining of education, with a greater focus on teaching critical thinking, creativity, and adaptability – skills that AI is unlikely to replicate anytime soon.

So, What is the Future of Work in the Age of AI?

This is a subject of significant interest and debate among economists, technologists, and policymakers alike. As AI and automation technologies continue to advance, the landscape of work is undergoing a profound transformation.

One of the most discussed aspects of AI's influence on work is its impact on employment levels. There is a dual narrative that unfolds here. On the one hand, AI and automation are poised to displace a considerable number of jobs, particularly those involving routine, manual, and clerical tasks. For example, self-service kiosks and automated checkout systems have already begun to replace cashiers in retail environments. Meanwhile, AI-driven software increasingly performs tasks traditionally done by entry-level legal assistants and paralegals.

However, it's crucial to recognise that AI also creates new jobs and industries, many of which we might not yet be able to fully envisage. These include roles in AI development and maintenance, data analysis, cybersecurity, and more. Furthermore, AI can augment human capabilities, making workers more efficient and enabling them to focus on higher-value tasks that require creativity, emotional intelligence, and complex problem-solving.

The displacement and creation of jobs by AI underscore a significant shift in the skills demanded by employers. There is a growing need for technical skills related to AI, machine learning, data science, and robotics. At the same time, soft skills such as critical thinking, creativity, and interpersonal communication are becoming increasingly important. These skills enable workers to excel in roles that AI is unlikely to usurp soon, as they involve nuanced human judgement, empathy, and innovation.

The evolution of skills necessitates a rethinking of education and training systems. Lifelong learning becomes not just an asset but a necessity for workers aiming to stay relevant in a rapidly changing job market. Educational institutions, employers, and governments must collaborate to develop flexible learning pathways that can adapt to the pace of technological change. In doing so, they will provide workers with the opportunity to continuously upgrade their skills.

AI is also transforming the structure of the workplace itself. Remote work, facilitated by digital communication and collaboration tools, has become increasingly viable and popular. It's a trend dramatically accelerated by the COVID-19 pandemic. AI-powered tools can enhance remote work by automating routine tasks, facilitating project management, and improving communication among distributed teams.

Additionally, the gig economy is expanding, partly driven by AI-enabled platforms that match freelance workers with short-term tasks and projects. This shift towards more flexible work arrangements offers workers greater autonomy but also presents challenges related to job security, benefits, and labour rights.

I spoke to Gabriel Luna-Ostaseski, Co-Founder of Braintrust, a "user-owned" talent network, on the podcast[6] about the opportunity for people to move from employees to becoming "gig workers". Gabriel believes that the future of work is distributed and augmented with "gig workers". There is also the opportunity to use Distributed Ledger Technology (DLT) and tokenisation to run the networks on which we are now working.

The integration of AI into the workplace raises several ethical considerations. These include concerns about privacy, as AI systems often rely on large datasets that may include sensitive personal information. There's also the risk of bias in AI algorithms, which can perpetuate or even exacerbate existing inequalities in the workplace. Ensuring that AI systems are transparent, accountable, and fair is crucial.

Moreover, as AI transforms the nature of work, questions arise about the distribution of the economic benefits generated by increased productivity. Addressing potential disparities in income and opportunities will require thoughtful policy interventions, including perhaps the exploration of concepts like universal basic income or reimagined social safety nets.

The future of work in the age of AI is complex and multifaceted, presenting both challenges and opportunities. While AI and automation pose risks to certain jobs, they also pave the way for new forms of employment and ways of working that can enhance human capabilities and creativity.

Navigating this transition requires a concerted effort from all stakeholders, including policymakers, educators, businesses, and workers themselves. This will ensure that the benefits of AI are broadly shared and that the workforce is equipped to thrive in this new era. As we move forward, the focus must remain on harnessing the potential of AI to improve the quality of work and life, while also addressing the ethical and social implications that arise.

Curious Five

Here are five things you can do to prepare for the future of work in the age of AI.

1. Read the *Harvard Business Review* and their articles on the future of work. The one entitled "AI is Changing Work – and Leaders Need to Adapt"[7] is a good place to start.

2. Audit your current role. What tasks could you automate now with AI and which tasks are likely to be replaced by AI in 2 to 5 years?

3. Prepare for new forms of employment. As discussed in this chapter, the rise of AI could lead to new industries and job roles. Keep an eye on emerging sectors and consider how your skills could be applied in innovative ways. Additionally, understand the implications of gig work, including the need for self-management and the potential lack of traditional job security and benefits, and prepare accordingly.

4. Listen to the entire podcast with Mark McCrindle on the future of work under AI.[8]

5. Read the latest thinking from the World Economic Forum on AI and jobs of the future. The article "These are the Jobs that AI can't Replace"[9] is an excellent piece.

CHAPTER 20
QUANTUM COMPUTING

This is probably one of the most futuristic topics in the book. Although quantum computing may be a few years from becoming a mainstream technology, the opportunities it offers, as well as the threat it poses to existing security systems and encryption, make it a future technology well worth being digitally curious about.

What is Quantum Computing?

Quantum computing is a revolutionary approach to computation that uses the peculiar principles of quantum mechanics, a branch of physics that describes the behaviour of particles at the microscopic level.

Unlike traditional computers, which process bits of information as 0s or 1s, quantum computers use quantum bits (qubits). Qubits have the remarkable ability to exist in a state of 0, 1, or both simultaneously, thanks to a phenomenon known as superposition. This allows quantum computers to process vast amounts of data simultaneously, potentially solving complex problems much faster than current computers.

The implications of quantum computing are vast. By offering solutions that are currently beyond the reach of classical computing technologies, quantum computing promises breakthroughs in fields such as cryptography and drug discovery.

Practical and widespread use of quantum computing still faces significant technical challenges. These include maintaining qubits in a stable state and scaling up the number of qubits to a level where they can outperform traditional computers on a wide range of tasks.

To drill down further in what it means for enterprises, I spoke with Richard Hopkins from IBM[1] and Chris Johnson from Nokia[2] on the podcast.

When Richard first introduced me to the study of quantum computing, I was surprised to learn that quantum computers are very large structures and require cooling to −273°C, nearly −450°F, just above "absolute zero". Something this cold does not exist naturally on Earth, where the coldest temperature on record is −89.2°C (−128.6°F).[3] This is not something that will be available in a desktop configuration anytime soon.

The reason quantum computers need to be so cold is because, for a qubit to work, it needs to be as stable as possible. Even the slightest external disturbance, from vibration, heat, or electromagnetic waves, could disrupt a qubit. When this happens, a qubit loses its quantum properties through a process called decoherence and introduces errors into the result.

By cooling the system to near absolute zero, quantum computers minimise these thermal vibrations, helping to preserve the qubits' quantum states and ensure that they can operate correctly. Maintaining such low temperatures is one of the many challenges in the development and scaling of quantum computing technologies.

> "What you're trying to do is insulate the whole thing from the real world as much as you can so that the actual quantum qubits can continue to work and do their job as a quantum computer. Most of what you see in a quantum computer, this beautiful chandelier made of gold, wires, and so on, are all there to cool everything down. They're attenuating the signals as they go in and amplifying them as they come out so they don't heat up the machine."
>
> —*Richard Hopkins, IBM*

Figure 20.1 A quantum computer. Credit: IBM Research / CC BY-ND 2.0

Who is Developing Quantum Computers?

One of the notable players in the quantum computing industry is IBM. They have made their quantum computers accessible via the cloud to the broader research community, fostering innovation and research in quantum computing applications.[4]

Google's quantum computing project, known as Quantum AI,[5] claimed a major milestone by achieving quantum supremacy. This term refers to a quantum computer solving a problem that is practically impossible for a classical computer to solve in a reasonable amount of time. Intel, known for its leadership in traditional computing technologies, is also investing in quantum research by exploring various types of qubits and how to manufacture them at scale.[6]

Microsoft's quantum computing initiative, called Quantum Development Kit,[7] includes a programming language for quantum algorithms. The company is developing a topological quantum computer, a novel approach that aims to provide more stable qubits.

Honeywell has made headlines with its claims of having the most powerful quantum computers regarding quantum volume, a metric that considers the number and quality of qubits, connectivity, and error rates.[8]

Richard at IBM had a particular perspective as to IBM's journey to quantum.[9]

> "IBM is pushing hard to get to a position of quantum advantage, where a quantum computer can do a real-world, real-life problem that a normal classic computer would never be able to do and do more cost-effectively than a normal computer."
>
> —*Richard Hopkins, IBM*

Of course, just like with AI, quantum computers are not going to automatically be the best option for every problem. The reason why building a quantum computer requires such specific conditions (and therefore costs so much) is that they are extremely sensitive to their environment.

Often the cost of implementing proper quantum error correction negates the potential benefits offered by speeding up, unless the task itself does not require quantum capabilities. Add to this the fact that modern computing infrastructure and the internet aren't designed around a quantum computer's architecture, which means they can't interface with these systems directly.

What quantum computers specialise in are specific tasks that rely on their ability to process multiple possibilities simultaneously. This means that you need to be aware of the problem to be solved, and possibly take a hybrid approach.

> "Hybrid algorithms and hybrid ways of working are going to be around for quite a long time. For example, they are not superb at dealing with large amounts of data.

So if you had to deal with an algorithm where you have to process large amounts of data against a quantum computer algorithm, you might start using the classical computer to divide the problem down. Spread that out, have multiple quantum runs, and then assemble the problem back and then make a decision based on that result and do it again."

—*Richard Hopkins, IBM*

Many industries could benefit from the power of quantum computing. In our interview, Richard mentioned several specific industries in particular: material sciences, pharmaceuticals, and the finance industry. The following are some other areas in which quantum computing would be beneficial.

Better Understanding of the Natural World

Richard Feynman, an American theoretical physicist known for his work on quantum mechanics, brought scientists together at an MIT conference in the 1980s because, as a longtime user of computers, he was frustrated. He knew by mathematics and quantum mechanics that the computers we use today wouldn't be able to simulate or understand nature. He said that if we really want technology to understand nature, we need a quantum computer.

It is understandable, therefore, that one of the applications that excited Richard most was the potential to understand the world we live in better. Richard explains that the process by which we create fertiliser is expensive and inefficient, requiring a phenomenal amount of energy. We need fertiliser to grow food. Without it, billions would starve. But what if we could discover another, more efficient way to make it?

"The enzyme the process requires isn't that large and exists in plants already. It is possibly amenable to being modelled by quantum computers in the near future. If you could turn that enzyme into a catalyst, you could save a lot of energy and reduce the environmental impact of feeding lots of people. Imagine if we could lop off one and a half per cent of the world's gas consumption in one go!"

—*Richard Hopkins, IBM*

Beyond this, there are lots of exciting opportunities in the world of molecular engineering, through which quantum computing could make a real difference to the world. They could perform carbon capture more efficiently, improve our ability to store solar and wind energy in batteries, or allow us to create new medicines.

Quantum Finance

In the finance sector, quantum computing could solve several significant problems as well. Financial institutions have to manage countless variables to monitor and track the state of thousands of transactions and the greater economy. Applying quantum computing could allow them to more efficiently handle questions like:

- Is this transaction fraudulent or not?

- What could be done to optimise this portfolio of stocks and shares for my client?

- How can I model the movements around my bank and understand future conditions so I can look after my risk stance and ensure it retains liquidity?

- Could I create a more precise picture that allows me to free up more cash and do more exciting things?

Quantum computing is also being considered in areas where complex calculations are required, such as helping airlines with revenue management and recovering from service disruptions caused by bad weather.[10]

Quantum AI

As a planet, the energy we expend on AI and machine learning doubles every 3.5 months. Quantum computing could help tackle some of this work in a more efficient way, but as I said earlier – it is only really effective for certain types of tasks, such as optimisation or classification of data.

"There's every possibility that quantum computing will find areas where it can accelerate machine learning. Quantum has that ability to sit alongside large natural language models, symbolic models, and quantum models, and they can all work together – this is what we are currently building towards. This, maybe, will help us reach AGI faster, but I don't know."

—Richard Hopkins, IBM

There are risks associated with this, however. As we have discussed already, protecting our data is important and the main tool we have in our arsenal is cryptographic encryption. Unfortunately, one application that quantum computing may become well suited to in future is breaking these encryptions. This is something worth planning for now. If you hold data that might be valuable 20 to 30 years in the future, ask yourself if it is going to be protected.

"There are some organisations around the world that do care about that level of cryptography that far out in advance. So we've been working for years with NIST, which is the standards body of the States, and others to establish new cryptographic frameworks that we think we were pretty certain are not crackable by quantum algorithms, or by quantum computers, or by conventional computers, for that matter, either.

In our current batch of mainframes that we just announced, the banks used to do all the big processing and everything else; they have got quantum-safe algorithms built into them now."

—Richard Hopkins, IBM

Since cryptography is baked into almost everything, changing it is one of the hardest things you can do. Imagine needing to re-engineer an entire telecoms network or bank. Richard predicts that technology will be coming that will help us become more cryptographically agile. This means we will be able to switch a cryptographic regime or algorithm more easily to keep ourselves and our data secure, even if quantum computer power finds its way into the wrong hands.

Q-Day

Due to the issue of cracking existing encryption with quantum computing, the threat of a "Q-Day" could be as soon as 2030, according to some experts. To find out more, I spoke with Chris Johnson from Nokia.[11]

> "We've got to start branding the threat of Q-Day in the same way that ESG needs to be prominent. We need to understand who are the companies that are supporting the journey and those that are not."
>
> —*Chris Johnson, Nokia*

Chris explains that Nokia divides networks into three categories.

- *Mission-critical*: Networks underpinning key infrastructure like energy, utilities, transport, public safety, defence, etc.

- *Business-critical*: The enterprises and industries leveraging connectivity to their advantage.

- *Social-political*: Connections between people, for example our ability to access the internet.

The advent of quantum computing, AI, and other advances promises to increase the volume of data being moved across these networks 100-fold. The key question Nokia is trying to answer is how to take advantage of that, while protecting this data from being deciphered by those who should not be able to access it.

> "We can see the impact of quantum, or Q-Day as it's sometimes called, rapidly coming. So, what we're trying to do is create a quantum-ready ecosystem and quantum-safe network. Right now, we use encrypted networks, such as VPNs. We have the padlock on our website when we're doing our banking.
>
> But if someone's recording all of that encrypted traffic, there will be a day when someone can replay that and decrypt it using quantum. It's therefore imperative now to start building quantum-safe networks."
>
> —*Chris Johnson, Nokia*

Chris estimates this danger point could be as early as 2030. This is why Nokia is planning ahead about how to protect their networks – not only at that point in time, but also to protect their data from "retrospective attack".

But what could you do to protect yourself? Chris and I agree: educating yourself and being digitally curious is a vital first step. However, 2030 is not far away. The key is to take steps and measures to anticipate and protect against it sooner rather than later.

Quantum needs to be accounted for in the design of any new network or network strategy you are deploying. Have you identified which networks are mission-critical in your organisation and in society at large? What have you done to protect them against quantum? Is everyone in your organisation aware of the fact that an unprotected email or file sent yesterday might become vulnerable without the right measures?

Future-proofing here relies on awareness. Perhaps we might get to the point where quantum readiness is a network or infrastructure safety standard. But we need to be talking about and preparing for this now.

Preparing for Quantum Computing

The threat of Q-Day is real – companies need to have it on their cybersecurity and risk assessment lists. However, the timeline for quantum computing to become mainstream is fluid. Experts agree that we are likely a decade or more away from seeing widespread adoption.

The journey to mainstream quantum computing is dependent on several key triggers, including:

- Significant advancements in qubit stability and error correction.

- Scalable quantum architecture.

- Development of quantum algorithms that can solve practical, real-world problems more efficiently than classical computers.

- Integration of quantum computing into existing technological infrastructures.

- Development of a skilled workforce capable of working with quantum technologies.

The industries in which quantum computing particularly promises to deliver significant advantages are finance, pharmaceuticals, and materials sciences, as I mentioned earlier. Readers in those fields should stay informed about technological advancements to capitalise on quantum computing's potential when it matures.

Once quantum computing becomes a viable mainstream technology, the early adopters stand to benefit significantly.

> "We've now got modular technology that allows us to start building bigger and bigger machines. We think it gives us the roadmap to get a lot bigger than that. It's really putting those fundamental building blocks in place to get us away from just being in a single chip. It's doing all the work on how you get many chips to work together, and many fridges [cooling chambers] to do it together."
>
> —*Richard Hopkins, IBM*[12]

Be prepared to invest in quantum skills and partnerships with leading quantum computing firms. Companies like Google, IBM, and Intel, which are at the forefront of quantum computing research, along with startups and academic institutions, are playing vital roles in advancing the technology.

Curious Five

Here are five things that you can do to investigate quantum computing.

1. Invest in quantum literacy. You could start by educating your leadership and key personnel about quantum computing and its potential impact on your industry. This includes understanding the basics of quantum mechanics as it applies to computing, current developments in the field,

and realistic timelines for breakthroughs. Workshops, courses, and partnerships with academic institutions or quantum computing firms can facilitate this knowledge-building. A good place to start is the IBM Basics of Quantum course.[13]

2. Watch a TED talk on quantum computing. Talks by researchers and experts in the field, such as Shohini Ghose,[14] John Preskill, and Michelle Simmons, offer fascinating insights into quantum computing, its potential impacts, and the challenges that lie ahead. All explained in a way that's accessible to general audiences.

3. Think about how quantum computing might change the world for you and your business. Consider the changes it will bring to your domain and in your sphere.

4. Contact your risk department to see if they are aware of "Q-Day" and have a strategy to deal with this. Begin transitioning to quantum-safe cryptography. This process, known as Post-Quantum Cryptography (PQC), involves adopting cryptographic systems that are believed to be secure against both quantum and classical computers.

5. Develop a quantum strategy. Integrating quantum computing into your company's strategic planning is essential. This strategy should address how the company intends to leverage quantum computing for competitive advantage, protect against its threats, and adapt its business model to the quantum era.

CHAPTER 21
SOVEREIGN IDENTITY

In today's digital world, much of people's sensitive personal information is collected and stored by organisations, without individuals fully understanding or consenting to how it is used. With the rise of Web 3.0 and growing awareness of the value of our data, people are becoming more interested in being in control of their own data, rather than letting it be controlled by centralised companies or governments.

This has led to the development of an online space known as "self-sovereign identity" or "digital identity". Self-sovereign identity (SSI) aims to put people back in charge of their data through decentralised identity systems and verifiable credentials. This gives individuals greater privacy, security, and autonomy over their digital lives in an increasingly data-driven world. It ties in closely with data sovereignty, which we explored in Chapter 8.

While the concept is not new, widespread adoption is some distance away. There are many entities and organisations that will have to change and adapt their platforms to accommodate this, and there is currently no real financial incentive to do so. Over time, greater consumer demand for access to and control of their own data will be key to making self-sovereign data a reality.

The Risk of Centralised Data Storage

A good example of where companies store more information than they need is the Optus data breach[1] of September 2022, which I shared with you in Chapter 17. As you'll recall, one of the major issues was that the breach included customers' names, birthdates, home addresses, phone numbers, email contacts, and passport and driving licence numbers. In other words, a great deal of highly sensitive information.

The question is, why did Optus have so much data from so many people stored on their servers? Even if having a copy of a driver's licence and passport details was necessary to confirm identities during onboarding and account creation, why was this data kept? It wasn't needed to manage the customer relationship and should have been deleted once the identity was verified.

In the EU, the GDPR prohibits the retention of this sort of information[2] when it is not required to deliver the service provided.

This scenario is the perfect example of why self-sovereign data will become more important going forward. In a self-sovereign world, if Optus required a new customer to prove their identity with a driving licence and/or a passport, they could get what they needed without the customer losing control over their data.

The customer could present the required details using cryptographically signed verifiable credentials for attributes like their driver's licence provided (and digitally signed) by the government authorities issuing these documents. At no time would the actual licence or passport number be shared. Instead, the company would simply be sent "official proof", in digital format, that these were official, current documents.

Optus would verify the minimum required attributes (valid licence) without storing sensitive details like licence numbers long-term. If a breach occurred, no private details would be at risk as Optus would not have collected and stored that personal data in the first place. This reduces the risk of breaches impacting individuals while still enabling necessary identity verification in a privacy-preserving manner.

Marie Wallace on SSI

This was covered in detail on The Digitally Curious Podcast when I interviewed Marie Wallace, Digital Identity Lead at Accenture.[3] Marie and I worked together at IBM and she has been pioneering some of the work in this space. She also has a no-nonsense approach when explaining complex technologies such as this, something I find quite refreshing.

Marie explained the concept of SSI by comparing streaming music services such as Spotify to "streaming trust" services that we will see in a self-sovereign world. Before services like Spotify and Apple Music, you had to buy entire CDs to get the few songs that you actually liked. This means that the data belonging to the songs that you're not interested in is still available on the CD.

This is perfectly fine for music, but if the CD held your entire set of personal information – from where and when you were born to your health records – you would not want that falling into the wrong hands. The "whole-CD" scenario is analogous with companies collecting unnecessary personal data today. Music streaming allows on-demand access to only the songs needed, without ownership.

This is similar to identity credentials only being shared when necessary, not stored long-term. Individuals can verify credentials directly between each other (like streaming a song) without an intermediary storing/transferring the underlying data.

In the case of a company needing to confirm your date of birth, you would "stream" just that piece of information to them, rather than all of your records, in the same way that you can stream just the song or songs you like. The pieces of information the company is not interested in never leave the server, so there is no risk of them being compromised.

Indeed, the drive for SSI has come from the public sector. We will see companies wanting to provide these services to mitigate the effects of any data breaches as cybercrime increases. Beyond the benefits for the consumer, it reduces costs for companies by eliminating unnecessary data collection and storage.

The Impact of SSI

While the streaming model transformed the music industry, Marie believes that SSI can similarly transform how companies and individuals approach digital identity and personal data. She believes that verified credentials provide a lot of flexibility in terms of how consumers are sharing their data. She cautions though that it is not a magic wand, and there are going to be a lot of issues around ethics.

Marie explained how verifiable credentials can streamline processes like onboarding by reducing the need for companies to store large amounts of personal data, while allowing individuals to exchange credentials on demand. Importantly, trust is still placed in trusted issuers of credentials, like the government, which issues licences and passports. Once trustworthy organisations are agreed upon, the verification of these documents can then become decentralised.

Empowering people with their own data, and putting pressure on companies to release our own data back to us, is key. She also believes that it has a positive side-effect on the ethics of AI. Driving mainstream adoption will require focusing on frictionless user experiences to meet real business and industry needs, as well as grassroots consumer demand for data privacy and safety.

One good example is when you wish to rent a car. Currently, when renting a car from a company such as Hertz, an individual has to provide a lot of personal information upfront, like proof of driver's licence, insurance, and residential address. Hertz then has to verify this data by contacting separate entities like the licensing agency, insurance company, and so on. This leads to delays and the company storing unnecessary customer data, as in the Optus case.

With verifiable credentials, the individual would have cryptographic proofs of their driver's licence and insurance stored digitally on their phone. When renting a car, they could quickly share just these credentials with Hertz through a verification process, without Hertz storing any underlying personal details.

It's the digital equivalent of being asked for ID when you're buying alcohol in the supermarket. The cashier just needs to see your ID and know it's real and valid before they can sell you the wine or beer. They don't need to store a copy of it once the transaction is complete.

This provides a more seamless, privacy-preserving experience for both the customer and the company by reducing friction and limiting data collection/storage. It also reduces the cybersecurity risks for the company because they store less sensitive information, reducing their risk and reputation profile should a cyber breach occur.

Other important use cases for SSI include worker credentialing, organisational identity verification, and enabling new AI applications through increased individual control and transparency over personal data.

Bring Your Own Identity

Ultimately, SSI will empower individuals with their own data, and allow them to monetise this information in a more equitable way. Let's imagine that we could ask a company to release all of the insights they have generated about us. With the amount of data we give away to companies, and the amount of AI that is being applied across this to infer our behaviour, it is likely that a company knows more about me than I know about myself.

While companies may perform a credit check on potential customers, imagine if I was able to obtain a verified credential that showed I always paid my account on time. This would be of value to a company, and might lead to more favourable terms, or dynamic pricing. All of these verifiable credentials could be stored on my phone, backed up to the cloud.

Another example of how you could leverage your own identity and data better is through your CV. After all, your CV is a collection of data about your professional experience and history. Imagine if you could get full control of all this data. As an individual, you could receive personalised career advice and development from a specifically tailored AI.

Professionally, it could allow employers to hire with more confidence. A verified CV credential could allow a potential hire to prove that they have the required skills, experience, and qualifications without needing to invest in extensive background checks.

Currently, on LinkedIn, all the information about someone's previous employment – dates of employment, roles held, and responsibilities – are user-generated, potentially leading to misinformation. LinkedIn has created a feature that allows you to verify your current employment by sending a verification email to your company email, however, this only works for your current position. More recently, they have introduced a service powered by Persona[4] that allows you to use the RFID chip in your passport to verify your identity – bringing us a step closer to SSI-powered verification.

I would welcome the ability to have all of my previous positions verified by the companies I worked for. All that would be needed is for the HR departments of each of the companies I worked for to issue me a "digital proof" confirming dates employed and roles held.

Then, all LinkedIn needs to do when updating my profile is to verify the digital proof against the digital credentials provided. The platform could place a "Verified by LinkedIn" badge against each of the roles that have been digitally verified. Going beyond simple employee tenure information, any awards or certifications gained while at each of these organisations could also be provided as a digital proof.

Moving trust away from central organisations such as governments and big tech companies into everyday transactions will be the key for SSI to work. However, interoperability between different identity systems and wallets will be a key challenge. This is where global standards will come into play.

Things to Look For When Exploring SSI Solutions at Your Workplace

1. *Global standards and protocols emphasis*: Does the solution or vendor adhere to global standards such as the W3C's Decentralised Identifiers (DIDs) and Verifiable Credentials (VCs)? These standards are the backbone of interoperability in the SSI domain, facilitating the seamless exchange of credentials across diverse systems and wallets. Assess their commitment to these standards and its involvement in shaping future protocols.

2. *Cross-blockchain compatibility*: Investigate the solution's capability to operate across multiple blockchain platforms. Since interoperability hinges on the ability to communicate across different identity systems and ledgers, a solution's support for a wide range of blockchains is crucial.

3. *Support for interoperable identity wallets*: Understand how the SSI solution supports interoperability among different digital wallets. This is essential for enabling users to use their digital identities across various services and platforms without friction. Explore the wallet technologies the project supports and how it ensures secure, seamless credential exchange.

4. *Active participation in global SSI communities*: Gauge the SSI provider's involvement in global SSI initiatives, standards bodies, and interoperability working groups. Active participation in these communities indicates a commitment to fostering interoperability and shaping a universally compatible SSI landscape.

5. *Demonstrated ecosystem collaborations*: Look for proven examples of ecosystem partnerships that highlight the solution's interoperability with other identity systems and services. Successful collaborations can serve as evidence of the solution's capability to function within a globally interconnected digital identity network.

The intersection of open source and SSI presents a pivotal movement in digital identity management. Open source will play a crucial role in the SSI ecosystem by providing transparent, auditable, and collaborative frameworks for developing identity solutions. This transparency is essential for building trust among users, developers, and stakeholders, as it allows for the rigorous inspection and verification of the security and functionality of SSI systems.

The open-source community has a key role to play in the SSI landscape by developing and refining protocols, standards, and software that facilitate these capabilities. Projects like Hyperledger Indy,[5] Sovrin,[6] and Veramo[7] exemplify the collaborative efforts to create robust, scalable SSI solutions. Open-source contributions ensure that these projects remain adaptable and resilient against evolving threats, benefiting from the collective expertise of a global developer community.

Moreover, the principles of open source align with the ethos of self-sovereignty, emphasising freedom, transparency, and community collaboration. This synergy fosters innovation and accelerates the adoption of SSI technologies, potentially transforming how we perceive and manage digital identities.

As more organisations and individuals recognise the benefits of SSI, supported by open-source development, we can anticipate a more secure, privacy-respecting digital world where individuals hold the key to their personal data.

Where is SSI Being Used Already?

- *Government IDs*: Countries like Estonia have long issued digital IDs to citizens that can be used for e-voting, taxes, etc. The EU is working on a digital wallet for all citizens.[8]

- *Healthcare*: Systems for provider credentialing, digital health passes for COVID-19 vaccination status verification. A good example is New York's Excelsior Pass.[9]

- *Education*: Universities issuing and verifying student credentials for transcripts, qualifications proofs.

- *Finance*: Banks exploring use of verifiable credentials for Know Your Customer (KYC)/Anti-Money Laundering (AML) checks, reducing data collection needs.

- *Workforce management*: Companies like LinkedIn supporting credentials for automated profile verification and job applications.

- *Supply chain integrity*: Projects aiming to reduce fraud through verifiable identities of organisations and certifications.

- *Travel*: Pilot programmes exploring the use of credentials for seamless airport security/check-ins to reduce physical contact.

Here are some real-world examples of SSI projects:

- Dock.io[10] offers an SSI solution that emphasises privacy and control by enabling users to share selected data with verifiers without revealing more information than necessary. This approach ensures that only authentic, verifiable credentials are recognised and utilised, underscoring the importance of trust and privacy in digital interactions.

- Cheqd[11] explores a wide range of SSI use cases, from banking and KYC applications to travel and decentralised finance. The project highlights how SSI can streamline identity verification processes, enhance privacy, and offer a more seamless and secure experience across various sectors.

- European Union digital wallet.[12] The EU is working to issue digital IDs to all citizens via a digital wallet by 2024/5.

- LinkedIn (owned by Microsoft) is using Microsoft Entra to verify LinkedIn credentials.[13]

- NYC COVID-19 passes. Digital health passes were implemented in several countries as decentralised credential systems, like New York's Excelsior Pass,[14] developed by IBM.

These projects illustrate the versatility and potential of SSI in addressing the current challenges in digital identity management. They also emphasise the importance of user control, privacy, and interoperability in developing a more secure and efficient digital world.

Curious Five

Here are five things you can do to better understand the digital identity space.

1. Research SSI and decentralised identity models. Read whitepapers and articles to understand the concepts and how they differ from traditional identity systems. A good place to start is "Introduction to Self-Sovereign Identity" by Walt ID.[15]

2. Follow leaders in the space, such as Marie Wallace, on LinkedIn[16] to stay up-to-date on projects, use cases, and developments.

3. Try out digital wallet and credential apps. Download wallet apps such as Selfkey[17] to see decentralised identity in action and understand the user experience.

4. Listen in full to the podcast with Marie Wallace.[18] She explains the concepts in an easy-to-understand way.

5. Try creating your own verifiable identity. dock.io allows you to do this for free.[19]

CHAPTER 22
EVERYTHING AS A
SERVICE

In 2000, while at Telstra, I was involved in a very early variant of Software-as-a-Service (SaaS) called the Application Service Provider (ASP) model. This was an early precursor to the modern cloud service models, particularly SaaS.

ASPs allowed businesses to access and use software applications over the internet rather than purchasing and installing them on individual computers. Our first project was with Microsoft to offer versions of Office over a "thin client". This meant renting the software to an end user without having to download the full version to their computer.

This initial service transitioned into the Microsoft 365 product family we are all familiar with today. In this scenario, we "rent" versions of Microsoft Word and PowerPoint for a yearly fee, with promises of product updates and security improvements over the subscription period. Thus, we use Microsoft Office "as a service".

In the 2000s, the limited internet bandwidth available to end users was a major issue, and the ASP model was not commercially successful. However, it did lay the groundwork for the cloud-computing revolution that followed.

Since the early days of the ASP model, as-a-service models have expanded beyond software, delivering a wide range of products and services across various industries. The "as-a-Service" (aaS) subscription model has become a cornerstone of the modern digital economy, encapsulating a wide range of services delivered over the internet. Some of the most common types include the following.

- *Software as a Service (SaaS)*: This is the most well-known and widely adopted service model, where software applications are hosted by a service provider and made available to customers over the internet. Examples include email services like Gmail, office tools like Microsoft 365, and CRM systems like Salesforce.

- *Platform as a Service (PaaS)*: PaaS offers a cloud-based platform that allows customers to develop, run, and manage applications without dealing with the underlying infrastructure. It provides a framework that developers can build upon to develop or customise applications. Examples include Google App Engine and Microsoft Azure.

- *Infrastructure as a Service (IaaS)*: IaaS provides virtualised computing resources over the internet. It offers foundational computing resources such as virtual server space, network connections, and bandwidth, allowing businesses to scale and shrink resources as needed. Examples include Amazon Web Services (AWS) and DigitalOcean.

Companies have embraced Everything as a Service (XaaS) for everything from IaaS and PaaS in the IT world to vehicles (VaaS) and furniture (FaaS) in the physical world. These models represent the flexibility and scalability of cloud computing, enabling businesses and individuals to access sophisticated services without significant upfront investment in hardware, software, or maintenance resources.

The subscription economy and the XaaS concept represent a transformative shift in how businesses and consumers interact. With it, we're moving away from traditional one-off sales to ongoing subscription-based relationships.

The Subscription Economy

The phrase "subscription economy" was coined by Tien Tzuo, the CEO and co-founder of Zuora, a company that provides software solutions for subscription-based businesses. He was an early employee at Salesforce, one of the pioneers of the SaaS model. I spoke with John Philips, head of Alliances and Partner Ecosystems at Zuora, on the podcast[1] and he gave me a behind-the-scenes look at how the subscription economy is evolving.

The subscription economy's roots can be traced back to the early days of newspaper and magazine subscriptions. However, the model has evolved dramatically with the advent of the internet and digital technologies.

Services you subscribe to already, like Netflix and Spotify in entertainment, Stitch Fix in fashion, Dollar Shave Club in personal grooming, or Hello Fresh in food, are examples of how the subscription model has permeated nearly every aspect of consumer life.

The subscription model offers numerous benefits for both businesses and consumers. It provides a steady, predictable revenue stream for businesses, which can help with cash-flow management and financial planning. It also fosters closer customer relationships as businesses continuously engage with subscribers, collect data on their preferences and behaviours, and adapt their offerings accordingly.

Subscriptions offer consumers convenience, flexibility, and often a more personalised experience. Instead of making large upfront investments, customers can access a wide range of services and products for a recurring fee, typically with the option to cancel anytime. This model also caters to the increasing consumer preference for access over ownership, particularly in digital content and services.

The subscription economy is not without its challenges and criticisms. For businesses, continuously delivering value to prevent churn requires constant innovation and customer engagement efforts.

The Rise of the Super-Subscription

The competition in popular subscription categories is fierce, and differentiating offerings can be challenging. On top of this, the accumulation of subscription fees can lead to "subscription fatigue" among consumers, who may become overwhelmed by the number of subscriptions they manage and seek to cut back.

This means that a company offering subscription services needs to think very carefully about the value they are offering their customers. In our interview, John pointed out that the subscription economy is a huge change from what came before:

> "This is not the world of the finance systems of the last 20–30 years, which were there to record a finite transaction. These systems didn't like things that lasted a long time. In our world, we are dealing with a recurring evergreen contract – ideally, you want the customer to be for life."
> —John Phillips, head of Alliances and Partner Ecosystems, Zuora

Attracting customers and keeping them means you should think carefully about what causes "subscription fatigue". There are several factors that you need to consider and account for when designing your subscription services. These include the flexibility of your service, the value you are giving your client, and your relationship with your client.

The best services you subscribe to are flexible and open to your changing needs. This includes upgrading, downgrading, or making modifications to your contract in real time as you need. The example John used was the family Spotify account – you would want the ability to modify it as needed, for example when your children go to university or come back for the holidays. Why would you want to be charged for more than you are actually using?

As a business, offering this is easier said than done. After all, you need to be able to predict your recurring revenue. If you have countless customers constantly changing their contracts, this becomes a challenge. It means that you need to have accounted for this on the back-end and made sure you have a system in place to manage it. This is a service that Zuora provides.[2]

Designing a flexible service leads to another question. Offering a subscription for a service is one thing, but XaaS is not limited to the abstract or digital. What if the product being offered is something physical? As I mentioned already, physical objects like vehicles and machinery can be offered as a subscription.

Companies which used to operate as leasing companies are now offering subscription services instead. These mean that the customer can enjoy a more flexible form of financing. You can offer them the choice between paying a fixed amount per month or a flexible amount based on how much you use the item in question per month.

Integrating AI and machine learning into XaaS will further personalise subscription offerings, making them more appealing to consumers. Additionally, the expansion of 5G and improvements in IoT technology will enable new subscription services, particularly in areas like smart homes and connected vehicles.

> "This is where things like the world of IoT and connected devices really have changed the world and the subscription economy. For example, one of our biggest customers, Caterpillar, uses sensors in their products. They can actually measure the amount of earth that you move. ... Or in the case of a fertiliser company, they put sensors into the farm into the land to see how the land is being irrigated."
> —John Phillips, head of Alliances and Partner Ecosystems, Zuora

As John points out, this has several benefits. Customers only get charged for what they've been using. Businesses can get a lot of valuable information. You can understand how much your customers are using your products, where, and the product's maintenance needs.

This allows you to better control your production and operate more sustainably and efficiently – without hurting your revenue. Not only is this more cost-effective for you, but it is also better for the environment.

Sustainability and circular economy principles are also becoming intertwined with subscription models, as they offer opportunities for businesses to reduce waste through reuse and recycling initiatives. For instance, subscription models in fashion and electronics can facilitate the return and refurbishment of products, extending their lifecycle and reducing environmental impact.

Having this level of connection to the client also lets you build a stronger relationship with them. Where previously a car manufacturer might not have had a direct relationship with the people driving their cars, this technology opens the door to interacting more closely with their end users. John uses the guitar company, Fender, as an example of this in action.

> "The problem was people – particularly in phases of their life where they thought they wanted to be a rock star – were buying guitars. Then they would go home and never learn how to play. Within about two or three months, they felt pretty stupid that there was a 300-pound guitar getting just dust on it. Fender realised that they needed to do something otherwise that person would never buy another guitar."
> —*John Phillips, head of Alliances and Partner Ecosystems, Zuora*

Their answer was to focus on the outcome, rather than the physical product. They started looking for ways to build a direct digital relationship with their customers that could form the base of a subscription. The result was that they started to provide a service that met their customers' desire to become rock stars and helped teach them how to play the guitar.

"Subscription fatigue" is driving the rise of the "super-subscription", in which a single company buys subscription services at a wholesale rate and bundles them into one monthly subscription. The advantage for consumers is that they only have to make one monthly (usually discounted) payment, rather than having multiple subscriptions coming out at different times.

Examples of this include Optus SubHub[3] in Australia and Sky Ultimate[4] in the UK, which offer their own subscription TV programmes and then bundle in other popular services such as Netflix.

The decision by Netflix in late 2022 to introduce a lower-cost "ad-supported" plan met with some resistance from the subscription industry. Since its launch, Netflix has been vindicated and said in an earnings call following the introduction of the plan:

"Adoption of our ads plan continues to grow – with ad plan memberships up almost 70% quarter-over-quarter. On average, 30% of sign ups in our ads countries are to our ads plan, with more work to do to scale this business."

—Netflix Q3 2023 letter to shareholders[5]

The company says its $6.99-per-month ad-supported plan "continues to support our ads plan growth" in the US.

Netflix says they have been able to "do what traditional TV has never been able to do ... deliver relevant ads to reach audiences at scale".

The coffee chain Pret in the UK launched a subscription programme in April 2023 called "Club Pret"[6] to provide members up to five drinks per day, as well as a discount on food for a monthly fee. In April 2024, they had to make changes, as subscribers were sharing their membership QR codes with friends, costing the company money,[7] in the same way that Netflix had to clamp down on password sharing to stop revenue leakage.[8]

This is the downside of subscriptions, and something that also needs to be considered when designing a subscription programme.

Curious Five

Here are five ways you can explore the power of subscriptions.

1. Look at your own existing subscriptions – how many do you have, and is there scope to combine them into a "super-subscription"?

2. Look at your current business model to see if a subscription model would make commercial sense.

3. Review the data you collect on your customers' current use of the product, and consider how more detailed usage data could drive the development of new products.

4. Investigate how IoT subscriptions might work in your business, renting sensors or home/office appliances that are connected to the internet for a monthly fee.

5. Look at how physical goods could be offered on a subscription basis.

CONCLUSION
CURIOUS ABOUT ...
WHAT'S NEXT?

In the last 22 chapters, we've looked at platforms and tools that are here now and will be important in the next 10 years. But what other technologies were not covered here, and what can we expect even further ahead?

As mentioned in the Introduction, the range of technologies covered in this book was deliberately not meant to be exhaustive. I selected the ones that corporate audiences ask me about the most, so what are some of the things I'm still curious about and I think you should be?

What Am I Still Curious About?

The rise of "big tech" is something that I'm fascinated about. It impacts us every day, perhaps without us realising it.

Just a few years ago, analysts started talking about the "FAANG" group of companies.[1] Facebook (now Meta), Amazon, Apple, Netflix, and Google being the big tech companies that control most of the things that we see and do online. Many simply refer to them as "big tech".

One could argue now that this list could be expanded to include Microsoft and Nvidia, creating a gang of seven tech companies – perhaps called FAANNGM?

As AI takes more of a foothold in the enterprise and consumer spaces, we can expect that these companies will become even more important globally. They will most certainly attract the attention of regulators as they seek to ensure that these seven companies don't overstep the mark when it comes to the flow of global information.

AI Evolution This Year and Next

Writing a physical book about technologies, and an industry that seems to change daily, has been a challenge. While I'm reading hundreds of articles each week to ensure I'm up-to-date when in front of my corporate audiences, I suspect that many readers just won't have the time to do this.

In my more than 30 years in this industry, I've never seen a technology take off so quickly and drive so much innovation. The issue though for you, the reader, is what should you be concerned about and focus on, and how can you filter out the noise and focus on what is important for you and your business?

I believe that 2024 was the year that the AI conversation moved from "What is AI?" to "How do we deploy AI?" I'm hoping that the preceding pages have helped you to formulate a plan, or at least ask the right questions of your team to take the next steps with AI.

The risk is that companies rush into an AI project without carefully considering the multitude of issues that have been discussed in detail in the preceding pages.

While there was a disproportionate level of hype around Bitcoin, NFTs, and the metaverse when these technologies were launched and covered in the media, when it comes to AI I've never quite seen anything like it. From where I sit as a Master's degree-qualified engineer, and someone who is engaged by some of the largest companies in the world to advise them about their technology strategy, it's quite amusing to see the same people on platforms such as LinkedIn morph from "social media experts" in 2015 into Bitcoin/blockchain/metaverse and now AI experts.

The real concern I have for this sudden rise in GenAI platforms (and experts) is that there is now the ability for almost anyone to publish well-written and intelligent-sounding copy about AI. This means we risk being flooded with AI content, to the point where we may no longer be able to distinguish between human and AI-generated writing.

Tech website CNET has been writing about technology since 1992, and I noticed they now have an AI policy which says: "None of the stories on CNET have been or will be completely written by an AI." They do go on to say, though: "If that changes, as technology and our processes evolve, we will disclose it here."[2]

I'll make a prediction that within a year of this book being published, many tech sites and even mainstream websites will have experimented heavily with this technology, and articles will be labelled "created by AI".

So, what does this mean for human creativity, and importantly, your role in this?

Creative technologist Prakhar Mehrotra perfectly articulates this in his article "ChatGPT and the Magnet of Mediocrity".[3] He speaks about how indeed we will be flooded with AI-generated content, and there will be a "magnet of mediocrity".

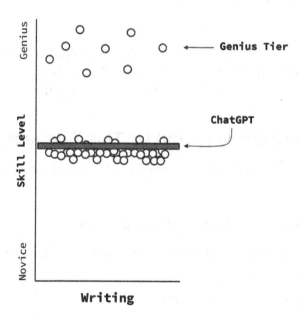

Figure Conclusion.1 A graph representing skill levels in relation to writing post-GPT. Credit: Prakhar Mehrotra

Prakhar argues that there will only be two tiers of skills – the ChatGPT "good enough" skill and a top-tier, genius-level skill.

A topic that I've been engaged with at my corporate talks has centred around graduates being able to learn the intermediate writing skills and reasoning skills that can now be done by GenAI.

With GenAI capable of handling tasks that require median skills, the middle-tier opportunities that traditionally help individuals progress from novice to expert are vanishing. This absence of intermediate work makes it difficult for individuals to gain the varied experiences and incremental improvements needed to achieve genius level.

This may mean that we have fewer "geniuses" and more mediocre content.

Author Malcom Gladwell argued in his book *Outliers* that it takes 10,000 hours of intensive practice to achieve mastery of complex skills and materials.[4] So, if ChatGPT takes away our ability to exercise our skills over 10,000 hours, what should we do?

My advice is not to use GenAI content directly. Instead, use it to form part of your research. Think about GenAI tools as that "always on, enthusiastic intern" and outsource some, but not all, of your tasks to these tools.

Where is AI Likely to End Up This Year and Next?

Several factors are holding back enterprise adoption of GenAI today. These include:

- Uncertainty about the most effective use cases.
- Rapidly evolving capabilities that are not yet stable enough for large-scale IT projects.
- Scarcity of AI engineering talent.
- Regulatory issues that haven't yet been integrated into major AI tools.
- Difficulty building a viable business case given all the unknowns.

This will continue in the years after this book is published, so I encourage you to look at the issues above and formulate a strategy to overcome them now, rather than wait.

Other technical shifts that we will see more of this year and next are likely to include the following.

AI Watermarks Will Become Mandatory

As it is now becoming very simple to clone audio and video, we can expect more regulation around labelling AI-generated content. This won't stop "bad actors" (read criminals or foreign governments) from using this content, but humans will be able to see what content is definitely AI-generated.

AI-Generated Intellectual Property Becomes a Legal Minefield

The controversy surrounding OpenAI's "Sky" voice model and its similarity to actor Scarlett Johansson, coupled with the revelation that OpenAI had approached Johansson to provide her voice to the ChatGPT 4o product,[5] is an example of how tricky AI-generated IP will become.

An actor's voice is integral to their brand and can be considered intellectual property. The legal implications of using someone's voice without proper licensing or agreements are complex and could lead to litigation. We can expect to see more issues such as this, where the technology constantly challenges existing regulations.

AI Will Allow Reasoning

One area of GenAI that has been lacking is the ability to reason. The hallucinations from platforms such as ChatGPT "making things up" occur because the platform currently has no way of understanding if the response it is producing is reasonable, accurate, or even legal. As discussed previously, it is providing a mathematically correct answer, not necessarily a well-reasoned one.

In early 2024, *The Financial Times* reported that OpenAI and Meta are developing new AI models capable of "reasoning".[6]

OpenAI's Chief Operating Officer Brad Lightcap told *The Financial Times* that the next generation of GPT would show progress on solving "hard problems" such as reasoning. Meanwhile, Meta's chief AI scientist Yann LeCun said it was working on AI "agents" that could, for instance, plan and book each step of a journey, from someone's office in Paris to another in New York, including getting to the airport.

Prompt Engineering Won't Become a Career Option

In the early months of the OpenAI ChatGPT hysteria in the media, I kept hearing about a new type of job for the future – "prompt engineering". This is where a human is deployed to create the perfect "prompt" to allow a GenAI system to return useful content based on the input.

You've probably also seen the multitude of "ChatGPT cheat sheets" circulating on LinkedIn and other platforms. I believe that this skill will never be taught in schools, because this too will be augmented by AI tools.

Rick Battle and Teja Gollapudi at California-based cloud computing company VMware argue that "Prompt Engineering Is Dead".[7] I think they are right, and if we mix in the reasoning ability of AI, then this is likely to happen relatively soon.

The Rise of Industry LLMs

I believe that we will start to see more industry-specific LLMs that have been carefully trained and audited with trusted content and fed industry terminology and nomenclature. A good example would be a Law LLM that has been trained on every case brought before the UK High Court.

The Chip War

As we have seen with Nvidia's rise to become one of the world's most valuable chip manufacturers, expect to see Google, OpenAI, Meta, and Amazon start producing their own chips. This means that the cost of AI servers may come down as the reliance on a small number of chip manufacturers, and the scarcity of AI-ready servers, reduces.

AI Regulation Will Take Hold

The finalisation of the EU AI Act that has taken years to ratify will mean that in late 2024 and early 2025, these regulations will come into place. GenAI providers will need to be compliant, as will your organisation, so your legal and risk teams should be reviewing this legislation now.

AI Consulting Will Become a Massive Industry

My former employer IBM has been at the forefront of AI for many years. More lately, I've seen the rise of new consulting offerings built around GenAI.

In the first quarter of 2024, consulting giant Accenture reported $600M of revenue related to GenAI consulting,[8] proving that consulting in this emerging space can be big business. I've seen this personally, with 2023 being the busiest I'd ever been, thanks to the hunger from corporates to learn more about AI and what they need to do next. We can expect to see the Big 6 (Accenture, IBM, PwC, Deloitte, KPMG, EY) develop sophisticated AI consulting offerings and tools for their clients.

We Are Likely to See the Rise of Personal AI-Powered Digital Agents

Following on from the example from Meta's LeCun, I believe that GenAI technologies will mature in 2025 to allow useful digital agents. When I first predicted this, few of the components were available to make this a reality.[9] Now I'm more convinced that soon I will have my very own digital agent that can do all of the personal tasks I'd rather not. I'd be happy to pay in the order of $1000 a year to have this function. Expect them to be commercially available soon.

AI Will Become Able to Cheat

Proving how dynamic this GenAI space is, in the days before I submitted this manuscript, I came across an article that suggested that LLMs can strategically deceive their users when put under pressure[10] (they can cheat). It naturally made me curious to learn more, and made me think – do we want AI systems to emulate all the components of a human, to include the bad traits such as cheating and lying? This will be something to watch closely.

Robotics Meets GenAI

Robotics is an interesting space that I've been researching, but has a more narrow focus so I chose not to cover it in this book. One interesting development from Google is the intersection of robotics and GenAI, called RT-2.[11] This is a breakthrough as it allows ChatGPT-like commands to a robot that hasn't been trained on a particular move or object. Commands such as "I've spilled a cup of coffee, help me clean it up" are now a reality, without the robot ever having seen the environment in which it is being asked to operate.

What Else Should You Keep an Eye Out For?

We have listed some of the predictions related to the fast-moving world of AI, but what other areas of technology should you be keeping an eye on?

Regulations Around Cryptocurrency

With the recent prosecution of former founder of the FTX crypto exchange Sam Bankman-Fried, we can expect that regulators globally will take a stronger view on all technologies that deliver alternative finance instruments.

Autonomous Vehicles

We've seen a lot of progress with driverless cars, and can expect to see more autonomous vehicle examples. I've previously mentioned UK company

Aurrigo; they have developed autonomous cargo and baggage facilities for airport operators.[12]

In 2018, Australian mining company Rio Tinto developed an autonomous train,[13] which regularly travels 280 km to deliver iron ore without a human driver.

Wireless Charging

Those of you who have taken advantage of the wireless charging available in many mobile phones will realise the benefits of having fewer cords. We will start to see more "things" that can be charged wirelessly, from eBikes through to electric vehicles.

We may start to see more charging loops buried in the roadway underneath dedicated charging spots. In the future, we can expect to see charging loops in major roads, charging devices as they move along, removing the need for dedicated charging stations.

In late 2023, an experimental stretch of road in Detroit was used to prove the concept.[14]

Space-Based Solar Power

Extending this concept, we are a decade or so away from beaming power generated in space down to Earth. I first came across the notion of space-based solar power when I moderated an Engineers Australia event in London in 2022.[15] The concept is indeed a futurist's dream – collecting solar power in space then beaming it back down to Earth. Since then, two of the panellists, Martin Soltau and Sam Alden, have set up Space Solar. In 2024, they demonstrated an innovative wireless energy transmission system.[16]

While many years away from commercial reality, this, like quantum computing, is an area you should be aware of now.

Space-Based High-Speed Internet

You're likely to have come across Elon Musk's Starlink[17] platform, a constellation of thousands of low-earth orbit satellites, located between 160 km and 2000 km above Earth, that are providing broadband-speed internet to the entire planet. You should also keep an eye on what Project Kuiper[18] from Amazon are planning, as well as Visat.[19]

What's Next For You?

How can you possibly keep up with all of the topics mentioned in this book, and will you commit to remain digitally curious a year from now?

To help with this challenge, why not hand this book (or send it as a physical or digital gift) to a friend or colleague? As a challenge for you, pick your three most interesting chapters and do at least ONE thing listed in the Curious Five for each.

Your own LinkedIn newsfeed can become a good source of useful content. You can "follow", instead of connect, with interesting people outside of your direct industry, and this will mean that their content will appear in your feed. Much of the thinking that challenged me over the last 12 months came from someone on LinkedIn that I follow but have never met.

Looking Further Ahead

I've deliberately styled myself as The Actionable Futurist and concentrated on the near-term corporate impacts from technology in the 6 to 12-month time-frame. From time to time though, I'm asked to look further ahead, sometimes 20 or 50 years.

I often resist this, but sometimes I like to dream big and think about what might be around when I'm not.

Some of the technologies that I believe I will see in my lifetime include a "digital pill" that we will swallow. It will then complete a full-body analysis to predict our future health. Our smartwatch will work in conjunction with this pill, and AI powered by hundreds of millions of other devices, all sharing their health data (with consent, and in exchange for something of value), will help to predict and mitigate the next global pandemic, as well as help doctors diagnose, manage, and treat individual issues such as cancer, diabetes, and mental health issues.

Information will be beamed to our retinas using a thin-film technology that is yet to be developed. The internet will be always on and superfast everywhere. Quantum computing coupled with AGI will be put to good use to find a cure for fatal diseases such as cancer from the point of diagnosis.

These are more personal wishes than firm predictions. However, if we look at the pace of technical developments over the last 5 years and extrapolate this, then perhaps these will all become a reality in my lifetime.

At the launch of the 2024 Emerging Tech Trends report at South By South West (SXSW), Founder and CEO of the Future Today Institute, Amy Webb, spoke about the rise of AI and its impact across different industries, the development of connected ecosystems of things like wearables, extended reality devices, the IoT, and sensors that will collect more data to fuel AI advancement.[20]

She also predicted advancements in biotechnology like new materials science, generative biology, and the development of organoid intelligence and biological computers made from human cells.

Finally, she mentioned the convergence of AI, biotechnology, and connected devices forming a "technology supercycle" that is reshaping society and the economy in unprecedented ways.

In many ways, this could be the path for technology over the next 10 years, and these are all areas that you should remain curious about.

Why Should You Be Curious About What's Next?

If you've experimented with items listed in each of the Curious Five over the last 22 chapters, then congratulations! You've done more than most of your colleagues and friends have done in their lifetime to investigate the world around you.

I'd now invite you to return to the list of the six traits of the highly digitally curious that I shared in Chapter 1. As a reminder, these traits are:

1. Willingness to experiment.

2. Proactive learning.

3. Engagement with digital trends.

4. Problem-solving.

5. Creativity and innovation.

6. Adaptability.

Do you remember how you scored yourself on a scale of 1–5 before you read most of this book? I encourage you to repeat this exercise now and see if simply reading this book and implementing some of the Curious Five has increased your score in any, or all, of these areas.

Can you also identify ways in which becoming more digitally curious has benefited your personal or professional life?

Perhaps only the most curious of you reading this book will continue in your journey. In this final section, I provide a range of resources to continue your curious journey in the world of technology.

I hope you enjoy what's yet to come.

Getting in Touch With the Author

I'd love to hear from you as you embark on your journey of digital curiosity.

Here are several ways to connect with me to ask questions or stay up-to-date with my latest talks and thinking.

LinkedIn: I post multiple times during the week, and this is one of the primary ways I challenge my own thinking and learn from my peers in my news feed:

https://curious.click/linkedin

Twitter: I've been on Twitter (I still can't seem to bring myself to call it "X") since 2009. I've found myself using it very sparingly of late, but you can contact me here:

https://curious.click/twitter

Instagram: I started using Instagram to see what all the fuss was about back in 2016, and it propelled my love of photography. You can see a mix of artistic photos from the places I visit and futurist-focused content here:

https://curous.click/instagram

My speaking website also has a wide range of information on all the topics discussed:

https://curious.click/speaking

My podcast, which has been the source of much of the content in this book, can be found by searching for "digitally curious" in your favourite app, or listen to all the episodes and subscribe here:

https://curious.click/podcast

And finally, as mentioned in the sections above, I have used ChatGPT to create **CuriousGPT**, which has been trained on this book, and which I am also updating on a regular basis as new tips and tools evolve. You can ask it anything here:

https://curious.click/gpt

I'd love to hear from you if you found the book useful and it helped you to become even more digitally curious. Thank you for coming on this journey with me.

GLOSSARY

1G: The first generation of wireless cellular technology, focusing on voice communication. It used analogue voice technologies and had limited coverage and capacity.

2FA (Two-Factor Authentication): A security process where two different authentication methods are used to verify the user's identity, enhancing account security.

2G: Second-generation wireless telephone technology. It introduced digital encryption and data services such as SMS and MMS.

3G: The third generation of mobile telecommunications technology, improving mobile data bandwidth and support for multimedia applications like video calling and mobile internet.

4G: The fourth generation of mobile communications systems, offering higher data speeds and supporting advanced mobile services such as HD mobile TV and 3D television.

5G: The fifth generation of mobile network technology, succeeding 4G, with capabilities that significantly improve the speed, coverage, and responsiveness of wireless networks.

5G NSA (Non-Standalone): A deployment method for 5G networks that relies on existing 4G systems and architecture.

5G SA (Standalone): A deployment where 5G networks operate independently of existing systems with all new architecture, allowing for new features and efficiencies.

6G: The anticipated next generation of mobile telecommunications standards beyond the current 5G networks. Although still in the early stages of research and development, 6G aims to deliver even faster data speeds, lower latency, greater reliability, and higher capacity than 5G.

Actionable Futurist: A professional who not only studies trends and predicts future developments but also provides practical, actionable advice to businesses or individuals on how to prepare for and leverage these future trends and delivers insights that can be directly applied to achieve strategic advantages, innovate products and services, and navigate potential challenges effectively in the near term.

AGI (Artificial General Intelligence): AI that can understand, learn, and apply intelligence across a broad array of tasks, much like a human's cognitive abilities.

AI (Artificial Intelligence): The simulation of human intelligence processes by machines, especially computer systems, including learning, reasoning, and self-correction.

Airdrop: The distribution of cryptocurrency tokens to a large number of wallet addresses, often for free, as a marketing strategy to promote a new project or to reward loyal community members.

Ambient Intelligence: A digital environment that proactively, but sensibly, supports people in their daily lives by surrounding them with intelligent and intuitive interfaces embedded in all kinds of objects.

AMPS (Advanced Mobile Phone System): An early analogue mobile phone system standard developed by Bell Labs, and widely used in North America and other locales before being replaced by digital standards.

API (Application Programming Interface): A set of rules and tools for building software applications, specifying how software components should interact. Most often used for automated machine-to-machine interactions.

AR (Augmented Reality): An enhanced version of the real world achieved through the use of digital visual elements, sound, or other sensory stimuli delivered via technology.

ASP (Application Service Provider): An early form of cloud services that allowed businesses to access software applications over the internet, a precursor to modern cloud services like SaaS.

Autonomous Vehicles: Vehicles equipped with advanced autonomous systems that can operate without human intervention under certain conditions.

Avatar: A digital representation of a user in virtual environments or online communities. Avatars can range from simple 2D icons to complex 3D models.

AWS (Amazon Web Services): A subsidiary of Amazon providing on-demand cloud computing platforms and APIs to individuals, companies, and governments, on a metered pay-as-you-go basis.

BBS (Bulletin Board System): An online communication system used before the rise of the internet, where users could connect via a dial-up modem to post messages, share files, and chat.

Big Data: Extremely large datasets that may be analysed computationally to reveal patterns, trends, and associations, especially relating to human behaviour and interactions.

Biometrics Authentication: The measurement and statistical analysis of a person's unique physical and behavioural characteristics, used for identification and authentication purposes.

Bitcoin: The first decentralised digital currency, invented in 2009 by an unknown person using the alias Satoshi Nakamoto. It operates on a decentralised network using blockchain technology to manage and record transactions.

Black Box: In technology and engineering, a device, system, or object which can be viewed in terms of its inputs and outputs without any knowledge of its internal workings.

Blockchain: A decentralised digital ledger that records transactions across many computers so that the records cannot be altered retroactively without the alteration of all subsequent blocks.

Blockchain Provenance: The use of blockchain to trace the history and ownership of an item, enhancing transparency and trust in the supply chain.

BYOAI (Bring Your Own AI): A policy or environment where employees are encouraged or allowed to use their own AI tools and solutions at work.

BYOID (Bring Your Own Identity): A system where individuals bring their verified digital identity to various services rather than creating new credentials for each service.

CAPTCHA (Completely Automated Public Turing test to tell Computers and Humans Apart): A type of challenge–response test used in computing to determine whether the user is human. It typically requires users to perform tasks that computers find difficult, such as recognising distorted text, identifying images, or solving a simple puzzle.

CBDC (Central Bank Digital Currency): Digital form of fiat money issued and regulated by a country's central bank, intended to replace traditional banknotes and coins.

CDN (Content Delivery Network): A system of distributed servers that deliver web content and pages to a user based on their geographic locations, speeding up the delivery of content on the internet.

Chatbot: Software applications that use AI and natural language processing to understand what a person wants and guide them to their desired outcome with as little work for the end user as possible.

ChatGPT: An AI model developed by OpenAI that specialises in understanding and generating human-like text based on the input it receives, often used in customer service and other interactive applications.

Cloud Computing: Technology that allows data and applications to be stored on remote servers, and accessed over the internet, providing scalability and flexibility in computing resources.

Cloud Storage: Internet-based computing that allows users to store data and files in remote servers that are accessible through the internet, enabling easy access and backup.

Co-Pilot: An artificial intelligence system designed to assist users in performing tasks by providing suggestions, automations, or enhancements based on the context of the user's activities. These systems are often integrated into software applications to improve productivity and efficiency.

Conscious Bias: Known prejudices in decision-making processes that can affect judgement and actions, typically requiring active management to mitigate.

CMS (Content Management System): A software application used to manage the creation and modification of digital content.

Conversational AI: AI technologies that enable software to understand, process, and respond to human language in a conversational manner.

CRM (Customer Relationship Management): Software that manages a company's interactions with current and potential customers by using data analysis about customers' history with a company to improve business relationships.

Cryptocurrency: Digital or virtual currency secured by cryptography, making it nearly impossible to counterfeit or double-spend. It is typically decentralised, operating on a blockchain.

Cryptography: The practice and study of techniques for secure communication in the presence of third parties called adversaries. It involves constructing and analysing protocols to prevent adversaries from reading private messages.

Cybersecurity: The practice of protecting systems, networks, and programs from digital attacks aimed at accessing, changing, or destroying sensitive information, extorting money from users, or interrupting normal business processes.

DALL-E: An AI program developed by OpenAI that creates images from textual descriptions, utilising a version of the GPT architecture to generate novel, diverse visual content.

DAOs (Decentralised Autonomous Organisations): Blockchain-enabled organisational structures where control is spread out rather than centralised, often governed by smart contracts and organisational tokens.

DApps (Decentralised Applications): Applications that run on a blockchain or P2P network of computers instead of a single computer, aiming to avoid any single point of failure.

Data Analytics: The science of analysing raw data to make conclusions about that information, often using specialised systems and software.

Data Mining: The process of discovering patterns and knowledge from large amounts of data, using statistical methods, machine learning, and database systems.

Data Privacy: The aspect of information technology that deals with the proper handling, processing, storage, and dissemination of personal data and ensuring individuals' privacy preferences are complied with.

Data Sovereignty: The concept that digital data is subject to the laws of the country in which it is located or stored.

Data Visualisation: The graphical representation of information and data, which uses visual elements like charts, graphs, and maps to provide an accessible way to see and understand trends, outliers, and patterns in data.

Deep Learning: A subset of machine learning in AI that has networks capable of learning unsupervised from data that is unstructured or unlabelled.

Deepfake: Synthetic media in which a person in an existing image or video is replaced with someone else's likeness, using powerful techniques such as machine learning and neural networks to manipulate or generate visual and audio content.

DeFi (Decentralised Finance): Financial services offered on public blockchains, especially Ethereum, that operate without traditional financial intermediaries.

DevOps: A set of practices that combines software development (Dev) and IT operations (Ops) aimed at shortening the systems development lifecycle while delivering features, fixes, and updates frequently in close alignment with business objectives.

DID (Decentralised Identity): An identity that is not tied to any centralised organisation, giving users full control over their personal information.

Digital Curiosity: An interest in understanding and utilising digital technologies and their potential impacts.

Digital Ethics: The branch of ethics that studies the moral issues surrounding digital technology use, including questions about privacy, data security, and information accuracy.

Digital Ethnography: The study of social interactions, behaviours, and perceptions that occur through digital media, used to obtain insights into the communities and cultures formed through such media.

Digital First Impression: The online presence or image that one presents, often considered before face-to-face interactions in personal and professional contexts.

Digital Footprint: The unique set of digital activities, actions, and communications that leave a trace of personal data that can be traced back to an individual.

Digital Identity: An online or networked identity adopted or claimed by individuals, organisations, or electronic devices.

Digital Legacy: The digital information available about someone after they pass away, including social media profiles, online accounts, and other data stored on digital platforms.

Digital Literacy: The ability to effectively and critically navigate, evaluate, and create information using a range of digital technologies. It encompasses a variety of skills, including the ability to use digital devices, communicate and collaborate online, understand and utilise digital content, and manage digital identity and security.

Digital Native: A person born or brought up during the age of digital technology and thus familiar with computers and the internet from an early age.

Digital Proof: A method of verifying information through digitally authenticated evidence, commonly used for confirming credentials in digital identities.

Digital Sovereignty: The concept that data or digital information is subject to the laws and governance of the country in which it is located.

Digital Transformation: The integration of digital technology into all areas of a business, fundamentally changing how businesses operate and deliver value to customers.

Digital Twin: A digital replica of a physical entity that can be used for various purposes including simulation, monitoring, and optimisation, often in industrial and manufacturing and healthcare contexts.

Digital Wallet: A software-based system that securely stores users' payment information and passwords for numerous payment methods and websites. It can be used for transactions in stores or online using a mobile device.

DLT (Distributed Ledger Technology): A digital system for recording the transaction of assets in which the transactions and their details are recorded in multiple places at the same time, providing transparency and security.

DR (Disaster Recovery): Strategies and processes put in place to recover technology infrastructure and systems following a serious incident or disaster.

DRM (Digital Rights Management): A technological solution that allows software publishers, copyright holders, and individuals to control the use of digital content and devices after sale.

E-commerce: The buying and selling of goods and services over the internet, and the transfer of money and data to carry out these transactions.

E-learning: Learning conducted via electronic media, typically on the internet, involving educational content that is more interactive and tailored to individual learning speeds.

Edge AI: AI that processes data at the edge of the network, near the source of the data, reducing latency and bandwidth use in networks.

Edge Computing: A method of optimising cloud computing systems by performing data processing at the edge of the network, closest to the source of the data.

ELIZA: An early natural language processing computer program created at the MIT Artificial Intelligence Laboratory in the mid-1960s, designed to simulate conversation by using a pattern-matching and substitution methodology.

ERP (Enterprise Resource Planning): Software systems used by organisations to manage and integrate the important parts of their businesses. An ERP software system can integrate planning, purchasing inventory, sales, marketing, finance, human resources, and more.

Ethereum: A decentralised, open-source blockchain system that features smart contract functionality. It is the second-largest cryptocurrency platform by market capitalisation, after Bitcoin.

EU AI Act: Legislation proposed by the European Union aimed at regulating the use of AI in various sectors, ensuring AI systems are safe, transparent, and accountable.

Explainability: In AI, the ability to explain the processes and decisions made by machine learning models to human users.

FaaS (Function as a Service): A cloud computing service that allows developers to execute code in response to events without the complexity of building and maintaining the infrastructure typically associated with developing and launching an app.

Fintech: A portmanteau of "financial technology". It refers to new tech that seeks to improve and automate the delivery and use of financial services.

Flash Storage: A type of non-volatile storage that can be electronically erased and reprogrammed, known for its fast access times and better shock resistance than hard drives.

Futurist: A person who studies the future and makes predictions about it based on current trends. This can involve a range of disciplines, including technology, economics, and sociology.

Gamification: The application of game-design elements and game principles in non-game contexts to improve user engagement, organisational productivity, flow, learning, crowd sourcing, and more.

GB (Gigabyte): A unit of digital information that equals approximately 1 billion bytes. Commonly used to measure storage capacity in computing and consumer electronics.

GB/s (Gigabytes per Second): A unit of data transfer rate that indicates the amount of digital data (measured in gigabytes) that can be moved or processed per second.

Gen Alpha (Generation Alpha): Refers to the demographic cohort born from 2010 through 2025. They are the children of Millennials and are the first generation to be born entirely in the 21st century. This generation is characterised by its significant exposure to technology, digital devices, and social media from a very young age, influencing their learning, communication, and play.

Gen X (Generation X): This demographic cohort follows the Baby Boomers and precedes Millennials. Generation X typically includes individuals born from the early 1960s to the early 1980s. Members of this generation are known for their independent attitudes, having grown up during times of shifting societal values and economic change.

Gen Y (Generation Y): Also known as Millennials, follows Generation X and precedes Generation Z. This group includes individuals born from the early 1980s to the mid-1990s to early 2000s. Millennials are characterised by their familiarity and integration with communication, media, and digital technologies.

Gen Z (Generation Z): A demographic grouping that follows Millennials and precedes Generation Alpha. This cohort includes those born from the mid-to-late 1990s through the early 2010s.

GenAI (Generative AI): a type of artificial intelligence that can generate new content, ranging from text and images to music, code, and video based on the patterns and information it has learned from training data. An example is ChatGPT.

General AI: Often used interchangeably with AGI (Artificial General Intelligence), referring to a type of AI capable of understanding or learning any intellectual task that a human being can.

GDPR (General Data Protection Regulation): A regulation in EU law on data protection and privacy in the European Union and the European Economic Area, which also addresses the transfer of personal data outside the EU and EEA areas.

Gig Economy: A labour market characterised by the prevalence of short-term contracts or freelance work as opposed to permanent jobs.

GPT (Generative Pre-trained Transformer): A type of AI developed by OpenAI and others that uses deep learning to produce human-like text based on the input it is fed.

GPU (Graphics Processing Unit): A specialised electronic circuit designed to accelerate the processing of images and complex calculations in parallel. AI developers favour GPUs because of their ability to handle large-scale computations simultaneously, significantly speeding up the training and execution of deep learning models.

Green Computing: The practice of designing, manufacturing, using, and disposing of computers, servers, and associated subsystems – such as monitors, printers, storage devices, and networking and communications systems – efficiently and effectively with minimal impact on the environment.

GSM (Global System for Mobile Communications): A standard developed by the European Telecommunications Standards Institute to describe the protocols for second-generation digital cellular networks used by mobile devices such as mobile phones and tablets.

Hackathon: An event, typically lasting several days, in which a large number of people meet to engage in collaborative computer programming.

Hallucinations: In the context of AI, refers to instances where AI generates false or misleading information, often due to limitations or flaws in the underlying model.

Hybrid Cloud: A computing environment that uses a mix of on-premises, private cloud, and third-party, public cloud services with orchestration between the two platforms.

Hybrid Cloud Storage: A storage solution that combines on-premises data storage with cloud storage services, enabling data and applications to be shared between them.

IaaS (Infrastructure as a Service): A form of cloud computing that provides virtualised computing resources over the internet.

Internet Governance: The development and application of shared principles, norms, rules, decision-making procedures, and programs that shape the evolution and use of the internet.

IoT (Internet of Things): The network of physical objects – "things" – that are embedded with sensors, software, and other technologies for the purpose of connecting and exchanging data with other devices and systems over the internet.

IP (Internet Protocol): The method or protocol by which data is sent from one computer to another on the internet. Each computer (known as a host) on the internet has at least one IP address that uniquely identifies it from all other computers on the internet. An example of an IP address is 45.32.183.112

IT (Information Technology): The use of computers to store, retrieve, transmit, and manipulate data or information. IT is typically used within the context of business operations as opposed to personal or entertainment technologies.

LEO (Low Earth Orbit): Refers to a satellite which orbits the earth at altitudes between 160 kilometres (99 miles) and 2000 kilometres (1200 miles).

LISP (LISt Processing): A family of programming languages with a long history and a distinctive, fully parenthesised prefix notation. Primarily known for its use in AI.

LLM (Large Language Model): AI models that process and generate natural language or other data in a human-like manner. These models are trained on vast datasets to improve their predictive capabilities.

M2M (Machine-to-Machine): Technology that allows both wireless and wired systems to communicate with other devices of the same ability, often used in industrial automation and IoT.

Machine Learning: A branch of AI that enables systems to learn from data, identify patterns, and make decisions with minimal human intervention.

MB (Megabyte): A unit of information equal to 1000 kilobytes or approximately 1,000,000 bytes. Megabyte is commonly used to describe data size or storage capacity.

MB/s (Megabytes per Second): A unit of data transfer rate equal to 8 megabits per second. It is used to quantify the rate at which data is transferred from one device to another or accessed from storage.

Mechanical Turk: Originally referring to an 18th-century automaton in the form of a chess-playing machine, the term describes platforms or services that use human labour to perform tasks that computers currently cannot do effectively on their own. An example is Amazon Mechanical Turk, a crowdsourcing marketplace that makes it easier for individuals and businesses to outsource their processes and jobs to a distributed workforce who can perform these tasks virtually.

Metaverse: A collective virtual shared space, created by the convergence of virtually enhanced physical reality, persistent virtual spaces, and the internet. It suggests a future integration of physical, augmented, and virtual reality in a shared online space.

MFA (Multi-Factor Authentication): A security system that requires more than one method of authentication from independent categories of credentials to verify the user's identity for a login or other transaction.

Midjourney: An AI-based image generation tool that allows users to create visual content by providing text descriptions. It uses advanced algorithms to interpret the text and generate detailed, high-quality images from the prompts.

Millennials: Also known as Generation Y, are the demographic cohort following Generation X and preceding Generation Z. Typically, this group includes individuals born from the early 1980s to the mid-1990s to early 2000s. Millennials are known for their comfort with digital technologies and the internet, having come of age during the rise of mass communication, social media, and the digital revolution.

Minecraft: A video game developed by Mojang Studios, known for its distinctive blocky, pixelated graphics, the game allows players to explore, gather resources, craft items, and build structures or earthworks in different game modes, including survival and creative modes. Players can modify the game with skins, textures, and custom maps to create new gameplay mechanics and experiences.

Multi-cloud: The use of multiple cloud computing and storage services in a single heterogeneous architecture. This strategy can help prevent data loss or downtime due to a localised component failure.

MVP (Minimum Viable Product): A product with just enough features to satisfy early customers, and to provide feedback for future product development.

Narrow AI: AI systems that are designed to handle a specific task or a narrow range of tasks, as opposed to General AI, which can handle any cognitive task.

Network Security: The protection of the underlying networking infrastructure from unauthorised access, misuse, malfunction, modification, destruction, or improper disclosure.

Neural Networks: Computational models that are designed to simulate the way the human brain analyses and processes information.

NFT (Non-Fungible Token): A type of digital asset that represents ownership of a unique item or piece of content, using blockchain technology to establish verified and public proof of ownership.

NLG (Natural Language Generation): The use of AI programming to produce written or spoken narrative from a dataset.

NLP (Natural Language Processing): The branch of AI focused on giving computers the ability to understand text and spoken words in much the same way human beings can.

NLU (Natural Language Understanding): A subset of natural language processing in AI that deals with machine reading comprehension. It is concerned with the machine's ability to understand the intent behind the text and the context in which it is used.

Observability: The capability to monitor and measure the internal states and outputs of AI systems in real time, enabling developers to gain insights into their behaviour and performance. This is essential for identifying issues, ensuring reliability, and maintaining optimal functioning of AI applications and compliance with relevant legislation and business rules.

Open Source: Software for which the original source code is made freely available and may be redistributed and modified. This allows anyone to inspect, modify, and enhance the software.

OpenAI: An AI research and deployment company that aims to ensure that AGI benefits all of humanity. OpenAI is known for its advancements in the field of AI with projects like GPT (Generative Pre-trained Transformer).

PaaS (Platform as a Service): A cloud computing model that provides customers with a platform allowing them to develop, run, and manage applications without the complexity of building and maintaining the infrastructure typically associated with developing and launching an app.

Passkey: A new kind of user authentication method designed to replace passwords with a more secure and easier to use solution. Passkeys involve cryptographic key pairings that are more resistant to theft and phishing than traditional passwords.

Phishing: A cybercrime in which a target or targets are contacted by email, telephone, or text message by someone posing as a legitimate institution to lure individuals into providing sensitive data.

PoS (Proof of Stake): A type of algorithm by which a cryptocurrency blockchain network aims to achieve distributed consensus. In PoS-based cryptocurrencies, the creator of the next block is chosen via various combinations of random selection and wealth or age.

PoW (Proof of Work): A consensus mechanism in blockchain technology that requires participants to do a computationally intensive task to validate transactions and create new blocks.

PQC (Post-Quantum Cryptography): Cryptographic systems that are secure against an attack by a quantum computer. This field is evolving rapidly as the advent of quantum computing presents new challenges to the security of current cryptographic techniques.

Predictive Analytics: The use of data, statistical algorithms, and machine learning techniques to identify the likelihood of future outcomes based on historical data.

Predictive Maintenance: Techniques designed to help determine the condition of in-service equipment in order to predict when maintenance should be performed, which promises cost savings over routine or time-based preventive maintenance.

Private Cloud: A cloud computing model where the infrastructure and services are maintained on a private network. These clouds are used by a single organisation and offer greater control and security.

Prompt: In the context of AI and programming, a prompt is an input given to an AI system to generate a specific output or perform a task. This is common in language models where prompts are used to guide the generation of text.

Prompt Engineering: The practice of crafting inputs (prompts) to get the best possible outputs from AI systems, especially large language models. It involves understanding how the model interprets inputs to optimise responses.

Public Cloud: A cloud computing model where services and infrastructure are hosted off-site by a cloud provider, available to the general public over the internet. Public clouds offer scalability and efficiency but may have less control and security than private clouds.

PWND: Slang derived from the word "owned", indicating domination or defeat. In gaming and internet culture, it means having decisively beaten or embarrassed someone, usually in a public manner. Used in the name of the website Have I Been Pwned to allow individuals to understand if their digital identity has been compromised in a data breach.

Q-Day: Refers to the hypothetical future date when quantum computers will break most of the cryptographic standards that are currently in use. This term highlights the potential impact of quantum computing on global security. Experts predict Q-Day could be as early as 2030.

Quantum AI: The application of quantum computing to enhance machine learning algorithms and AI capabilities, potentially leading to significant advancements in processing speeds and problem-solving abilities.

Quantum Computing: A type of computing that uses quantum bits (qubits) to perform calculations at much higher efficiencies than traditional computers.

Quantum Cryptography: The application of quantum mechanics to cryptographic protocols, which provides a level of security that is not possible through traditional algorithms.

Quantum Sensing: The use of quantum systems, phenomena, and methods to measure physical quantities with high precision, which could potentially revolutionise fields like navigation, imaging, and mineral exploration.

Quantum Supremacy: The potential ability of quantum computing devices to solve problems that classical computers practically cannot.

Qubit: Also called a quantum bit, it is the fundamental unit of quantum information, analogous to a bit in classical computing. Unlike a classical bit that can be either 0 or 1, a qubit can exist in a superposition of both states simultaneously, enabling quantum computers to perform complex computations more efficiently than classical computers.

RAM (Random Access Memory): A type of computer memory that can be accessed randomly; any byte of memory can be accessed without touching the preceding bytes.

RegTech: Regulatory Technology, a subclass of fintech that uses technology to help businesses comply with regulations efficiently and at a lower cost.

RFID (Radio-Frequency Identification): A technology that uses electromagnetic fields to automatically identify and track tags attached to objects. These tags contain electronically stored information, which can be read from a distance, making RFID useful for inventory management, asset tracking, and various other applications such as Apple Pay, Google Pay, and contactless card payments.

RLHF (Reinforcement Learning from Human Feedback): An AI training approach where models learn optimal behaviours through trial and error, guided by feedback from human trainers, to improve performance in complex environments.

Roblox: An online platform and storefront where users go to play games. Unlike traditional video game platforms, Roblox allows users to create and share their own games and experiences using Roblox Studio, its proprietary game development tool.

ROM (Read-Only Memory): A type of non-volatile storage that is used in computers and other electronic devices to store permanent data that does not change, such as firmware.

SaaS (Software as a Service): A software distribution model where applications are hosted by a third-party provider and made accessible to customers over the internet.

SDN (Software Defined Networking): An approach to network management that enables dynamic, programmatically efficient network configuration to improve network performance and monitoring.

Second Life: An online virtual world, developed in 2003, where users can create avatars, meet new people, chat, build, and create virtual property and trade goods.

Semantic Web: An extension of the World Wide Web through standards by the World Wide Web Consortium (W3C). The goal of the Semantic Web is to make internet data machine-readable, to facilitate data sharing and reuse across application, enterprise, and community boundaries.

Smart Buildings: Buildings that use automation technologies to automatically control the building's operations, including heating, ventilation, air conditioning, lighting, security, and other systems.

Smart City: An urban area that uses digital technology to enhance performance across the urban operation and services and connect to citizens.

Smart Contracts: Self-executing contracts with the terms of the agreement between buyer and seller being directly written into lines of code, which automatically execute and enforce themselves via a blockchain network.

Social Engineering: The psychological manipulation of people into performing actions or divulging confidential information. A common tactic in fraud and information theft.

Sovereign Identity: A digital identity model where individuals or businesses have the ability to control their own identity information and transactions securely, without depending on a central authority.

SSI (Self-Sovereign Identity): A digital movement that allows individuals to own, control, and present their identity data without relying on administrative authorities. SSI empowers individuals with the management of their own identity.

Subscription Economy: A business model where customers pay a recurring price at regular intervals for access to a product or service, rather than purchasing it outright.

Supply Chain Analytics: The application of analytics tools and processes to manage supply chain activities, aiming to improve efficiency and effectiveness as well as to ensure operational reliability and supply chain visibility.

Synthetic Media: Media content, such as videos, audio, and text, generated with AI techniques, often used for creating realistic simulations or modifications of real human behaviours.

TED Talk: A presentation at one of a series of conferences run by the non-profit organisation TED (Technology, Entertainment, Design) under the slogan "Ideas Worth Spreading".

Threat Intelligence: Evidence-based knowledge, including context, mechanisms, indicators, implications, and actionable advice, about an existing or emerging menace or hazard to assets that can be used to inform decisions regarding the subject's response to that menace or hazard.

Token Staking: In blockchain, the process of holding tokens in a cryptocurrency wallet to support network operations and security in return for rewards.

Tokenisation: The process of converting rights to an asset into a digital token on a blockchain, which can include everything from data security strategies to asset ownership.

Tokenomics: The economic policies and incentives designed to regulate the supply and demand of tokens within the ecosystem of a blockchain project.

TQ (Technology Quotient): A measure of an individual's ability to adapt, manage, and integrate technology based on their understanding of its current capability and potential.

UI (User Interface): The space where interactions between humans and machines occur, with the goal of effective operation and control of the machine from the human end, while the machine simultaneously provides feedback that aids the operator's decision-making process.

UX (User Experience): The overall experience of a person using a product, system, or service, especially in terms of how easy or satisfying it is to use.

Verifiable Credentials: Digital proofs of information about an individual that are secured and confirmed through blockchain technology, improving reliability and privacy.

Virtual Assistants: AI systems that can perform tasks or services for an individual based on commands or questions. Some popular virtual assistants include Apple's Siri, Amazon's Alexa, and Google Assistant.

Voice Assistants: Software agents that can perform tasks or services based on verbal commands or queries, integrating advanced AI technologies to interpret human speech.

VPN (Virtual Private Network): A service that allows you to connect to the internet via an encrypted tunnel to ensure your online privacy and protect your sensitive data. VPNs are commonly used to secure connection to public Wi-Fi networks.

VPS (Virtual Private Server): A virtual machine sold as a service by an internet hosting service. A VPS runs its own copy of an operating system, and customers have superuser-level access to that operating system instance, so they can install almost any software that runs on that OS.

VR (Virtual Reality): A simulated experience that can be similar to or completely different from the real world, typically achieved through head-mounted displays or multi-projected environments.

WAP (Wireless Application Protocol): A protocol launched in 1999 used for enabling access to the internet on mobile devices. WAP provided internet browsing speeds of around 14 kB/s on 2G networks.

Wearable Technology: Devices that are worn on the body as accessories or part of clothing that use advanced electronic technologies to assist with everyday activities.

Web 1.0: The first stage of the World Wide Web evolution. In Web 1.0, the web was mostly static HTML pages that were linked together, and users were mainly consumers of content.

Web 2.0: The evolution of Web 1.0, where the internet became more interactive and social. Web 2.0 involves user-generated content, usability, and interoperability for end users. It includes social networking sites, blogs, wikis, video-sharing sites, hosted services, and web applications.

Web 3.0: The next iteration of the internet, focusing on decentralised networks and enhanced user empowerment through ownership and control of data and digital identities.

XaaS (Everything as a Service): The broad category encompassing various services delivered over the internet, shifting from traditional product delivery to a service-based model.

XR (Extended Reality): A term referring to all real-and-virtual combined environments and human–machine interactions generated by computer technology and wearables, including augmented reality (AR), mixed reality (MR), and virtual reality (VR).

Y2K (Year 2000 problem): Refers to a class of computer bugs related to the formatting and storage of calendar data. Many programs represented the year with only two digits, making the year 2000 indistinguishable from 1900, which potentially led to errors when the date changed from 1999 to 2000.

Zero Trust Security: A strategic approach to cybersecurity that centres on the belief that organisations should not automatically trust anything inside or outside its perimeters and instead must verify anything and everything trying to connect to its systems before granting access.

RESOURCES

Listed here are the resources mentioned in each section, and some additional tools for you to investigate.

Introduction: Are You Digitally Curious?

The Digitally Curious Podcast – all episodes from my podcast series since 2019, available on all podcast platforms. Many of the guests on the show are featured in this book.

https://curious.click/podcast

Andrew Grill Speaking website – details of my previous speaking engagements and the topics I cover with a list of clients.

https://curious.click/website

The Scary Slide – the slide full of jargon that I show at events to scare executives into becoming more digitally curious. Which ones can you cross off the list after reading this book?

https://curious.click/scary

Accenture on Digital Fluency – great blog post from Andy Young at Accenture about the need for digital fluency.

https://curious.click/fluency

The Digital Advantage – Capgemini and MIT Sloan report which was one of the inspirations for this book. It examines how digital technology can create competitive advantage for organisations and leaders.

https://curious.click/mit

Raindrop.io – a fantastic website bookmarking service that allows you to categorise, search, and save a snapshot of a page for later recall. This is the one of the main tools I have been using with the footnotes for this book to create a snapshot of a web page in case they are removed or changed.

https://curious.click/raindrop

The Wayback Machine – a digital archive of the World Wide Web founded by the Internet Archive, an American nonprofit organisation. It was launched in 2001 and allows users to go "back in time" to see how websites looked previously and how they've changed over time. This can be useful if you have not taken a snapshot of the page using tools such as raindrop.

https://curious.click/wayback

Rebrandly – a custom website link shortener that can be used with your own domain. This is the tool I have used to create, monitor, and update all of the footnote links from the "curious.click" domain that direct you to resources featured in this book. The tool also uses AI to suggest the optimal time to share your branded link.

https://curious.click/rebrandly

BBC Tech Decoded Newsletter – a useful weekly digest of technology that is making the news.

https://curious.click/tech-decoded

Part I: Curious About ... AI

What is ChatGPT doing and why does it work? – a fantastic long read from Stephen Wolfram which explains the inner workings of ChatGPT.

https://curious.click/wolfram

Alan Turing paper from 1950 – this is entitled "Computing Machinery and Intelligence", where Turing asks: "Can machines think?"

https://curious.click/machines

Google Research – attention is all you need – the 2017 research paper that formed the basis of GenAI as we know it today.

https://curious.click/attention

ChatGPT data sources – a blog post from Dennis Layton which explains the possible sources of training data for ChatGPT 3.5.

https://curious.click/sources

Data Quality – a UK government paper explaining why data quality is important for AI projects.

https://curious.click/data-quality

Shaping the Future of Enterprise AI – the podcast episode with Umesh Sachdev, CEO of AI company Uniphore, where we discussed AI in the enterprise.

https://curious.click/uniphore

The Opportunity for Enterprise AI – the podcast episode with Darshan Chandarana and Julia Howes from PwC.

https://curious.click/pwc

ChatGPT Plus – detailed information on ChatGPT Plus subscriptions.

https://curious.click/chatgpt

Microsoft Copilot – detailed information on Copilot.

https://curious.click/copilot

Grammarly – AI-powered spelling and grammar checker.

https://curious.click/grammarly

Otter.ai – an AI-powered text-to-speech platform with a GenAI interface that interrogates every recording. I use this tool daily, and it transcribed all of the podcast interviews for the book.

https://curious.click/otter-ai

Luminance – Legal AI Co-Pilot example of an industry-specific LLM.

https://curious.click/luminance

Bing Chat – Microsoft's search engine powered by GenAI.

https://curious.click/bing

Google Gemini – a free and paid version of Google's GenAI tool.

https://curious.click/gemini

Meta Llama – an open-source GenAI model from Meta.

https://curious.click/llama

XAi Grok – Elon Musk's open-source GenAI tool.

https://curious.click/grok

Claude - Anthropic's GenAI tool. Amazon has invested $4Bn in Anthropic.

https://curious.click/claude

Jasper – a marketing-focused GenAI tool – with a free trial available.

https://curious.click/jasper-ai

AI Tools for Creativity

CopyAI – a sales-focused GenAI tool.

https://curious.click/copyai

Veed.io – a powerful AI video editing and avatar creation tool.

https://curious.click/veed

Eleven Labs – a powerful voice cloning tool which can even be used to create an audiobook.

https://curious.click/eleven-labs

Adobe Firefly – Adobe's free GenAI tool for creatives, some of which is already integrated into tools such as Photoshop.

https://curious.click/firefly

Shutterstock – useful to create stock images using GenAI.

https://curious.click/shutterstock

Midjourney – GenAI image creator – takes a while to understand how to use it. Currently accessed via a Discord server.

https://curious.click/midjourney

OpenAI Sora – text-to-video generator – at the time of writing, it was an internal preview; likely to be available for use by the time you are reading this.

https://curious.click/sora

Stability AI – an open-source GenAI company with open-access AI models with minimal resource requirements in imaging, language, code, and audio. Creator of Stable Diffusion.

https://curious.click/stability-ai

Dall-E 2 – part of the OpenAI tools. Available as part of ChatGPT Plus, or standalone. It's an AI system that can create realistic images and art from a description in natural language.

https://curious.click/dalle2

Canva – the Australian unicorn graphic design company. It competes with Microsoft PowerPoint to provide graphic design with AI-powered elements.

https://curious.click/canva

Descript – video and podcast editor that can be commanded with text.

https://curious.click/descript

Part II: Curious About ... Technology

Unifi – professional Wi-Fi platform and devices.

https://curious.click/unifi

Amazon Web Services – free tier where you can try out your own cloud projects for 12 months. Naturally, usage limits apply.

https://curious.click/aws-free

Vodafone 5G futurist report – written in early 2024 in partnership with Vodafone UK on the future of 5G Standalone.

https://curious.click/vodafone-5g

Zoom meetings OtterPilot – a plugin to allow Otter.ai to automatically record Zoom calls.

https://curious.click/otter-pilot

What3words navigation system – used to accurately locate any 3 m × 3 m space in the world using.three.words.

https://curious.click/w3w

Little Snitch – network monitoring for MacOS to see what services are connected to your PC from around the world.

https://curious.click/snitch

Netlimiter – a network monitoring tool for Windows to see what services are connected to your PC.

https://curious.click/netlimiter

Quic.cloud – a content delivery network for WordPress. It delivers content closer to the user requesting it, speeding up website response times globally.

https://curious.click/cdn

Surfshark VPN – allows you to securely connect to local or remote servers in 100 countries.

https://curious.click/surfshark

Part III: Curious About ... The Internet

Gartner Hype Cycle – explaining the methodology behind Gartner's yearly look at what technology is being hyped up. Good indicator of what's coming next.

https://curious.click/hype

Accenture Life trends 2023 report – a podcast with Katie Burke looking at emerging technologies.

https://curious.click/katie

Ethereum explained – a good introduction to the Ethereum protocol and how it works.

https://curious.click/ethereum

Crypto, Web 3.0, and the metaverse explained – provides a clear explanation of the core concepts of cryptocurrencies, blockchain, Web 3.0, NFTs, and the metaverse, and the policy implications from Sam Gilbert at the University of Cambridge.

https://curious.click/sam

Web 3.0, NFTs, crypto, DAO, and DeFi explained – a podcast with lawyer Nick Abrahams.

https://curious.click/nick

Bitcoin whitepaper – Satoshi Nakamoto's original paper from 2008 explaining the concept of a "A Peer-to-Peer Electronic Cash System".

https://curious.click/whitepaper

Ethereum Proof of Stake energy consumption review – an article looking at how a "Proof of Stake" consensus mechanism is more efficient than the "Proof of Work" method that Bitcoin currently uses.

https://curious.click/pos-energy

Deep dive into blockchain scalability – an analysis of why Bitcoin's global transaction speed is limited to just seven transactions per second.

https://curious.click/seven

The Creation Generation report – a report on how Gen Alpha's use of creation gaming platforms is enhancing learning and supporting development.

https://curious.click/creation-generation

Part IV: Curious About ... Your Data

Google Alerts – a Google platform to allow you to set up mentions of your name, brand, or a competitor, with results sent to you "as they happen" on email. Useful for monitoring your digital profile.

https://curious.click/google-alerts

Lifelock from Norton – provides a way to detect and manage identity theft.

https://curious.click/lifelock

Identity Plus from Experian – a similar service to Lifelock.

https://curious.click/experian

Reputation Defender – a tool from Norton to allow users to monitor and manage their online reputation.

https://curious.click/reputation-defender

RESOURCES

Andrew Grill's LinkedIn profile

https://curious.click/linkedin

Have I Been Pwned website – set up by Australian security researcher Troy Hunt, it lists billions of email and password breaches in a searchable database.

https://curious.click/pwned

1Password – the password manager I use, also integrated with Have I Been Pwned.

https://curious.click/1password

Day One Journal app – a Mac and iOS application for writing a daily journal.

https://curious.click/dayone

Elaine Kasket – a digital legacy podcast episode where we discuss what happens to your data when you die and what you can do to prepare.

https://curious.click/afterlife

EU AI Act – the European Commission's AI Act, ratified in 2024 after many years and multiple rounds of negotiations between the EU member states. A likely blueprint for other countries to follow.

https://curious.click/eu-ai

Susie Alegre – a podcast episode where we discussed our most fundamental human right, the freedom to think, and why it is in grave danger.

https://curious.click/freedom

Susie Alegre – GenAI, ChatGPT podcast episode. This was a follow-up episode after ChatGPT was launched to look at the issues around GenAI.

https://curious.click/susiegpt

Namecheap – useful for searching for and buying your own domain name.

https://curious.click/namecheap

Sitemaker – create a personal or small business website in just a few clicks. Whether you want to promote a restaurant, showcase your startup, or develop a one-page bio site, this website builder will help you every step of the way.

https://curious.click/site-maker

About.me – create a one-page website for free, and connect it to a custom domain for a small monthly fee.

https://curious.click/about-me

Fastmail – a company that allows you to host and create your own personalised email address, which you can link to your own domain name.

https://curious.click/fastmail

Part V: Curious About ... The Future

OpenAI blog – on their plans for Artificial General Intelligence (AGI).

https://curious.click/openagi

OpenAI and Microsoft – talk to *The Economist*. Replay of an interview with OpenAI CEO Sam Altman and Microsoft CEO Satya Nadella, with Editor-in-Chief of *The Economist*, Zanny Minton Beddoes.

https://curious.click/economist-ai

Corsera courses – on AI.

https://curious.click/coursera

edX Executive AI – education courses.

https://curious.click/edx

Khan Academy – free AI courses.

https://curious.click/khan

The Actionable Futurist AI Hub – a source of talks, podcasts, and articles focused on AI.

https://curious.click/ai-hub

MIT Technology Review – an excellent source of information and opinion on new technologies.

https://curious.click/tech-review

OpenAI blog – the latest thinking on AI from OpenAI.

https://curious.click/openai-blog

Google AI blog – the latest thinking on AI from Google.

https://curious.click/google-ai

Microsoft AI blog – the latest thinking on AI from Microsoft.

https://curious.click/microsoft-ai

Anthropic AI blog – the latest thinking on AI from Anthropic.

https://curious.click/anthropic-ai

TED talks – on AI, a collection of AI-themed TED talks.

RESOURCES

https://curious.click/ted-ai

Elements of AI course – a free online resource from The University of Helsinki.

https://curious.click/elements

The jobs that AI can't replace – World Economic Forum analysis on jobs of the future.

https://curious.click/wef-ai

The threat of Q-Day in 2030 – a podcast episode with Chris Johnson from Nokia on the threats from quantum computing.

https://curious.click/chris

IBM Quantum website – a great starting point to better understand quantum computing.

https://curious.click/ibm-quantum

The future of self-sovereign identity – a podcast episode with Marie Wallace from Accenture on the concepts around SSI.

https://curious.click/marie

EU Digital Identity – a paper from the EU Commission on their plans for a digital wallet using SSI.

https://curious.click/eu-wallet

LinkedIn identity verification by Persona – add a verified checkmark to your profile by using your mobile phone and an NFC-enabled passport.

https://curious.click/persona

Conclusion: Curious About ... What's Next

Future Today Institute – 2024 trends report with 700 technology and science trends that are likely to influence every industry. Useful for future scanning and understanding likely technology trends. Updated every year.

https://curious.click/2024-trends

These publications help me to stay on top of what's next:

Wired Magazine – one of my original "go-to" publications on all things tech.

https://curious.click/wired

The Information – a fresh take on industry news and views.

https://curious.click/the-information

Fast Company Magazine – something I've been reading since the "dot.com boom" in 2000.

https://curious.click/fast-company

MIT Technology Review – a fantastic resource from the team at MIT.

https://curious.click/technology-review

Techcrunch – another great source of technology news and views.

https://curious.click/techcrunch

NOTES

Introduction: Are You Digitally Curious?

1. Speaking Office website: https://curious.click/so
2. Digitally Curious Podcast: https://curious.click/podcast
3. Andrew Grill Speaking Engagements: https://curious.click/speaking

Chapter 1: Becoming Digitally Curious

1. Project Parakeet: https://curious.click/parakeet
2. Visions for the Future – Telstra Webcast 8 August 2000: https://curious.click/futurist-2000
3. Andrew Grill appointed CEO of property website PropertyLook: https://curious.click/propertylook

Chapter 2: Why Being Digitally Curious is Good for Your Career and Your Business

1. Augmented work for an automated, AI-driven world – IBM report: https://curious.click/ibm-ai
2. The Digital Advantage: How digital leaders outperform their peers in every industry. Capgemini & MIT Sloan: https://curious.click/digital-advantage
3. When will you cross the AI Chasm? https://curious.click/chasm
4. Discover Global Network keynote, Dubai, October 2023: https://curious.click/discover
5. Scary Slide: https://curious.click/scary
6. What is a hackathon? – TechTarget Definition: https://curious.click/hackathon
7. The New Elements of Digital Transformation – MIT Sloan Management Review: https://curious.click/mit
8. Technology's Battle for IQ, EQ, or Something Very Different – Psychology Today: https://curious.click/tq
9. Digital directors: Boost tech savviness of the board – Accenture blog: https://curious.click/digital-directors

10. Four keys to boosting digital fluency – Accenture blog: https://curious .click/fluency
11. The Digital Advantage: How digital leaders outperform their peers in every industry – Capgemini & MIT Sloan report: https://curious.click/leaders
12. The New Elements of Digital Transformation – MIT Sloane Management Review: https://curious.click/mit
13. Wired Magazine: https://curious.click/wired
14. The Information: https://curious.click/information
15. Oxford Artificial Intelligence Programme: https://curious.click/oxford-ai

Part I: Curious About . . . AI

1. Watson, *Jeopardy!* champion – IBM: https://curious.click/jeopardy
2. Talks at GS with Ginni Rometty – YouTube: https://curious.click/ginni
3. Grammarly AI-powered grammar checker: https://curious.click/grammarly
4. Otter.ai AI-powered transcription tool: https://curious.click/otter
5. Veed.io AI-powered video creation tool: https://curious.click/veed
6. What Is ChatGPT Doing . . . and Why Does It Work? Stephen Wolfram: https://curious.click/wolfram

Chapter 3: From Turing to Transformers

1. Creating Video from Text – Open AI: https://curious.click/sora
2. Mustafa Suleyman, DeepMind and Inflection Co-founder, joins Microsoft to lead Copilot: https://curious.click/mustafa
3. Alan Turing Paper (1950) – Computing machinery and intelligence: https://curious .click/machines
4. Arthur Samuel – IEEE Computing pioneers: https://curious.click/arthur
5. Dartmouth AI conference: https://curious.click/dartmouth
6. Lisp – Encyclopaedia Britannica: https://curious.click/lisp
7. Arthur Samuel, "Some studies in machine learning using the game of checkers" – IBM: https://curious.click/checkers
8. What is the Eliza Effect? Builtin: https://curious.click/eliza
9. The Stanford Cart – Stanford University: https://curious.click/cart
10. IBM's Deep Blue: https://curious.click/deep-blue
11. Attention is All You Need – Google research: https://curious.click/attention
12. Captcha if you can: How you've been training AI for years without realising it – TechRadar: https://curious.click/captcha
13. Bret Greenstein – The Digitally Curious Podcast: https://curious.click/bret
14. Mechanical Turk definition – PC Mag: https://curious.click/mechanical-turk
15. IBM's Deep Blue: https://curious.click/deep-blue
16. Watson, *Jeopardy!* champion: https://curious.click/jeopardy

17. MidJourney – AI-based image generation tool: https://curious.click/midjourney
18. ChatGPT – Show me the Data Sources – Dennis Layton – Medium: https://curious.click/sources
19. Attention is All You Need: https://curious.click/attention
20. Introducing ChatGPT – OpenAI: https://curious.click/chatgpt3
21. ChatGPT Plus: https://curious.click/chatgpt-plus
22. Introducing ChatGPT – OpenAI: https://curious.click/chatgpt
23. Claude from Anthropic: https://curious.click/claude
24. Jasper.ai – Marketing-focused AI tool: https://curious.click/jasper
25. Google Gemini: https://curious.click/gemini
26. Amazon and Anthropic announce strategic collaboration to advance generative AI: https://curious.click/anthropic

Chapter 4: Deploying AI in the Workplace

1. Exposing artificial intelligence's true costs – Baillie Gifford: https://curious.click/genai-costs
2. Jaeger Glucina – Luminance on The Digitally Curious Podcast: https://curious.click/luminance-podcast
3. Dr Mark Kennedy – Imperial College London – CEO Club talk: https://curious.click/kennedy
4. A guide to using artificial intelligence in the public sector – UK Government: https://curious.click/data-quality
5. Data Quality: The Better the Data, the Better the Model – Appen website: https://curious.click/appen
6. Italy says OpenAI's chatbot breaches data protection rules – BBC News: https://curious.click/italy
7. Pulitzer-winning authors join OpenAI, Microsoft copyright lawsuit: https://curious.click/lawsuit
8. Shaping the Future of Enterprise-Grade AI with Umesh Sachdev of Uniphore – The Digitally Curious Podcast: https://curious.click/uniphore
9. When it Comes to Gorillas, Google Photos Remains Blind – Wired: https://curious.click/google-photos
10. ChatGPT iterative deployment: https://curious.click/rlhf
11. Training language models to follow instructions with human feedback: https://curious.click/upwork
12. Shaping the Future of Enterprise-Grade AI with Umesh Sachdev of Uniphore – The Digitally Curious Podcast: https://curious.click/uniphore
13. The opportunity for Enterprise AI with Darshan Chandarana and Julia Howes from PwC – The Digitally Curious Podcast: https://curious.click/pwc
14. AI in Marketing – Debunking Myths and Exploring Opportunities with Isabel Perry of DEPT – The Digitally Curious Podcast: https://curious.click/dept

Chapter 5: Tools to Get You Started with AI

1. Predictions 2024: Where Will AI Go Next? – Forrester: https://curious.click/forrester
2. ChatGPT data controls: https://curious.click/data-controls
3. AI-Created Images Aren't Protected by Copyright Law According to U.S. Copyright Office – Forbes: https://curious.click/ai-copyright

Part II: Curious About . . . Technology

1. Unifi Wireless – Ubiquity website: https://curious.click/unifi
2. How I fixed my dodgy WiFi – Troy Hunt blog: https://curious.click/troy
3. AWS Free tier: https://curious.click/aws-free

Chapter 6: The Promise of 5G

1. Vodafone report examines how 5G SA could transform UK over next 5–7 years: https://curious.click/5g-report
2. UK public: 5G has more potential than AI to improve society – Vodafone: https://curious.click/vodafone-5g
3. 5G and Aviation Safety – FAA website: https://curious.click/faa
4. Futurist Andrew Grill predicts five ways 5G will supercharge the things the UK loves most in five years – Vodafone website: https://curious.click/5g-futurist
5. Shahid Ahmed from NTT on the opportunities for Private 5G networks – The Digitally Curious Podcast: https://curious.click/ntt
6. What's the Future of 5G with Paul Scanlan, CTO Huawei Carrier Group – The Digitally Curious Podcast: https://curious.click/scanlan
7. Vodafone report examines how 5G SA could transform UK over next 5–7 years: https://curious.click/5g-report
8. Makeup Virtual Try-on Nyx Looks Try It On – L'Oreal website: https://curious.click/nyx
9. Amazon's 'AI-powered' cashier-free shops use a lot of . . . humans – Guardian website: https://curious.click/amazon-go
10. Vodafone report examines how 5G SA could transform UK over next 5–7 years: https://curious.click/5g-report

Chapter 7: Let's Talk – The Power of Voice

1. Dragon Dictate: https://curious.click/dragon
2. Karen Jacobsen – the GPS Girl on her serendipitous role as the original Australian voice of Siri – The Digitally Curious Podcast: https://curious.click/karen
3. The Future of Voice with James Poulter – The Digitally Curious Podcast: https://curious.click/vixen
4. Put Your Zoom Meetings on OtterPilot: https://curious.click/otter-pilot

5. Google Duplex: An AI System for Accomplishing Real-World Tasks Over the Phone: https://curious.click/duplex
6. What3words navigation system: https://curious.click/w3w
7. Umang Patel from Microsoft and Dr Simon Wallace from Nuance on the future of healthcare – The Digitally Curious Podcast: https://curious.click/nuance
8. Enterprise-Grade AI with Umesh Sachdev of Uniphore – The Digitally Curious Podcast: https://curious.click/uniphore

Chapter 8: Cloud Computing

1. Top 10 Cloud Service Providers Globally in 2024 – Dgtlinfra: https://curious.click/cloud10
2. Warren Buffett CNBC Interview Omaha 2017: https://curious.click/warren
3. Apple's Data Center Locations: Enabling Growth in Services – Dgtlinfra: https://curious.click/apple-data
4. Little Snitch network monitoring tool for MacOS: https://curious.click/snitch
5. Netlimiter network tool: https://curious.click/netlimiter
6. What is Data Sovereignty? Cloudian: https://curious.click/data-sovereignty
7. Quic.cloud Content Delivery Network for Wordpress: https://curious.click/cdn
8. Surfshark Virtual Private Network: https://curious.click/surfshark
9. Cloud Migration "Saved the Ukrainian Government and Economy" – Nextgov: https://curious.click/ukraine
10. AWS Snowball – Accelerate moving offline data or remote storage to the cloud: https://curious.click/snowball
11. Multi-Cloud vs Hybrid Cloud Solutions: What's the Difference? – Digital Realty: https://curious.click/multi-hybrid
12. The Transformative Impact of Edge Computing with Mark Swinson from Red Hat – The Digitally Curious Podcast: https://curious.click/redhat
13. Aurrigo Autonomous Vehicles Podcast: https://curious.click/aurrigo
14. The Future of Multicloud Technology: A Deep Dive with Steve Young of Dell Technologies: https://curious.click/dell

Chapter 9: The Internet of Everything

1. Google Nest smart home products: https://curious.click/nest
2. Arlo security cameras: https://curious.click/arlo
3. Google Fitbit products: https://curious.click/fitbit
4. Apple Watch: https://curious.click/watch
5. Vodafone report examines how 5G SA could transform UK over next 5–7 years – The Actionable Futurist report: https://curious.click/5g-report
6. The future of the Internet of Things with Ron Rock from Microshare – The Digitally Curious Podcast: https://curious.click/ron

7. NB-IoT vs LTE-M: Comparing the two IoT technologies – OneMondo blog: https://curious.click/iot-m
8. The opportunity for Enterprise AI with Darshan Chandarana and Julia Howes from PwC: https://curious.click/pwc
9. What is IoT (Internet of Things)? – Amazon Web Services: https://curious.click/iot
10. SmegConnect ovens: https://curious.click/smeg

Part III: Curious About . . . The Internet

1. Visions for the Future – Telstra Webcast 8 August 2000: https://curious.click/futurist-2000
2. Community Fibre website: https://curious.click/fibre
3. What's New in the 2023 Gartner Hype Cycle for Emerging Technologies: https://curious.click/hype

Chapter 10: The New Internet

1. Tim Berners-Lee W3 website: https://curious.click/tim
2. The Internet Archive of andrewgrill.com from 18 October 2000: https://curious.click/2000
3. The Ethics and Implications of Data Privacy in the Digital World with Anton Christodoulou from Imagination – The Digitally Curious Podcast: https://curious.click/anton
4. Katie Burke from Accenture on their Life Trends 2023 Report – The Digitally Curious Podcast: https://curious.click/katie
5. Web 3.0 Explained: A Comprehensive Guide: IP With Ease: https://curious.click/web3-guide
6. Welcome to Ethereum: https://curious.click/ethereum
7. What is Web 3.0? Everything explained – Creative Tim: https://curious.click/creative-tim

Chapter 11: The Metaverse

1. Introducing Meta: A Social Technology Company – Facebook news: https://curious.click/meta
2. Neal Stephenson website: https://curious.click/neal
3. Crypto, Web3 and the Metaverse – University of Cambridge: https://curious.click/sam
4. Second Life: https://curious.click/second-life

5. Meta spent $10 billion on the metaverse in 2021, dragging down profit – NY Times: https://curious.click/meta-costs
6. How the Apple iPhone became one of the best-selling products of all time – CNBC: https://curious.click/apple-sales
7. Nick Abrahams from Norton Rose Fulbright on Web3, NFTs, Crypto, DAO and DeFi – The Digitally Curious Podcast: https://curious.click/nick
8. Thomas Bendenk – The opportunities for Extended Reality and the Metaverse – The Digitally Curious Podcast: https://curious.click/thomas
9. AI Magazine – Metaverse destined to become an impossible, dangerous place: https://curious.click/dice
10. The Creation Generation – How creating gaming is revolutionising educational engagement for generation alpha: https://curious.click/creation-generation
11. Apple Vision Pro headset – Apple website: https://curious.click/vision-pro
12. Apple Vision Pro EyeSight: https://curious.click/eye sight
13. Google Glass: https://curious.click/google-glass
14. Google Glass Wasn't a Failure. It Raised Crucial Concerns – Wired: https://curious.click/glass-concerns

Chapter 12: Bitcoin and Blockchain

1. Bitcoin: A Peer-to-Peer Electronic Cash System – whitepaper: https://curious.click/whitepaper
2. An Event Study of the Ethereum Transition to Proof-of-Stake: https://curious.click/pos-energy
3. A Deep Dive into Blockchain Scalability – Crypto.com: https://curious.click/seven
4. Everledger Diamond provenance history: https://curious.click/diamonds
5. Walmart, JD.com, IBM and Tsinghua University Launch a Blockchain Food Safety Alliance in China – Jingling: https://curious.click/wallmart
6. What was the DAO? Cryptopedia: https://curious.click/dao-hack
7. The Future of Crypto Payments – Nuvei whitepaper: https://curious.click/crypto-whitepaper

Chapter 13: Tokenisation and NFTs

1. Beeple's opus – Christie's website: https://curious.click/beeple
2. Nick Abrahams from Norton Rose Fulbright on Web3, NFTs, Crypto, DAO and DeFi – The Digitally Curious Podcast: https://curious.click/nick
3. Seatlab website: https://curious.click/seatlab

4. The National Football League to Offer Limited Edition NFTs to Celebrate Super Bowl LVI: https://curious.click/superbowl
5. Top 11 Most Expensive Bored Ape Yacht Club NFTs – Crypto blogs: https://curious.click/bored
6. How Did the Bored Ape Yacht Club Get So Popular? – Wired magazine: https://curious.click/banana
7. The Starbucks Odyssey Begins – Starbucks website: https://curious.click/odyssey
8. 'MetaBirkins' NFT creator loses trademark fight with Hermès – The Verge: https://curious.click/hermes
9. Power of the Purse – Hermès Prevails in NFT Trademark Trial – Baker McKenzie: https://curious.click/birkin
10. Nick Abrahams from Norton Rose Fulbright on Web3, NFTs, Crypto, DAO and DeFi – The Digitally Curious Podcast: https://curious.click/nick

Chapter 14: Your Digital First Impression

1. Speakers for Schools website: https://curious.click/schools
2. Actionable Futurist Keynote Speaking showreel: https://curious.click/showreel
3. Set up Google Alerts: https://curious.click/google-alerts
4. Surfshark VPN: https://curious.click/surfshark
5. Lifelock from Norton: https://curious.click/lifelock
6. Identity Plus from Experian: https://curious.click/experian
7. Join Delete Me: https://curious.click/delete-me
8. Reputation defender by Norton: https://curious.click/reputation-defender
9. Namecheap domain search: https://curious.click/namecheap
10. Fastmail email hosting: https://curious.click/fastmail
11. About me – free one page website: https://curious.click/about-me
12. Namecheap site maker – build a website in minutes: https://curious.click/site-maker

Chapter 15: Staying Safe in the Age of AI

1. You Should Probably Change Your Password! – Michael McIntyre Netflix Special – YouTube: https://curious.click/passwords
2. Have I Been Pwned website: https://curious.click/pwned
3. 1Password password manager website: https://curious.click/1password
4. Trend Micro – spear phishing definition: https://curious.click/spear-phishing
5. Preparing for a passwordless future – 1Password blog: https://curious.click/1p-survey
6. IBM Cost of a Data Breach Report: https://curious.click/data-breach
7. 2023 Cost of Insider Risks Global Report – DTEX Systems: https://curious.click/ponemon

Chapter 16: Creating Your Digital Legacy

1. Elaine Kasket website: https://curious.click/elaine-kasket
2. All the Ghosts in the Machine: The Digital Afterlife of your Personal Data: https://curious.click/ghosts
3. The Future of your digital afterlife with Dr Elaine Kasket – The Digitally Curious Podcast: https://curious.click/afterlife
4. 1Password app: https://curious.click/1password
5. Day One Journal app: https://curious.click/dayone
6. Digital Legacy Association – Social Media Will: https://curious.click/legacy-resources
7. Facebook Legacy Contact: https://curious.click/facebook-legacy
8. Inactive Google Account Policy: https://curious.click/google-inactive
9. Yahoo releases e-mail of deceased Marine: Cnet: https://curious.click/marine

Chapter 17: Data Privacy and Regulation

1. Cambridge Analytica Data Scandal – The Guardian: https://curious.click/ca
2. The Ethics and Implications of Data Privacy in the Digital World with Anton Christodoulou from Imagination – The Digitally Curious Podcast: https://curious.click/anton
3. Optus: How a massive data breach has exposed Australia – BBC News: https://curious.click/optus
4. Susie Alegre website: https://curious.click/susie
5. The Ethics and Implications of Data Privacy in the Digital World with Anton Christodoulou from Imagination – The Digitally Curious Podcast: https://curious.click/anton
6. EU AI Act: First regulation on artificial intelligence – European Parliament: https://curious.click/eu-ai
7. The Digital Privacy Advocacy Group – Trust 3.0: https://curious.click/trust
8. EU AI Act: First regulation on artificial intelligence – European Parliament: https://curious.click/eu-ai
9. Susie Alegre – Freedom to Think: https://curious.click/freedom
10. Susie Alegre on Generative AI, ChatGPT and the freedom to think – The Digitally Curious Podcast: https://curious.click/susiegpt

Chapter 18: The Future of AI

1. Microsoft Now Claims GPT-4 Shows 'Sparks' of General Intelligence – Vice: https://curious.click/microsoft-agi
2. Planning for AGI and beyond – OpenAI blog: https://curious.click/openagi
3. David Shrier – The Digitally Curious Podcast: https://curious.click/shrier
4. New College Oxford – The Tutorial System: https://curious.click/oxbridge-tutorial

5. Bret Greenstein on Evolutionary Artificial Intelligence – The Digitally Curious Podcast: https://curious.click/bret

6. The bosses of OpenAI and Microsoft talk to The Economist: https://curious.click/economist-ai

7. Amazon and Anthropic announce strategic collaboration to advance generative AI: https://curious.click/anthropic

8. Navigating the World of General Artificial Intelligence with Peter Voss – The Digitally Curious Podcast: https://curious.click/voss

9. What Is ChatGPT Doing . . . and Why Does It Work? Stephen Wolfram: https://curious.click/wolfram

10. Why GPUs Are Great for AI – Nvidia blog: https://curious.click/nvidia

11. Amazon and Anthropic announce strategic collaboration to advance generative AI: https://curious.click/anthropic

12. Microsoft Rations Access to AI Hardware for Internal Teams – The Information: https://curious.click/ration

13. Nvidia market share 2024 – Yahoo Finance: https://curious.click/nvidia-share

14. Coursera – Learn without limits: https://curious.click/coursera

15. edX – Executive Education: https://curious.click/edx

16. Khan Academy – Free online courses: https://curious.click/khan

17. Actionable Futurist AI Hub: https://curious.click/ai-hub

18. MIT Technology Review: https://curious.click/tech-review

19. OpenAI blog: https://curious.click/openai-blog

20. Google AI blog: https://curious.click/google-ai

21. Microsoft AI: https://curious.click/microsoft-ai

22. Anthropic AI: https://curious.click/anthropic-ai

23. TED Talks on AI: https://curious.click/ted-ai

Chapter 19: The Future of Work

1. The Future of Work – The Digitally Curious Podcast: https://curious.click/future-work

2. Four-Day Workweek Pilot Project Abandoned at Hungarian Telecom Company – Bloomberg: https://curious.click/4day

3. The Future of Work with Dom Price from Atlassian – The Digitally Curious Podcast: https://curious.click/dom

4. The opportunity for Enterprise AI with Darshan Chandarana and Julia Howes from PwC – The Digitally Curious Podcast: https://curious.click/pwc

5. Helsinki University – The Elements of AI course: https://curious.click/elements

6. Gabriel Luna-Ostaseki on distributed working – The Digitally Curious Podcast: https://curious.click/gabriel

7. AI is Changing Work – and Leaders Need to Adapt – Harvard Business Review: https://curious.click/hbr-ai

8. Mark McCrindle on AI's impact on the future of work – The Digitally Curious Podcast: https://curious.click/mccrindle-work
9. These are the jobs that AI can't replace – World Economic Forum: https://curious.click/wef-ai

Chapter 20: Quantum Computing

1. Richard Hopkins from IBM on the future of Quantum Computing – The Digitally Curious Podcast: https://curious.click/richard
2. The new Y2K? Quantum computing and the threat of Q-Day in 2030 with Chris Johnson from Nokia – The Digitally Curious Podcast: https://curious.click/chris
3. World's lowest temperature: https://curious.click/cold
4. IBM Quantum website: https://curious.click/ibm-quantum
5. Google Quantum AI: https://curious.click/google-quantum
6. Intel Quantum: https://curious.click/intel-quantum
7. Microsoft Quantum kit: https://curious.click/microsoft-quantum
8. Honeywell Quantum Solutions: https://curious.click/honeywell-quantum
9. Richard Hopkins from IBM on the future of Quantum Computing – The Digitally Curious Podcast: https://curious.click/richard
10. Application of quantum computing in airline revenue management – Amadeus: https://curious.click/quantum-airlines
11. The new Y2K? Quantum computing and the threat of Q-Day in 2030 with Chris Johnson from Nokia – The Digitally Curious Podcast: https://curious.click/chris
12. Richard Hopkins from IBM on the future of Quantum Computing – The Digitally Curious Podcast: https://curious.click/richard
13. IBM Quantum website: https://curious.click/ibm-quantum
14. Shohini Ghose – A beginner's guide to quantum computing – TED talks: https://curious.click/ted-quantum

Chapter 21: Sovereign Identity

1. Optus Data breach – BBC News: https://curious.click/optus
2. For how long can data be kept and is it necessary to update it? European Union: https://curious.click/eu-data
3. Unraveling the Future of Self-Sovereign Identity with Marie Wallace from Accenture – The Digitally Curious Podcast: https://curious.click/marie
4. LinkedIn Identity verification by Persona https://curious.click/persona
5. Hyperledger Foundation: Hyperledger Indy https://curious.click/indy
6. Sovrin: Trust Anchor for Verifiable Credentials https://curious.click/sovrin
7. Veramo: Performant and modular APIs for Verifiable Data and SSI https://curious.click/veramo
8. European Digital Identity – European Commission: https://curious.click/eu-wallet

9. Opening New York State for business with the power of blockchain – IBM: https://curious.click/excelsior-pass
10. Dock.io – Issue, Verify and Monetise Reusable Digital Identities: https://curious.click/dock
11. Cheqd – Infrastructure for Trusted Data markets: https://curious.click/cheqd
12. Digital Identity for all Europeans – EU Commission website: https://curious.click/eu-wallet
13. LinkedIn and Microsoft Entra introduce a new way to verify your workplace: https://curious.click/entra
14. Opening New York State for business with the power of blockchain – IBM: https://curious.click/excelsior-pass
15. Introduction to Self-Sovereign Identity – Walt ID: https://curious.click/ssi-intro
16. Marie Wallace LinkedIn page: https://curious.click/marie-linkedin
17. What is Self-Sovereign Identity? Selfkey website: https://curious.click/selfkey
18. Unraveling the Future of Self-Sovereign Identity with Marie Wallace from Accenture – The Digitally Curious Podcast: https://curious.click/marie
19. Create Reusable Digital ID credentials – dock.io: https://curious.click/dock-id

Chapter 22: Everything as a Service

1. John Phillips from Zuora on the subscription economy – The Digitally Curious Podcast: https://curious.click/subscription-economy
2. Zuora website: https://curious.click/zuora
3. Optus SubHub: https://curious.click/subhub
4. Sky website: https://curious.click/sky
5. Netflix ad-supported subscribers rise 70% in just three months – performance marketing world: https://curious.click/netflix-ads
6. Club Pret: https://curious.click/club-pret
7. Pret A Manger introduces new system 'so Club members can't share perks' – The Standard: https://curious.click/pret-sharing
8. Free Netflix Sharing is Over – CNET: https://curious.click/netxflix-passwords

Conclusion: Curious About . . . What's Next?

1. FAANG Stocks: Definition and Companies Involved – Investopedia: https://curious.click/faang-stocks
2. CNET's AI policy, updated March 2024: https://curious.click/cnet-policy
3. ChatGPT and the Magnet of Mediocrity – Prakhar Mehrotra: https://curious.click/magnet
4. Malcolm Gladwell "Outliers. The Story of Success": https://curious.click/outliers
5. Scarlett Johansson 'shocked' by AI chatbot imitation – BBC News: https://curious.click/scarlett

6. OpenAI and Meta ready new AI models capable of 'reasoning' – Financial Times: https://curious.click/ai-reasoning
7. AI Prompt Engineering is Dead – IEEE Spectrum: https://curious.click/prompt-engineering
8. Accenture books $600m in AI revenue as tech consulting push continues – Financial news: https://curious.click/accenture-revenue
9. The rise of the Digital Agents – The Digitally Curious Podcast: https://curious.click/digital-agent
10. Large Language Models can Strategically Deceive their Users when Put Under Pressure: https://curious.click/cheating-ai
11. RT-2: New model translates vision and language into action – Google DeepMind: https://curious.click/rt2
12. Aurrigo Aviation products: https://curious.click/aurrigo-aviation
13. How did one of the world's largest robots end up here? Rio Tinto website: https://curious.click/rio-tinto
14. Detroit's road of the future will charge your car as you drive on it – Fast Company: https://curious.click/road-charging
15. Space Based Solar Power – a Futurist's dream or a real option for net-zero? Engineers Australia event: https://curious.click/space-power
16. Breakthrough in Space-Based Energy: Space Solar Demonstrates World's First 360° Wireless Power Transmission – Space Solar: https://curious.click/space-solar
17. SpaceX Starlink: https://curious.click/starlink
18. Project Kuiper – About Amazon: https://curious.click/kuiper
19. Viasat website: https://curious.click/viasat
20. Amy Webb Launches 2024 Emerging Tech Trend Report – SXSW 2024 YouTube: https://curious.click/sxsw-2024

Acknowledgements

1. Return on Influence – Mark Schaefer: https://curious.click/influence-book
2. Critical Assumption Planning Methodology: https://curious.click/cap
3. Mezzo-Soprano Deborah Humble – from Wagner to Wine: https://curious.click/humble

ACKNOWLEDGEMENTS

First of all, thank you to Carolanne Reissiger for your love, support, and patience to allow me to finish the book over the last few months.

A huge thanks to my agent, Michael Levey, who provided the inspiration for this book back in 2019. He suggested I start a podcast series that could become the basis of a book. Over 90 published episodes later, and with more than 120 people interviewed, this has become a reality.

Thank you, Michael, for pushing me to get the book over the line, and providing me with a podcast and a platform to speak around the world and appear on TV and radio to talk about new technologies.

Thank you to my family – Mum, Dad, Madeleine, and Matthew – for your love and constant support.

Special thanks also to my "Christmas 2020" team – Britt-Karin Oliver, Lucinda Szebrat, Nina Beebe, and Christina Healy – who helped me get through lockdown.

My first podcast guest was Martin Brooks, who has also provided me with invaluable insights around my speaking style and delivery. I'd also like to thank Minter Dial, who had me on his podcast back in 2012 – my first podcast appearance. James Poulter, an expert on the power of voice, was also an early guest, and I remember fondly interviewing Dom Price from Atlassian on stage in front of 200 Australians during Tech Week 2019 at Australia House. Tiffany St James provided some great tips on digital transformation, and Ethan McCarty has been a great support from our time at IBM.

ACKNOWLEDGEMENTS

A special thank you to Adrian Talbot, who has supported me over the years, and Rob McCargow, who helped secure the PwC podcast and is always a delight to chat with about all things tech. Thank you John Clay and Rohan MacMahon from my Telstra days, and Scott McCallum who hosted my first world technology trip in 1999 as well as Leica Ison who I worked with in the same team at Telstra in 1999, and more recently we reconnected in London.

Thanks to Peter Shore, who was at Telstra at the same time as I was, and more recently we've reconnected about life in London.

Also thank you for the support and inspiration from Melissa Jenni, Suzy Fox, Ruth Mac Gowan, Noreen Boyhan, Rachelle Rowe, Selena Adams, Elspeth Lynn, Amy D'Eugenio, Lisa Barash, John Carroll, Yvonne Maher, Irena Popovic, Alison Payne, Stephen Vineberg, Mike Gazdar, James Kevin Flanaghan, Sylvia Mas, Jennifer King, Hazlitt Eastman, Lisa Coomey, Dennis Muirhead, Helen Anderson, Natalie Baynes, Dick Porter, Richard Basil-Jones, Julie Atkinson, Martin Rast, Melissa Nagy, and Elizabeth Carr.

Thank you to Melissa Cadzow for being on the other end of the Angle Park Computing Centre bulletin board back in 1993.

The first ever IBMer I met was Isabel Schwerdtfeger, at CeBit 1999. Twenty-five years later we're still in touch. Other notable IBMers include Guy Stephens, who recommended me into IBM, the always inspirational Jeremy Waite, along with Matt Candy and Luq Niazi, who hired me as a Partner in London. Paul Crick also provided invaluable support as I transitioned from a 12-year startup veteran into a large behemoth multinational organisation.

Thanks to Matt Russell and the team at Jolt website hosting who have kept me online for over 12 years.

I've been fortunate to interview people on the podcast who are also great friends, such as Lynn Gribble, who holds the record to date as a three-time guest, constantly challenges my thinking, and keeps me curious.

Lauren Walker and I became friends while at IBM and what she knows about data is second to none. Nicole Yershon and I met when she was running

ACKNOWLEDGEMENTS

Ogilvy Labs and we've stayed in touch since. Andy Lopata has been a great friend and connector.

Sue Walter and I became instant friends when, as the new CEO of the Hospital Club, I was at a meeting where she was soliciting feedback from existing members about how to improve the club. I know she will bring something similar to the Roof Gardens, which opens in 2024, and where I am a founding member.

Mark Schaefer and I met around the time he wrote his book *Return on Influence*[1] and I was the CEO of Kred. He was rightfully sceptical about yet another influencer measurement platform, and we became firm friends. Each time he's on the podcast, I learn so much from him.

Marty Gupta and David Dunham were instrumental in my early telecommunications career while I was at Optus. They introduced me to a revolutionary product development methodology called Critical Assumption Planning (CAP),[2] which helped me present and win funding for a $44 million project to launch one of Australia's fastest data networks at the time. Marty saw something in me and invited me to visit BellSouth in Atlanta to look at job opportunities.

Deborah Humble is my long-time mezzo-soprano friend, and I was humbled (no pun intended) to have her on the podcast[3] to talk about her journey from singing to winemaking. It was also a treat to interview Karen Jacobsen, the "original Australian voice of Siri", who I actually had the chance to meet in New York. Her fascinating story is included in this book.

Susie Alegre has been on the show twice and her book and the way she thinks constantly challenges me when it comes to data as a human right. She makes me think beyond the technology to better understand its impact on society.

Nick Abrahams has always been a genius at explaining difficult concepts around Web 3.0. Marie Wallace and I met while at IBM and her new area of focus around digital identity has opened my eyes to the art of the possible.

ACKNOWLEDGEMENTS

Interviewing Sanjay Srivastava, Chief Digital Officer at Genpact, as well as Tiger Tyagarajan, Genpact's CEO, while at the London Formula E Grand Prix was a real highlight.

Guarav Rao was an excellent podcast guest on the topic of AI ethics and has shaped much of my thinking in this area since. Stephanie Antonian and I recorded a podcast walking around Regent's Park in spring 2023, which has also shaped my thinking on AI ethics.

Thank you to Brian Solis, Jodee Rich, and Jeffrey Hayzlett, who I met around the same time, when social media started to become a thing that brands needed to pay close attention to in the early 2010s.

James Bunn from Engineers Australia in the UK was very supportive during the pandemic, and Damian Walsh and Louise Mulley at the Britain–Australia Society have also been strong supporters, and I now sit on their board.

The former South Australian Agent General and ad-man extraordinaire Bill Muirhead has always been so supportive to me in London. Thanks also go to Katie Keith and Pier Paolo Mucelli for being great connectors over the years.

Ben Kay and I met when he was at EE and I was a blogger who had an issue with a new 4G connection and dared to blog about it. Years later I managed to convince him to join me at IBM and he's been a strong supporter ever since.

Simon Welburn was my boss at British Aerospace Australia and gave me the confidence to go beyond engineering and move into management.

Paul Richardson was the head of technical training at Optus and took a risk hiring me, which led to the start of my telecommunications career. Brian Bailey also took a risk taking on a work experience student from Adelaide in their high-stakes satellite broadcast business.

Australian friends Darren and Lisa Gossling, and Emma Toohey, have always been there for me. A special thanks to my friend of over 30 years Natalie Ward, who mentioned me in her maiden speech to the Upper House of the NSW Parliament, so I must mention her here.

ACKNOWLEDGEMENTS

Networking extraordinaires Sophie de Schwarzburg-Gunther and Janine Stow from the Quorum Network, and Elizabeth Vega whom I met very serendipitously, have been very helpful in connecting me to the best people in London.

I owe a great deal of gratitude to Bill Chillingworth. While I was a member of the Rotary Club of Sydney, where he was President and also CEO of commercial property company CB Richard Ellis, he suggested I would be a good fit for a new online venture – PropertyLook. This began my 12-year startup career that would also get me to London. Garry Browne is another Rotarian who has been a huge supporter.

Thank you to Karen Saba for suggesting I audition for London Business School's TEDx in 2014 and then helping select me to deliver my first TEDx talk.

Thank you to PR expert Liam Rawson who has been a constant source of excellent podcast guests – many of whom appear in this book.

I'm grateful to the speaker bureaus who constantly book me – such as Speaker's Corner, London Speaker Bureau, JLA, Gordon Poole, Performing Artistes, Great British Talent, Raise the Bar, Champions Speakers, and VBQ Speakers – as well as the team at Speaking Office who keep the show on the road.

My team at Wiley deserve a special mention – Annie Knight who saw a market for my digitally curious idea, alongside Alice Hadaway and Susan Cerra, who have helped get it to press.

A huge thanks to the fast-moving team from Write Business Results – Georgia Kirke, Christopher Acheson, Katherine Lewis, and George Cox – who have helped me get this book over the line in the last 6 weeks with thorough proofreading, edits, and suggestions around content and launch marketing.

I'd like to acknowledge all of my podcast guests, who provided not only much of the content for this book but challenged my thinking about a range of technologies and concepts, including Peter Hopwood, James Varga, Julian Fisher, Jeremy Epstein, Nick Coleman, Dan Ziv, Jeremy Thomson,

ACKNOWLEDGEMENTS

Gabriel Luna-Ostaseki, Bret Greenstein, Steve Cadigan, Raj Samani, Tom Smith, Mark Sweeney, Michael Kaczmarek, Helena Nimmo, Muhi Majzoub, Dr Elaine Kasket, Phil Sorsky, Wayne Snyder, Aaron Goldman, James Walker, Charlotte Gregson, James Cridland, Tom Morley, Stephanie Buscemi, Chris Waiting, Umang Patel, Dr Simon Wallace, Jessica Gioglio, Christina Kosmowski, Euan Moir, Richard Hopkins, Byron Reese, Samantha Humphries, Paul Scanlan, Ron Rock, Trevor Hutchings, Sophia Matveeva, Thomas Bedenk, Andie Wood, James Butland, Katie Burke, Maya Moufarek, Mark Pinsent, Shahid Ahmed, John Philips, Heather Dawe, Guarav Rao, Mark McCrindle, Jochen Apel, Isabel Perry, Helen Armstrong, Jaeger Glucina, Steve Young, Mark Swinson, Chris Johnson, Jason Mander, Nicki Lyons, Darshan Chandarana, and Julia Howes. Thank you for your time and insights on every episode and making me more curious about your area of expertise.

Finally, I'd like to thank the people who develop and innovate the products I use every day, such as Adobe Audition for podcast editing, Adobe Premiere for video editing, Grammarly for grammar and spell checking, Otter.ai for transcripts, and ChatGPT, my always-on intern who never complains when I hand them endless research tasks with impossible deadlines.

If I've missed anyone, you can find the latest list of acknowledgements at https://curious.click/thankyou.

ABOUT THE AUTHOR

AI expert and leading futurist Andrew Grill is a dynamic and visionary tech leader with over three decades of experience steering technology companies towards innovative success.

Known for his captivating global keynotes, Andrew offers practical and actionable advice, making him a trusted advisor at the board level for companies such as Vodafone, Adobe, DHL, Nike, Nestlé, Bupa, Wella, Mars, Sanofi, Dell Technologies, and the NHS.

A former Global Managing Partner at IBM, five times TEDx speaker, and someone who has performed more than 550 times on the world stage, he is no stranger to providing strategic advice to senior leaders across multiple industries.

Andrew's unique blend of an engineering background, digital advocacy, and thought leadership positions him as a pivotal figure in shaping the future of technology.

Since 2000, Andrew has been providing advice, opinion, and the latest thinking on all things digital and the impact on business and society on his blog. He also contributes to a wide range of media outlets, including *The Drum*, *Changeboard*, and *ANZ BlueNotes*, along with numerous other online publications.

An in-demand futurist speaker, he has appeared on *BBC Television*, *BBC Radio*, *Sky News*, *Channel 4*, and *UKTV*, in *The Financial Times*, *The Telegraph*, *The Guardian*, *Sydney Morning Herald*, *The Australian*, *The Economist*, and *Australian Financial Review*, and on stage at over 550 in-person events in over 40 countries.

Engagements include senior executives from Vodafone, NHS, DHL, Nike, Nestlé, Adobe, Bupa, Worldpay, Euler Hermes, Mars, Arriva, Johnson Matthey, Taylor Wessing, Bunzl, De Beers, Sanofi, European Central Bank, L'Oréal, LinkedIn, Thomson Reuters, Royal London, ANZ, KPMG, Schroders, Mercer, British Airways, Finnair, UK government, Westpac, Qantas, Aon, American Airlines, and Shell. He also delivers workshops and provides strategic advice at the C-suite and board levels.

Andrew has hosted The Digitally Curious' Podcast series since 2019, which is available on all podcast platforms.

If you've liked the content of this book, then any of this can be delivered in a way that will inspire and delight audiences of any size or level.

Speaking enquiries can be directed to Michael Levey at Speaking Office:

michael@speakingoffice.com

For more on Andrew, you can visit the following sites:

Website: https://curious.click/website

LinkedIn: https://curious.click/linkedin

Podcast: https://curious.click/podcast

Instagram: https://curious.click/instagram

INDEX

About.me 168, 287
Abrahams, Nick 129–130, 148–150, 153
Accenture 21, 226, 249, 277, 284, 289
Actionable Futurist AI Hub 288
Actionable futurists 9–11, 252, 258
Adams, James L. 31
Adobe 281
ADSL (asymmetric digital subscriber line) 109
Advanced mobile phone system (AMPS) 63, 258
AGI *see* Artificial general intelligence
Ahmed, Shahid 68
AI *see* Artificial intelligence
AI models 28, 36, 42, 44, 49, 203, 248
Airdrop 258
AI training 25, 33, 34, 39, 42, 44–49, 279
AI watermarks 247
Alden, Sam 251
Alegre, Susie 186–187, 192
Alexa 61, 73, 75, 76, 100, 107
All the Ghosts in the Machine (Kasket) 179, 180
Altman, Sam 29, 196–197, 200
Amazon:
  Alexa voice assistant 61, 73, 75, 76, 100, 107
  as chip manufacturer 248–249
  digital curiosity at 86
  in FAANG group 243
  Project Kuiper at 252
  in Web 2.0 116
Amazon Go 70
Amazon Prime 37
Amazon Web Services (AWS) 85, 259, 282
  free cloud computing access 61–62, 96
  GPU chips 202, 203

infrastructure as a service from 236
on IoT system components 101
Ukrainian government's use of 90
Ambient intelligence 258
Ambient voice technologies 74–77
AMPS (advanced mobile phone system) 63, 258
Andrew Grill Speaking website 114, 115, 160, 255, 277
Anthropic 29, 38, 201, 202, 204, 288
API (application programming interface) 258
Apple:
  cloud use 86–87
  in FAANG group 243
  iPhone 64, 128, 183, 200
  Siri voice assistant 31, 61, 73–75, 81, 100
  Vision Pro headset 133–135
  in Web 2.0 116
Apple Music 227
Apple TV 37
Apple Watch 99
Application programming interface (API) 258
Application service providers (ASPs) 235, 258
AR (augmented reality) 68, 258
Archive.org 115
Artificial general intelligence (AGI) 193, 195–203, 258
  Sam Altman on 196–197
  for autonomous systems 198
  careers working with 198, 199
  defined 195–196
  predictions about 198–200
  process for developing 200–202
  technology required for 202–203

Artificial intelligence (AI). *See also* EU
    Artificial Intelligence (AI) Act
  beneficial applications of 42–44
  bias 45–47
  business case for products using 50
  business impact of 27–28
  careers working with 198, 199
  change management with AI projects
    47–50
  conversational (*see* Conversational AI)
  edge 264
  future of 195–203
  future of work with 207–211
  generative (*see* Generative AI [GenAI])
  history of 30–31
  implementing AI projects 47–51
  investments in 128, 194
  for IoT 100, 101
  legal issues 44
  limitations of using 39–42
  narrow 195, 269
  near-term developments in 246–250
  pilot projects, prototypes and MVP
    tests of 47
  planning for use of 39–40
  quantum computing applications in
    218–219
  terminology related to 31–35
  upcoming evolution 244–246
  winning new business 17–19
  workers displaced by 15, 208
  workplace deployment of 39–51
  in XaaS 239
Artificial intelligence (AI) tools 53–58
  ethical and legal issues 54
  quality and reliability concerns 55
  security and data risks 53–54
Art NFTs 149
ASPs (application service providers) 235, 258
Asymmetric digital subscriber line (ADSL)
  109
Atlassian 206, 207
Augmented reality (AR) 68, 258
Aurrigo 94, 95, 251
Automotive industry:
  autonomous vehicles 94, 95, 250–251, 259
  IoT use 102, 104–105

Autonomous systems 198
Autonomous vehicles 94, 95, 250–251, 259
AWS *see* Amazon Web Services

Bailenson, Jeremy 131, 132
Banking system 139–140, 173
Bankman-Fried, Sam 250
Bard 201
BBS *see* Bulletin board system
Bedenk, Thomas 130
Beeple 148
Berners-Lee, Tim 113
Bezos, Jeff 86
Bias, with AI 41, 45–47
Big Data 259
Big Tech 115, 117, 119, 180, 182, 243
Bing Chat 280
Biometric authentication 174, 259
Bitcoin 284
  blockchain technology 138
  buying and selling 141–142, 145
  defined 259
  as fungible token 148
  history of 137
  hype around 110, 244
  mining 140–141
  supply dynamics for 154
Black box 259
Blockchain 137–145, 259. *See also* Bitcoin
  accessibility issues 120
  creating consensus 139–141
  in DAOs 144–145
  data ownership and 121
  for decentralisation 117
  environmental impact 121
  financial transactions using 119, 122
  and IoT 101
  and metaverse 129
  and NFTs 147, 148
  power of 142–143
  for smart contracts 143–144
  SSI solutions 231
  for supply chain management 122
  and tokenomics 154, 155
  in Web 3.0 116
Bored Apes NFTs 149, 150
Born Digital tribe 19

Braintrust 210
Brand NFTs 150–153
Bridges, John 150
Bring your own AI (BYOAI) workplaces 53–55, 259
Bring your own identity (BYOID) system 229–230, 259
British Aerospace Australia 8
Broadband 66–67, 252
Buffett, Warren 86
Bulletin board system (BBS) 7–8, 59, 109, 259
Burke, Katie 121–122
BYOAI (bring your own AI) workplaces 53–55, 259
BYOID (bring your own identity) system 229–230, 259

Cambridge Analytica scandal 185, 187
Canva 282
Capgemini 16, 21–22, 278
CAPTCHA (completely automated public Turing test to tell computers and humans apart) 260
Caterpillar 239
Cattelan, Maurizio 150
CBDC (central bank digital currency) 260
CDN (content delivery network) 89, 260
CeBit Exhibition 133, 134
Central bank digital currency (CBDC) 260
Centralised data storage 225–226
Champions Speakers 165
Chandarana, Darshan 50, 101, 207
Change management 47–50
Charging loops, roadway 251
Chatbots 260
ChatGPT 57
    AI technologies prior to 25
    data sources 279
    defined 260
    development of 29
    EU AI Act implications 191
    evolution of 36
    GDPR compliance for 44
    limitations of 41

neural networks and function of 201–202
    opportunities to improve skills 245–246
ChatGPT 1, 36
ChatGPT 2, 36
ChatGPT 3, 36
ChatGPT 3.5, 1, 29, 34, 46, 195, 201
ChatGPT 4, 29, 196
ChatGPT 4o 29, 36, 38, 55–56, 195, 247
ChatGPT 5, 29
ChatGPT Enterprise 54
ChatGPT Plus 36, 55–56, 280
Christodoulou, Anton 117–118, 185, 188
Circular economy 239
Claude 38, 281
Cloud bursting 93
Cloud computing 83–97
    benefits of 95–96
    business impact of 84–85, 88–90
    data sovereignty in 88
    defined 84, 260
    and edge computing 93–96
    hybrid clouds 91–93
    for Internet of Things 100
    multi-cloud 91–92
    private vs. public clouds 90
    security and privacy issues with 85
    service providers 85–86
Cloud storage 86–87, 260
CMS (content management system) 260
CNET 245
Code Dependent (Murgia) 32
Coinbase app 141
Collaboration 48
Collectible NFTs 150
Commodore 64 computer 61, 73
Completely automated public Turing test to tell computers and humans apart (CAPTCHA) 260
Connected cars 102, 105
Connected clothing 69–70
Connected home 102–103. See also Smart devices
Conscious bias 45, 260
Content delivery network (CDN) 89, 260
Content management system (CMS) 260
Continuous improvement 48
Continuous learning 76

Conversational AI 75–81
  artificial general intelligence and 200, 202
  defined 75–77, 261
  Google Duplex 77–78
  in healthcare sector 78–79
  human–machine interactions with 79–81
  for IoT 100
Co-pilot systems 260. *See also* Microsoft
    Copilot
CopyAI 281
Copyrights 54, 190
Coursera 203, 287–288
The Creation Generation report 132–133, 285
CRM (customer relationship management)
    261
Crypto 124, 144, 145, 155, 250, 284. *See also*
    Cryptocurrency
Cryptocurrency 120, 122, 124, 155, 250, 261.
    See also Bitcoin
Cryptography 219–221, 261
Culture of innovation 48
Curious.click website 4, 6, 30
Curious GPT 26–27, 55, 88–89, 255
Customer relationship management (CRM)
    261
Customer service, AI in 42, 80
Cybersecurity 261

DALL-E 29, 55, 261, 282
DAOs *see* Decentralised autonomous
    organisations
DApps *see* Decentralised applications
Dartmouth Summer Research Project 30
Data analytics 261
Data breaches 170–171, 175–176, 186,
    225–226
Data localisation 88
Data mining 261
Data ownership:
  after death 180
  in Web 3.0 116–118, 121, 123, 148
Data privacy 185–190, 261
  BYOAI approach 53–54
  with cloud computing 85, 89–90
  and digital legacy 180, 182–183
  as human right 182, 186–188
  for implicit data 185–186

regulating 188–190
  self-sovereign identity for 225, 226, 228
  with voice technologies 80
  with Web 3.0 117–119, 122, 123
  with XR technology 133
Data protection laws 187
Data quality 40, 43, 49
Data residency 88
Data security:
  business impact of failure 175–176
  BYOAI approach 53–54
  with cloud computing 85, 89–90
  multi-factor authentication 173
  passwords for 169–175
  and quantum computing 219–221
  self-sovereign identity 225, 229
  with voice technologies 80
  with Web 3.0 117–119, 122, 123
  with XR technology 133
Data sovereignty 87, 88, 262
Data visualisation 262
Day One app 181, 286
Decentralisation 116–123, 137, 140
Decentralised applications (DApps) 143,
    154, 261
Decentralised autonomous organisations
    (DAOs) 122, 144–145, 261
Decentralised finance (DeFi) 119, 122, 262
Decentralised identity (DID) 230, 262
Deep Blue 31, 33
Deepfakes 262
Deep learning (DL) 195–196, 262, 289–290
DeepMind 29
DeFi *see* Decentralised finance
Deloitte 249
Democratic governance models, Web 3.0
    122
DEPT 51
DevOps 262
DICE framework 131, 135
DID (decentralised identity) 230, 262
Digerati (digital maturity) 21–22
The Digital Advantage 278
Digital afterlife 179–180
Digital agents 77
Digital assistants *see* Voice assistants
Digital capability 22

Digital curiosity 7–12, 262
  about AI 25–28
  about Big Tech 243
  about cloud computing 83
  about the internet 109–111
  about longer-term developments 252–253
  about technology 7–9, 59–62
  about the future 193–194
  about your data 157–158
  assessing your 12
  author's journey 7–9
  business/career benefits 15–22
  defined 1–2
  maintaining 252–254
  traits of digitally curious people 11–12, 254
Digital ethnography 262
Digital first impression 3, 158–168, 262
  analogue networking 159–160
  examining your own 160–162
  managing your online presence 166–167
  online strategy 162–163
  private vs. public persona 163–166
Digital footprint 120, 160, 167, 263
Digital identity 263. *See also* Self-sovereign
  identity (SSI)
Digital intensity 16
Digital legacy 158, 179–184, 263
Digital Legacy Association 182
Digital literacy 20, 21, 263
The Digitally Curious Podcast 2, 23, 56,
  192, 255
Digital maturity 16, 21–22
Digital native 263
Digital pill 252–253
Digital Privacy Advocacy Group
  Trust 3.0 192
Digital proof 263
Digital rights management (DRM) 264
Digital skills, demand for 21
Digital sovereignty 263
Digital transformation 92, 263
Digital twins 263
Digital wallets 231–234, 263
Digital will 181, 184
Disaster recovery (DR) 89–90, 93, 96, 264
Distributed ledger technology (DLT) 138,
  139, 210, 263

Distribution strategy, in tokenomics 154
Diversity, on AI project teams 46–47
DL *see* Deep learning
DLT *see* Distributed ledger technology
Dock.io 233, 234
Documentation 49, 190–191
Dolce & Gabbana 130, 150
Domain name 162–163
DR *see* Disaster recovery
Dragon Dictate 31, 73, 78
DRM (digital rights management) 264

E-commerce 264
The Economist 200, 287
Edge AI 264
Edge computing 93–96, 264
Education 132–133, 232
edX 203, 288
E-learning 264
Elements of AI course 208, 289
Eleven Labs 281
ELIZA and Eliza effect 31, 264
Ellsworth, Justin 183
Email address 162–163
Emergency Kit 1Password 172, 181
Emotional intelligence 81
Employee token option plans 153
Endava 130
Enterprise resource planning (ERP)
  264
ERP (enterprise resource planning) 264
Ethereum 124, 141, 143–144, 264, 284
Ethical issues 49, 54, 190–191, 210
ETSI (European Telecommunications
  Standards Institute) 64
EU Artificial Intelligence (AI) Act 189–192,
  249, 264, 286
European Telecommunications Standards
  Institute (ETSI) 64
European Union 232, 233. *See also* EU
  Artificial Intelligence (AI) Act
Everledger 143
Everything as a service (XaaS) 89, 193,
  235–242, 276
Evolutionary Artificial Intelligence 33
Excelsior Pass 232, 233
Explainability 44, 264

Extended reality (XR) 130, 133–134, 276
EY 249

FAA (Federal Aviation Authority) 66
FAANG group 243
FaaS (function as a service) 265
Facebook 184. *See also* Meta
  AI investments 201
  digital legacy 182–184
  in FAANG group 243
  Horizon Worlds 128
  memorialising accounts 179
  metaverse hype at 110, 125
  in Web 2.0, 115
Family password 177
Fashionistas (digital maturity) 21
Fast Company 290
Fastmail 167, 287
Federal Aviation Authority (FAA) 66
Fender 240
Feynman, Richard 217
Finance industry 218, 232
Financial institutions, hybrid clouds for 92
Financial transactions, DeFi 119, 122
Fintech 265
First impression:
  digital (*see* Digital first impression)
  in-person 159
5G 61, 71
  business benefits of 67–69
  connected clothing 69–70
  defined 63, 257
  non-standalone (NSA) 66, 257
  private 67–69
  RFID tags 70–71
  standalone (SA) 66–67, 69–71, 257
  vs. 4G 66–67
Flash storage 265
Flex club NFTs 149
Food Trust 143
Forrester 53
4G 65–67, 257
Four Ls exercise 206
Function as a service (FaaS) 265
Fungible tokens 148
Future of work 205–211
Future Today Institute 290
Futurist, defined 265

Gamification 265
Gaming 127–133, 150
Gartner Hype Cycle 110
GB (gigabyte) 265
GB/s (gigabyte per second) 265
GCP *see* Google Cloud Platform
GDPR *see* General Data Protection
    Regulation
Gemini 29, 38, 201, 280
GenAI *see* Generative AI
Gen Alpha (Generation Alpha) 132–133,
    265
General AI 266
General Data Protection Regulation (GDPR)
    44, 188, 226, 266
Generation Alpha (Gen Alpha) 132–133, 265
Generation X (Gen X) 265
Generation Y (Gen Y) 164, 266
Generation Z (Gen Z) 164, 266
Generative AI (GenAI) 38, 266
  consulting 249
  data privacy issues 188
  defined 34, 35
  digital agents 77, 249
  enablers 50, 55–57 (*See also specific*
    tools by name)
  evolution of 35–37, 244
  future of work 205
  Gartner Hype Cycle 110
  GPUs 202–203
  hallucinations 34–35
  hybrid cloud 93
  models of reasoning 247–248
  need for regulation 186, 191
  power of 37
  resources consumed by 39
  robotics 250
  skills 245–246
  use cases 49
  voice synthesis 74
Generative pre-trained transformer (GPT)
    35, 200, 266. *See also specific*
    ChatGPT versions
Gen X (Generation X) 265
Gen Y (Generation Y) 164, 266
Gen Z (Generation Z) 164, 266
Ghose, Shohini 223
Gigabit 109

Gigabyte (GB) 265
Gigabyte per second (GB/s) 265
Gig economy 210, 266
Gilbert, Sam 126
Gladwell, Malcolm 246
Global system for mobile communications (GSM) standard 63, 64, 267. *See also* specific generations, e.g.: 1G
Glucina, Jaeger 41
Gmail 236
Going Digital tribe 19, 20
Google 288
  AGI 204
  biased image recognition system 45–46
  digital first impression 160–167
  in FAANG group 243
  Fitbit wearables 99
  Gemini AI 29, 38, 201, 280
  GPU chips 203, 248–249
  Inactive Account Manager 182–184
  quantum computing research 215, 222
  RT-2 project 250
  transformer development 31, 35
  Wayback Machine archive 115
  in Web 2.0, 116
Google Alerts 166, 285
Google Assistant 73, 75, 81, 100
Google Chrome 160, 171
Google Cloud Platform (GCP) 85, 86, 90
Google Duplex 77–78
Google Glass 133
Google Maps 37
Google Nest 99
Governance *see* Regulation and governance
Governance tokens 144–145
Government IDs, SSI for 232
GPT *see* Generative pre-trained transformer
GPU (graphics processing unit) 202–203, 266
Grammarly 26, 56, 57, 280
Graphical user interface (GUI) 101
Graphics processing unit (GPU) 202–203, 266
Green computing 266
Greenstein, Bret 33, 199–200
Gribble, Lynn 306

GSM standard *see* Global system for mobile communications standard
GUI (graphical user interface) 101

Hackathon 19, 47–50, 267
Hallucinations 34–35, 267
Harvard Business Review 211
Have I Been Pwned website 170–171, 176, 286
Healthcare sector:
  Internet of Things 106
  SSI applications 232
  voice technology 78–79
Helsinki University 208
Hermès 152
Hertz 228
High-risk AI systems 189, 190
Honeywell 216, 222
Hopkins, Richard 214, 216, 217, 219, 222
Horizon Worlds 128
Howes, Julia 50–51, 207
Huawei 68
Human rights 182, 186–188
Humble, Deborah 307
Hunt, Troy 60, 170, 286
Huxley, Aldous 9, 169
Hybrid approach to quantum computing 216–217
Hybrid cloud 91–93, 267
Hybrid cloud storage 91–93, 267
Hyperledger Indy 231

IaaS (infrastructure as a service) 236, 267
IBM 163, 164, 249
  Excelsior Pass development 233
  Food Trust initiative 143
  metaverse presence 127
  quantum computing projects 215, 216, 222
  RedHat 93
  XR headset prototype 133
IBM Basics of Quantum course 223
IBM Cloud (Kyndryl) 85
IBM Quantum website 289
IBM Watson 25–26, 31, 33
iCloud 86
ICOs (initial coin offerings) 155
Identity theft protection 167

Identity tokens 144
Imperial College 41, 198
Implicit data 185–186
Inactive Account Manager, Google 182–184
Incentive models, in tokenomics 154
Information technology (IT) 267
The Information website 23, 290
Infrastructure as a service (IaaS) 236, 267
Initial coin offerings (ICOs) 155
Innovation 11, 155, 191
Insider attacks 176
Instagram 162, 166, 255
Integrated services digital network (ISDN) 109
Intellectual property (IP) rights 54, 151–152, 190, 247
Internet. *See also* Blockchain; Metaverse; Non-fungible tokens (NFTs); Tokenisation; Web 1.0; Web 2.0
    business impact 110–111
    governance 267
    new (*see* Web 3.0)
    space-based high-speed 252
Internet Explorer 113
Internet of Everything 99–108
Internet of things (IoT) 68, 99–108, 110, 267
    components 101
    connected cars 105
    edge computing 93–94
    importance of 101–104
    industries benefitting from 104–107
    subscription economy 239
    technologies required 100–101
Internet protocol (IP) address 267
Interoperability 118, 126–127, 129, 230, 231
"Introduction to Self-Sovereign Identity" (Walt ID) 233
IoT *see* Internet of Things
IP (internet protocol) address 267
iPhone 64, 128, 183, 200
IP rights *see* Intellectual property (IP) rights
ISDN (integrated services digital network) 109
IT (information technology) 267

Jacobsen, Karen 74
Jasper 38, 57, 281

Jeopardy! (TV series) 25, 31, 33
JLA 165
Johansson, Scarlett 247
Johnson, Chris 214, 220–221

Kasket, Elaine 179–181, 183
Kasparov, Garry 31, 33
Keene, David 94
Kennedy, Mark 41
Key performance indicators (KPIs) 49
Khan Academy 203, 288
Know your customer (KYC) checks 232
KPIs (key performance indicators) 49
KPMG 249
KYC (know your customer) checks 232

Large language models (LLMs):
    defined 268
    for GenAI 34
    hybrid cloud environment 93
    industry-specific 248
    legal applications 40
    for voice transcription 79
LastPass 170, 172
Leadership capability 22
LeCun, Yann 248, 249
Ledgers 138–139
Legal issues 44, 54, 151–153
Legal sector, AI use in 40–41
LEO (low earth orbit) 268
Levy, Michael 2, 305
Lifelong learning 208, 209
Lightcap, Brad 248
Limited-risk AI systems 189
LinkedIn 248
    digital first impression 3, 159, 160, 166, 167
    newsfeed 252, 255
    SSI applications 232, 233, 289
    user-generated data 229–230
List processing (LISP) 30, 268
Little Snitch 87, 97, 283
LLMs *see* Large language models
London Speaker Bureau 165
Long-term evolution for machines (LTE-M) 100

L'Oréal 70, 144–145
Low earth orbit (LEO) 268
LTE-M (long-term evolution for machines) 100
Luminance 280
Luna-Ostaseski, Gabriel 210

McCargow, Rob 306
McCarthy, John 30
McCrindle, Mark 207, 211
McDonalds 130
Machine learning (ML):
  conversational AI 75
  defined 32, 268
  history of 31
  quantum computing applications 218–219
  in Web 3.0 119
  in XaaS 239
Machine-to-machine (M2M) 268
McIntyre, Michael 169
Magnet of mediocrity 245
Magyar Telekom 205–206
MB (megabyte) 268
MB/s (megabytes per second) 268
Mechanical Turk 268
Megabit 109, 268
Megabyte (MB) 268
Megabytes per second (MB/s) 268
Mehrotra, Prakhar 245–246
Meredith, Tommy 198
Meta 110, 125, 128, 130, 243, 248–249.
  See also Facebook
MetaBirkin 151–152
Meta Llama LLM 280
Metaverse 110, 125–135
  defined 268
  evolution of 127–129
  extended reality headsets 133–134
  Gen Alpha 132–133
  hype around 244
  interoperability 129
  NFTs 129–130
  origin 125–127
  use cases 130–132
MFA see Multi-factor authentication
Microshare 100, 104

Microsoft 288
  AGI discussion at 204
  evaluation of GPT 4, 196
  FAANG group 243
  GPU chips 203
  Nuance acquisition 78
Microsoft 365, 55, 235, 236
Microsoft Azure 85, 90, 236
Microsoft Copilot 29, 56, 203, 280
Microsoft Entra 233
Microsoft Quantum Development Kit 216
Midjourney 17, 34, 54, 269, 281
Millennials 269
Minecraft 132, 269
Minimal-risk AI systems 189
Minimum viable product (MVP) 47, 269
Minton Beddoes, Zanny 200, 287
Mission-critical networks 220, 221
MIT Sloan 16, 21–22, 278
MIT Technology Review 203, 288, 290
ML see Machine learning
Mobile phones and technologies 60–61, 63–71
  4G vs. 5G 66–67
  business benefit of 5G 67–69
  connected clothing and 5G 69–70
  early history 63–64
  interoperability 129
  for IoT 100
  RFID tags for frictionless shopping 70–71
  rise of 4G 65–66
Molecular engineering 218
Multi-cloud approach 91–92, 269
Multi-factor authentication (MFA) 172, 173, 268
Murgia, Madhumita 32
Musk, Elon 252
MVP (minimum viable product) 47, 269

Nadella, Satya 200, 287
Nakamoto, Satoshi 137
Namecheap 167, 168, 287
Narrow AI 195, 269
Narrowband IoT (NB-IoT) 100
Natural language generation (NLG) 76, 269
Natural language processing (NLP) 75, 100, 197, 270

Natural language understanding
(NLU) 75, 270
NB-IoT (narrowband IoT) 100
Netflix 37, 237, 240–241, 243
Netlimiter 87, 97, 283
Netscape Navigator 113
Network security 269
Network slice 67
Neural networks 202, 269
NFTs *see* Non-fungible tokens
Nike 130
NLG (natural language generation) 76, 269
NLP *see* Natural language processing
NLU (natural language understanding)
75, 270
Nokia 220, 221
Non-fungible tokens (NFTs) 110, 116, 244
brand 151–153
categories 149–150
defined 148, 269
MetaBirkin controversy 151–152
in metaverse 129–130
popularity 147
potential value 148–150
as tickets 149
tokenomics 155
workplace applications 153
Non-standalone 5G (5G NSA) 66, 257
Norton Rose Fulbright 129–130, 148
NTT 68
Nuance Communications 73, 78
Nvidia 202, 203, 243, 248
NYX 70, 144–145

Observability 44, 270
Oculus headsets 126, 131
1G 61, 64, 257
1Password 170–172, 174, 176, 181, 286
Online strategy 162–163
OpenAI 204, 270, 288. *See also* ChatGPT
GPT model development 36
GPU chip manufacturing 248–249
reinforcement learning from human
feedback (RLHF) 46–47
Sora 29, 195, 282
Open source 231–232, 270

Optus 10, 61, 64, 186, 225–226, 228
Oracle Cloud 85
Otter.ai 26, 56–57, 81, 280
Outliers (Gladwell) 246
Oxford Artificial Intelligence Programme 23

PaaS (platform as a service) 236, 270
Passkeys 173–175, 270
Passwords 169–175
access after your death 181
family password 177
length and complexity 170–171
vs. passkeys 174–175
Passwordless access 174
Password managers 170–173, 181
Patel, Umang 78–79
Peer-to-peer networking 116
Perry, Isabel 51
Personal data. *See also* Data privacy
with BYOAI 53
definition 189
digital afterlife 179–180
individual control 229, 232
ownership 117–118, 123
protection 185, 187–188
unnecessary storage 225–228
Personal digital agents 249
Philips, John 236–240
Phishing 167, 172–173, 175, 270
Pilot projects, AI 47
Platforms, Web 2.0, 115–116
Platform as a service (PaaS) 236, 270
Ponemon Institute 175, 176
PoS (proof of stake) 141, 270
Post-quantum cryptography (PQC) 223,
271
Poulter, James 61, 76–77
PoW (proof of work) 140–142, 271
PQC (post-quantum cryptography) 223,
271
Predictive analytics 271
Predictive maintenance 271
Preskill, John 223
Pret 241
Pretexting 176
Pre-trained AI 35

Price, Dom 206–207
Private 5G 67–69
Private browsing 160
Private cloud 86, 90, 93, 271
Private persona 163–166
Professional digital legacy 184
Project Kuiper 252
Project Parakeet 8
Prompt engineering 248, 271
Proof-of-concept projects 47
Proof of stake (PoS) 141, 270
Proof of work (PoW) 140–142, 271
PropertyLook 10
Prototypes 47–50
Public cloud 90, 92, 271
Public LLM 35
Public persona 163–166
PwC 249
PWND 271

Q-Day 220–221, 272
Quantum AI project 215, 272
Quantum computing 193, 213–223
    for AI and machine learning 218–219
    for better understanding of the natural
        world 217–218
    defined 213–214, 272
    developers 215–217
    in finance sector 218
    preparing for mainstream adoption
        221–222
    threat of Q-Day 220–221
Quantum cryptography 272
Quantum Development Kit 216
Quantum supremacy 272
Qubits 213, 214, 272
Quic.cloud 283

Radio-frequency identification (RFID) tags
    70–71, 99, 272
Raindrop.io 278
Random access memory (RAM) 272
Read-only memory (ROM) 273
Read-only web 113–115
Read–write–execute web 116
Reasoning models, GenAI 247–248

Rebrandly 278
RedHat 93
RegTech 272
Regulation and governance:
    of AI 249
    of cryptocurrency 250
    data privacy 188–190
    ethical data use 190–191
    global standard for digital and AI
        technologies 191
    of NFTs 151–152
    with Web 3.0 120
Reinforcement learning from human
    feedback (RLHF) 46–47, 273
Reissiger, Carolanne 305
Remote and distributed work 205–206,
    208, 210
Remtulla, Sofia 69
Reskilling 208, 209
Retail industry 70–71, 106
RFID tags see Radio-frequency identification
    tags
Rio Tinto 251
RLHF (reinforcement learning from human
    feedback) 46–47, 273
Roblox 132, 273
Robotics 250
Rock, Ron 100, 104
ROM (read-only memory) 273
Rometty, Ginni 25–26
Rothschild, Mark 151–152
RT-2 project 250

SaaS see Software as a service
Sachdev, Umesh 45, 47, 79–80
Salesforce 76, 236
Samuel, Arthur 30, 31
ScaleAI 46
Scaman, Zoe 132–133
Scanlan, Paul 68
Scary slide 18–19, 277
Schaefer, Mark 307
SDN (software defined networking) 273
SeatLabNFT 149
Second Life 127, 128, 273
Selfkey 234

Self-sovereign identity (SSI) 225–234
  current applications 232–233
  defined 274
  exploring SSI solutions 230–232
  impact of 227–229
  risk of centralised data storage 225–226
  verified credentials for hiring 229–230
Semantic web 116, 118, 119, 273
Sensors 100, 103, 104
Short messaging service (SMS) 64
Shrier, David 198, 199
Shutterstock 281
Simmons, Michelle 223
Simpson, Mark 93–94
Sinclair ZX-80, 7, 9, 59
Siri 31, 61, 73–75, 81, 100
6G 257–258
Smart appliances 102–103
Smart buildings 103–104, 273
Smart cities 103, 273
Smart contracts 123, 143–144, 273
Smart devices 99–102
Smeg 103
SMS (short messaging service) 64
Snowball device 90
Snow Crash (Stephenson) 125–126
Social engineering 175, 274
Social media profile 163–164, 166
Software as a service (SaaS) 235, 236, 273
Software defined networking (SDN) 273
Solar power 251
Soltau, Martin 251
Sora 29, 195, 282
Sovereign identity 188, 193, 274
Speakers Corner 165
Speakers for Schools 163
Speaking Office 2
Spear phishing 172–173
Speech recognition 73, 75–76
Spotify 227, 237, 238
SRI International Artificial Intelligence Centre 73
Srivastava, Sanjay 308
SSI see Self-sovereign identity
Stability AI 282

Standalone 5G (5G SA) 66–67, 69–71, 257
Stanford Cart 31
Stanford University 131
Starbucks Odyssey programme 150, 151
Starbucks test 16–17, 137
Starlink 252
Stephenson, Neal 125–126
Subscription economy 236–237, 239, 274
Subscription fatigue 237–241
Suleyman, Mustafa 29
Super-subscription 240–241
Supply, in tokenomics 154
Supply chain management 105, 122, 142–143, 232, 274
Surfshark 89, 166, 283
Sustainability 48, 239
Synthetic media 274

Talbot, Adrian 306
Techcrunch 290
Technology. See also Cloud computing
  AGI 202–203
  business impact of 60–62
  future business impact 194
  hands-on experience 15–16
  for IoT applications 100–101
  mobile (see Mobile phones and technologies)
  near-term developments 250–252
  voice (see Voice technology)
Technology quotient (TQ) 20–21, 275
Technology supercycle 253
TED Talk 204, 223, 274, 288–289
Telstra 10, 61, 63–64, 84, 109, 235
Threat intelligence 274
3G 61, 64, 257
Tien Tzuo 236
Token burns 155
Tokenisation 147, 274. See also Non-fungible tokens (NFTs)
  defined 147
  in future of work 210
  and metaverse 129
  for ticketing 149
  tokenomics 154
  workplace applications 153
Tokenomics 154–155, 275

INDEX

Token staking 274
Tomchak, Ann-Marie 70, 71
TQ (technology quotient) 20–21, 275
Trademarks 151–152
Transformation management intensity 16
Transformer, AI 31, 35
Transportation and logistics industry,
    IoT for 105
Transportation-as-a-service model 105
Trust 137, 139, 140, 144
Trust 3.0 188
Turing, Alan 27, 30
Twin NFTs 150
Twitter (X) 2, 17, 159, 162, 163, 166, 255
2.5G 64
2G 64, 257
Two-factor authentication (2FA) 4,
    172, 177, 257
Tyagarajan, Tiger 308

UI (user interface) 275
Ukrainian government 89–90
UniFi 60, 282
Uniphore 79–80
Uniqlo 70
University of South Australia 8
Upwork 46
User experience (UX) 275
User experience, Web 3.0 120
User interface (UI) 275
Utility, in tokenomics 154
UX (user experience) 275

Veed.io 26, 281
Vehicle maintenance 105
Verifiable credentials (VCs) 227–230, 275
Viasat 252
Virtual assistants 275
Virtual private network (VPN) 62, 89,
    166, 220, 275
Virtual private server (VPS) 88–89, 275
Virtual reality (VR) 68, 126, 130–133,
    135, 275
Visa 142
Vision Pro headset 133–135
Vodafone 10, 66, 94
Voice assistants 61, 73–76, 79, 100

Voice recognition 74, 78–79
Voice synthesis 61, 73, 74
Voice technology 61, 73–81
    ambient 74–77
    conversational AI 75–81
    Google Duplex 77–78
    in healthcare sector 78–79
Voss, Peter 201
VPN *see* Virtual private network
VPS (virtual private server) 88–89, 275
VR *see* Virtual reality

W3C (World Wide Web Consortium)
    118, 230
Wallace, Marie 226–227, 234
Wallace, Simon 78–79
Walmart 143
Walton Family Foundation 132
Wang VS system 138
WAP (wireless application protocol) 64, 276
Warhol, Andy 152
Watermarks, AI-generated content 247
Wayback Machine 115, 278
Wearable technology 69–70, 107, 276
Web 1.0 113–115, 148, 276
Web 2.0 115–117, 148, 276
Web3 *see* Web 3.0
Web 3.0 110–111, 116–123, 276
    career opportunities 122
    challenges 120–121
    core components 116–118
    data ownership 116, 148
    embracing 121–123
    future of 118–120
    metaverse 129
    self-sovereign identity 225
Webb, Amy 253
Weizenbaum, Joseph 31
What3words navigation system 78, 283
WiFi 60, 62, 103, 166, 282
Wikipedia 34, 115
Wired 23, 290
Wireless application protocol (WAP) 64, 276
Wireless charging 251
Wolfram, Stephen 27, 201
World Wide Web (WWW) 113
World Wide Web Consortium (W3C) 118, 230

INDEX

X (Twitter) 2, 17, 159, 162, 163, 166,
    255
XaaS *see* Everything as a service
XAi Grok 280
XR *see* Extended reality

Y2K 276
Yahoo 183

Young, Steve 95
YouTube 115

Zero trust security 276
Zoom 89
Zuckerberg, Mark 125, 128
Zuora 236, 238
zzq: